The publisher and the University of California Press Foundation gratefully acknowledge the generous support of the Atkinson Family Foundation Imprint in Higher Education.

Making Global MBAs

Making Global MBAs

THE CULTURE OF BUSINESS AND THE BUSINESS OF CULTURE

Andrew Orta

UNIVERSITY OF CALIFORNIA PRESS

University of California Press, one of the most distinguished university presses in the United States, enriches lives around the world by advancing scholarship in the humanities, social sciences, and natural sciences. Its activities are supported by the UC Press Foundation and by philanthropic contributions from individuals and institutions. For more information, visit www.ucpress.edu.

University of California Press
Oakland, California

Cataloging-in-Publication Data is on file at the Library of Congress.

ISBN 978-0-520-32539-5 (cloth : alk. paper)
ISBN 978-0-520-32540-1 (pbk. : alk. paper)
ISBN 978-0-520-97425-8 (ebook)

28 27 26 25 24 23 22 21 20 19
10 9 8 7 6 5 4 3 2 1

For Natalie and Erik, who make all the difference
in the world

CONTENTS

FIGURES

ACKNOWLEDGMENTS

This project seems to be a departure from my longer arc of research as a Latin Americanist focused on Aymara communities of the Bolivian highlands. I sometimes reference my dual research focus, spanning indigenous Andean communities and MBA programs in the United States as evidence of the breadth of anthropology. "You really *can* study everything and anything as an anthropologist," has become part of my pitch to students in introductory classes I teach. The follow up is a "joke" that the more I learn, the more I think I am really studying the same thing. The Aymara I know sometimes evoke "pathways of memory," aligning the present with a series of places, experiences, and relationships over time. My own path to and through this project is one way to announce where I'm coming from with this book.

My earliest work in Bolivia focused on Aymara religious identity and experiences in the context of contemporary interactions with Catholic missionaries. The Catholic Church and the project of missionization constitute some of the foundational global institutions (if there is a rival for that position, it is surely in the practices of early modern capitalism). The missionaries I studied in the late 1980s and 1990s were in the curious position of evangelizing communities that, after centuries of missionization, already identified strongly as Catholic. And yet, this latest cohort of pastoral workers were committed to a vision of Catholic identity that embraced, and in some ways required, culturally varied engagements with what they believed to be a universal Christian truth. So the Aymara found themselves exhorted by European missionaries to become more authentic Christians by becoming more authentic Aymara through adopting "ancestral" practices, once considered idolatrous, but now to be embraced as a local expression of Christian meaning.

Suffice it to say that the Bolivia work has had me thinking about the push and pull of global and local forces—about the ways the global requires the local and the local is always produced in the context of the global. Add to that the timing of this pastoral turn (the "theology of inculturation"), which coincided with the implementation over the 1980s and 1990s of a swath of economic and political reforms in Bolivia (and elsewhere), dubbed "neoliberalism." Neoliberalism seemed to announce the post–Cold War triumph of capitalism and provide a new gear for intensified global integration. For Latin Americanists and other regional specialists, this was a vexing time. The regional units of academic area studies were decried as artifacts of a now passé Cold War era made further obsolete by the accelerating juggernaut of globalization.

In this context, my late colleague Nancy Abelmann invited me to participate in a panel titled "Area Studies Revisited" for the 2003 meetings of the American Anthropological Association. That collaboration provoked an ongoing scholarly interest in the history, politics, and practices of area studies; more importantly, it focused my attention on what I dubbed a "renaissance of regionalism"—an intensifying reconnection with local and regional differences evident programmatically on US college campuses through a welter of new international and global concentrations, including a trend in this direction at business schools. This book is based upon a little over a decade's worth of research and retraining building on that observation.

In following that trail, I did not travel very far. The complex entanglements of local and global, the ethnographic attention to the agents of globalization, and the understanding of globalization as always a cultural project, remain central to my work. And I have found that an anthropological focus on economics and capitalism shares much with an anthropological focus on religion and Christianity in that both capitalism and Christianity are at once objects of study and implicit foundations of much of Western culture. Thus my "joke" that these two projects have been different voicings of a single set of questions and concerns.

·   ·   ·

Three decades of work in the Andes, overlapping with a decade of research in MBA programs, have left me with a well-developed understanding of debt. So let me recognize a list of people, institutions, and opportunities that made this work possible.

I've already mentioned Nancy Abelmann, who was a profoundly generous colleague and friend, and who influenced me as a scholar and teacher in ways I continue to discover. I've benefitted and been sustained by many other colleagues (and friends), in academia and beyond, who have read portions of the manuscript, engaged with my published work on this project, organized conference sessions, brainstormed new ideas, put me in touch with relevant work or research contacts, and otherwise helped me down the path. I list them here with deep thanks: Rob Albro, Rob Borofsky, Marcelo Bucheli, Matti Bunzl, David Cassuto, Rudi Colloredo-Mansfeld, Jean Comaroff, Jane Desmond, Virginia Dominguez, Elizabeth Downes, Brenda Farnell, Paul Garber, Ilana Gershon, Zsuzsa Gille, Maria Gillombardo, Michael Goldman, Jessica Greenberg, Angelique Haugerud, Karen Ho, Craig Koslofsky, Steve Leigh, Andrew Lynch, Kora Maldonado, Ellen Moodie, Sasha Newell, Stuart Rockefeller, Gilberto Rosas, Rachel Schurman, Carol Symes, Rebecca Tolen, and Paul Vaaler. I want to make special note of two outstanding graduate research assistants. Jennifer Hardin helped me take my initial observation and develop it as a research project through a survey of international MBA programs around the United States. And, during the final stretch of this project, Liza Youngling helped me organize some of the field data and process voluminous material on the history of MBA programs, challenges to the MBA in the wake of the 2008 financial crisis, BRICS and MINTs, and other themes.

At the University of California Press, Kate Marshall and Enrique Ochoa-Kaup have made a welcoming home for this book. My thanks to them and other UCP staff who have helped guide the book toward publication.

This accounting of my debts necessarily excludes dozens of MBA faculty, students, and administrators who participated in the project by talking with me or by letting me participate in their daily lives. This book is possible thanks to their generous (and sometimes bemused) collaboration. Although not all would insist on anonymity, it was a condition of my research authorization, and an explicit condition of some of my research subjects, so I have tried to honor it scrupulously here.

. . .

An interesting class marker in the contemporary United States may be the number of degrees of separation between someone and an MBA. As we talked about this project, more than a few of my friends and colleagues would tell me about their brother-in-law, son, or daughter-in-law who have their

MBA degree. In my case, I've married into a family with a fairly high concentration of MBAs. None of them served as "natives" for this study, although they have listened to me talk about the project and been supportive as good family are when confronted with the strange work of anthropologists. Among those good family, I want to remember here my late brother-in-law André Melief. An MBA with a career that included consulting, banking, land development, and resort management, André was an outsized reminder that there is no single mold for an MBA. The last time I saw him, as I was finishing the manuscript of this book, André offered to put me up in his resort for what he called a "writing fellowship." I'd like to think he would be pleased with this final product.

Ingrid Melief (no MBA) has been a partner in every facet of my life. Ingrid read every word of this manuscript and helpfully called me to account when what I was trying to say didn't make sense or seemed so obvious that I needed to justify saying it. Our children, Erik and Natalie (no MBAs, yet), have been through middle school, high school, and much of college while this work has developed. I can't detail their contributions to this project, but I'm certain it would be impossible without them. Debt can be complicated that way.

Finally, this project has benefitted from a range of institutional support and opportunities. At the University of Illinois, the College of Liberal Arts and Science's Faculty Study in a Second Discipline Program afforded me an opportunity to train in the College of Business, which I approached as a step toward learning the native language of capitalism. Administrative stints as the Director of the Center for Latin American and Caribbean Studies and Head of the Department of Anthropology offered different sorts of immersion in the corporatizing culture of the neoliberal university, and should also be noted as part of the process of this research. Grants from the University of Illinois Research Board, from the Center for International Business Education and Research at the University of Illinois College of Business, and from the Wenner-Gren Foundation for Anthropological Research supported preliminary and longer periods of study at MBA programs around the country. A sabbatical leave during the 2016–17 academic year allowed me to complete the manuscript.

Despite all of this help and support, there are surely errors and shortcomings in this final work. I am responsible for those.

ONE

Wall Street Goes to the Ends of the Earth

THE 2011 TITLE OF A SPECIAL "DealBook" section of the *New York Times* announces a new day in international business. "Three of the largest markets for initial public offerings last year were Hong Kong, Shanghai and Shenzhen, China," reports the cover article.

> Private equity firms focused on emerging markets raised $22.6 billion in the first half of 2011, compared with $23.5 billion for all of last year. And Chile, Ukraine and Thailand are among the fastest-growing markets for deals. Wall Street titans can truly claim the title of Masters of the Universe—or at least the World. (Sorkin 2011)

The full-page illustration on the front page of the section underscores the message. In the foreground, a man stands at the edge of a dock in a light-colored suit with a panama hat, his jacket slung over his shoulder, his foot on a well-traveled suitcase bearing stickers indexing multiple destinations. In the shade of a palm tree, he looks across a body of water as a container ship steams toward him. On the other side of the water, a waterfall and verdant hills recede toward more mountainous terrain. An imposing and dramatically shadowed peak, backed by sunlit golden clouds against a blue sky, completes the scene.

Within this stock setting of raw, fertile, mysterious, and perhaps dangerous potential, other details complicate the story. The container-laden ship is steaming toward the dock. The smokestacks of a factory are onshore just behind the ship. And, sweeping across the mid-range of the image, the verdant hills and craggy mountains are dotted with wind turbines, a cell tower, and the skyscrapers of a distant city. The titles of some of the other articles in the section underscore this moment ripe with global opportunities for those able to manage the risks: "Think Globally, Deal Locally," "Untapped and Growing, Frontier Markets Beckon," "Emerging Markets Offer Banks Profits, but Headaches Too" (*New York Times* 2011).

The image (by Dan Cosgrove) conveys a strong "retro" feel: the handled suitcase, the Panama hat, the ship. The palm-treed scene echoes cinematic presentations of exotic locales, and harks back to a time when "emerging markets" were the "Third World" or "the Orient." Indeed, much of the story is not new. The Andrew Ross Sorkin article notes that firms that would later become Citigroup opened turn-of-the-century outposts in Shanghai, Calcutta, Manila, and Buenos Aires. The arc of international business is a long one; the "ends of the earth" have been a frequent destination for US capital.

Yet, there is something new to the twenty-first-century story being told here. The volume and value of global business is part of it: the intensification of internationalization. So too is a concern with the increased risk and volatility ascribed to international locales, particularly in the wake of a catastrophic financial crisis triggered by (largely homemade) risk in 2008.

The story is new in another crucial way. The recycled tropes of exotic difference conjure a purposeful rediscovery of the foreign. A generation ago, to judge by the reigning literature of the time, from the vantage of US business, the world was getting smaller and flatter. The business literature of the 1980s heralded a future of global standardization, with products designed to shape and meet the converging needs of consumers around the world. The trend toward multinational mergers and acquisitions, the proliferation of offshore production, all pointed to a historical moment of economic integration (e.g., Levitt 1983). In a corollary to other discussions of the time declaring "the end of history" (Fukuyama 1992), global capitalism was heady with the verge of the end of difference.

A generation ago, then, the world of stickers on your luggage and intrepid business travelers steaming to remote locales in tropical-weight suits seemed a quaint image from a rapidly receding earlier moment in the history of capitalism. How did it become the future again?

．　．　．

This book is about the rediscovery of the world of international business; the reimagining of global space as a space of difference, risk, and opportunity; and the redesigning of business managers as the subjects best prepared to see and seize these opportunities by managing the margins of a rediscovered world of difference. My focus is on the key sites for the production of business culture in the United States—business schools, and especially MBA programs. MBA programs are an exceptionally responsive barometer of the culture of capitalism in the United States—they at once chase and lead the field. They lead the field by distilling best managerial practices and leveraging an analytic historical perspective on the missteps and trends in business to shape a cohort of business leaders who will be managing capitalism's futures. In the process, they are acutely reactive to the trends and crises of the day. They aim to supply what corporate recruiters want. And they are keenly attuned to the expectations and concerns of their high-tuition-paying students. Their curricula often follow the news of the day: MBA ethics programs, for instance, mushroomed in the wake of the Enron and WorldCom scandals. As finance lost some of its luster in the wake of the 2008 crisis, MBA programs added new concentrations (social entrepreneurship, data sciences) or blended business with other professional degrees (medicine, engineering). And business programs have similarly led from behind in a drive to train a generation of MBAs prepared to manage a newly apprehended world of business: "masters of the world" if not "Masters of the Universe" in Sorkin's words.

MASTERS OF THE UNIVERSE

The story of the complex return to the complex world is slyly condensed by the "Masters of the Universe" reference. The gesture is to Tom Wolfe's 1987 novel *The Bonfire of the Vanities*, a dramatic depiction of high-flying Wall Street investment bankers in 1980s New York (Wolfe 1987). In this telling, Masters of the Universe are a younger generation of bankers whose soaring incomes reflect a new business environment pegged to a dramatic period of economic recovery in the United States. Wolfe's novel was one of a number of influential representations of the world of business during this time. That same year saw Michael Douglas's portrayal of Gordon Gekko in Oliver Stone's film *Wall Street*. These and similar characterizations helped to crystallize an image of audacious and dazzlingly lucrative business deals reflecting a definitive end to the economic doldrums of the 1970s and, the cautions of Gekko's fate notwithstanding, a born-again energized faith in the transcendent potential of markets. This was the moment of the ascendance of neoliberalism: a set of interlaced economic and sociopolitical policies emerging since the 1930s and 1940s under the influence of economists such as

Friedrich Hayek and Milton Friedman and consolidated through political programs associated with Thatcherism and Reaganism. In the United States, the period was marked by a rise of financialization, a disruption of a mid-century status quo of business practices and aspirations as the intensification of mergers and acquisitions and a variety of creative and aggressive innovations in financial securities, fueled by accelerating deregulation, changed the terms and the players of the game.[1]

I discuss this period as it figured in the development of US MBA programs in greater detail below. Here, I want to touch briefly on two features central to the story I aim to tell in this book. The first is that the arc from Wolfe's Masters of the Universe to Sorkin's "masters of the world" traces precisely this history: from the heady hubris of an early moment in globalization that saw a flat world aborning to the current rediscovery of a world of difference requiring the managerial talents embodied by the tropical-weight-suited man on the dock. The shift is from a faith in a standardized global market created by the triumph of capitalism[2] to the recognition that the connection of places across the world, rather than a foregone conclusion, is always an object of ongoing work.

Fortunately, we have heroic figures ready to undertake this work. This is my second point. The moment documented by Wolfe's novel was marked by the ascendance of a new cultural type. Brash young business hotshots came to embody the successes and the excesses of the late capitalist gilded age, and they became closely associated with the degree that many of them held: the MBA. "The MBA"—the credential and the person—were quickly melded in a powerful sign of the times.

THE MBA BOOM AND THE REFIGURING OF GLOBAL CAPITALISM

This *Bonfire* era was not the birth of the MBA degree, of business education, nor of the mythic figure of the "American"[3] businessman. These had been around since the turn of the twentieth century, a time shaped by the ascendance of managerial capitalism in the United States (Chandler 1977; see chapter 3). Yet the late twentieth century marked a profound recasting of the cultural figure of the MBA—a recasting that reflects the changing texture of capitalism within the current moment of globalization. Aspiring Masters of the Universe looked to MBA programs for the training, credentials, and networks that would constitute their "golden passports" to a life of suspenders and power ties (cf. McDonald 2017; Van Maanen 1983). Elite programs remained the primary gateways to the pinnacles of power and prosperity: Wall Street investment banks (e.g., Ho 2009). But they now stood as the market leaders of a booming industry as MBA programs sprung up as if guided by an invisible hand to meet the growing demand across the country. Between 1970 and 2008, the number of MBA and other masters-level business degrees granted annually increased sixfold: from 21,561 to 150,211 (Datar, Garvin, and Cullen 2010, 18). In 2016, 188,834 masters-level business degrees were awarded, down slightly from a high of 191,606 conferred in 2012. Business remains the most popular field of graduate training in the United States; the number of masters-level business degrees conferred in 2016 exceeded the number of masters degrees awarded in education (145,781) and in health professions (110,384), as well as the total number of doctor's degrees awarded in all fields (177,867).[4]

Against this backdrop of the rapid expansion of MBA education over the late twentieth century, this book examines the production of MBAs in the United States in the first decades of the twenty-first century, a moment marked by a refiguring of the international space of global capitalism. The boom in MBA production over the past generation connects in interesting ways with this latest moment of internationalization. For the MBA industry overplayed their hand. The growth in MBA programs over the 1980s and 1990s resulted in an overcapacity of the industry. This was compounded by periodic downturns in domestic demand related to moments of financial crises or scandal such as the dot-com bubble, Enron and WorldCom, and the Great Recession of 2008. As a result, seats in many MBA programs in the United States have been increasingly filled by applicants from abroad (e.g., AACSB 2011; Lieber 2016). Indeed, in convergence with the global hegemony of US business culture, demand for US MBA training soared around the world.

It is a particular irony of this convergence that as international applicants swarmed toward the global standard of business practice, US business programs became increasingly attuned to the intractable cultural and national differences that complicate the world of global capitalism. And it was not long before US MBA programs came to see the growing internationalization of the MBA cohorts (with international students composing nearly half of a given class in some programs) as a forward-looking strength rather than an inheritance of the irrational exuberance of the 1980s. Today MBA programs market themselves to domestic students as simulated international spaces—petting zoos of global capitalism, where aspiring MBAs will work closely with peers from China, India, Brazil, and so forth. It is now settled conventional wisdom that a manager of twenty-first-century capitalism will necessarily engage a world at once rife and rich with difference. Contemporary MBA programs are in the business of providing the corresponding worldview, along with a "starter kit" of international colleagues and experiences, the first of what are anticipated to be many stickers on the suitcases of aspiring managers of twenty-first-century capitalism.

The Necessity of the Foreign

Michael Porter, a professor of strategy at Harvard Business School, is among a select group of business school faculty whose research has at once helped set the terms of discussion in business school curricula and also helped to shape business practices "in the real world." Writing in 1990, Porter called attention to the increasing significance of national and local frameworks for global business.

> In a world of increasingly global competition, nations have become more, not less, important. As the basis of competition has shifted more and more to the creation and assimilation of knowledge, the role of the nation has grown. Competitive advantage is created and sustained through a highly localized process. Differences in national values, culture, economic structures, institutions and histories all contribute to competitive success. There are striking differences in the patterns of competitiveness in every country; no nation can or will be competitive in every, or even most industries. Ultimately, nations succeed in particular industries because their home environment is the most forward-looking, dynamic, and challenging. (Porter 1990)

Porter's essay, "The Competitive Advantage of Nations," harks back to David Ricardo's discussion of the comparative advantage of nations in his *Principles of Political Economy and Taxation* (1817). Advocating for the benefits of free international trade, and against protectionist mercantilist policies, Ricardo argued that national interests were better served by focusing on those industries in which they could produce commodities (say, corn) at the lowest cost relative to other nations, and trading with other nations for those commodities (say, wool) for which expanding production would be at a higher cost than importing them from other nations. Ricardo's foundational discussion extends the acquisitive pecuniary logic of capitalism across international space, scaling up Adam Smith's sense in *On the Wealth of Nations* ([1776] 1994) of the natural human propensity to truck, barter, and exchange.[5]

This propensity is an outwardly focused and social characteristic of Smith's *homo economicus* and it is a component of a broader expansive orientation toward space evident in these earliest articulations of the ethos of capitalism. Space appears laden with the interlaced potential of risk and opportunity: from the comparative advantages and salubrious effects of regional or national competitive differences to the promises of materials and markets in more distant colonies. The foundational texts also make clear that engagement with frontiers is an inexorable condition of capitalism's existence. As Karl Marx and Friedrich Engels observed, "The need of a constantly expanding market for its products chases the bourgeoisie over the whole surface of the globe. It must nestle everywhere, settle everywhere, establish connections everywhere" (Marx and Engels 1977, 224). In this light, global business is not only not new, it is inevitable.

Such expansion is an iterative process; as a cultural system, capitalism is ceaselessly productive of the very differences it struggles to transcend and realize as value. In Marx and Engel's just-so story of *homo faber*, the first historical act is the production of new needs (Marx and Engels 1970, 49). A corollary to that, crucial to the expansive ambitions of capital, concerns the production of new spaces: a development that has been energized under neoliberalism, which weds a universalizing faith in capitalist free markets with a localizing, niche-generating commitment to decentralization (e.g., Peck and Tickell 2002; Thrift 2006; cf. Orta 2013). As Nigel Thrift points out, "capitalism is not a fixed and unforgiving force. Rather, it is a heterogeneous and continually dynamic process of increasingly global connection—often made through awkward and makeshift links—and those links can be surprising, not least because they often produce unexpected spatial formations which can themselves have force" (2006, 280). Quite distinct from the flattening of global space posited by some discussions of globalized capitalism, what is at stake here is a limitless need for difference, "mystery," and "risk" as part of a chain binding the global to the local.

The Re-enchantment of the Local

The moment of Porter's writing, circa 1990, marks an important pivot point toward this "localizing, niche-generating" ethos. For much of the previous decade, the focus of business strategists, managers, and business school faculty had been on processes of globalization that were seen as integrating the world in an unprecedented way. Another member of the Harvard Business School faculty, professor of marketing Theodore Levitt, gave voice to this view of the promise of globalization in his 1983 article, "The Globalization of Markets." There he argued that marketing involved a mix of giving the customer what she wants and aligning those wants with an efficiently standardized repertoire of options. Thus, globalization generated an opportunity for "traditional multinational corporations" to think beyond national frameworks and innovate for a global market that would increasingly be served by, and indeed learn to be satisfied by, a standardized set of options. "Gone are accustomed differences in national or regional preference," declared Levitt. "The globalization of markets is at hand" (1983, 93).

Levitt reviews the case of a British subsidiary of Hoover, which in the 1960s undertook a study of consumer demand for automatic washing machines across a range of European countries. Hoover's study detailed a diversity of national preferences concerning such dimensions as machine capacity, water temperature, spin speed, drum material, etc. Hoover took the results of the study as a challenge to find ways to adapt washer design to meet different national preferences.

In Levitt's view, Hoover was asking the wrong questions. Instead of asking German, British, Italian, or French housewives what their ideal washer would look like, Hoover's market researchers ought to have been more attentive to global convergences in automated household clothes washing. He points out that in the German market, characterized by expensive machines designed to national tastes, low-priced basic machines manufactured in Italy were gaining market share. Conversely, in Italy, where the transition from traditional technologies of clothes washing was less advanced, households were eager to adopt any sort of automatic washing machine as an improvement over what were increasingly seen as outdated domestic practices. Finally, advances in detergent technology created increased performance in different water temperatures. Attention to these details might have shown Hoover executives that the better marketing strategy in this emerging global moment would have been to develop a standardized, low-cost, basic-featured washing machine that would compete on price in the German market, and provide Italian housewives if not everything that they dreamed of, at least recognizably more than they had (Levitt 1983).

Similar trends away from local specificity are also found in a good deal of the social science of the time, which was marked by a heady sense of an emerging global ecumene in which the significance of place was thought to be eroded by global cultural "flows" (e.g., Appadurai 1996; Hannerz 1989; cf. Rockefeller 2011). The vicissitudes of "the local" against the backdrop of shifting imaginings of "the global" is central to this book. In my home discipline of anthropology, the challenges of globalization have helped to provoke a critical reexamination of the central concept of "culture," even as MBA programs, post-Levitt, have taken up "culture" as key to effective business management (e.g., Hegeman 2012; see chapter 4). The changing apprehension of "global" and "local" in MBA curricula, as well as the conventional wisdom and business practices they reflect and shape, are a component of a broader and continuous reckoning of globalization and the nested scales of human activity that compose it.

Within these connected discourses, business-speak about the global is particularly influential. This stems from the authoritative status of economistic rhetoric under current conditions of neoliberalism (e.g., Bourdieu and Wacquant 2001; Mirowski 2014; Thrift 2000). It also reflects the material force of business practices in shaping the connections (through business networks and hierarchies) as well as the products and ideas that circulate and signify across the globe. These connective practices, networks, and circulating ideas and products are often cited as symptoms of a larger condition of globalization. But they also merit our careful attention as the local ideological, rhetorical, and material actions through which different actors conjure "the global" into being.

Globalization in this sense is aptly described by anthropologist Kalman Applbaum as "a social fact in the making" (Applbaum 2003, 76). It is "an abstraction that is developing thicker institutional moorings in the life world" (76). Moreover, globally oriented business practices require a particular kind of faith that global markets exist, or that they can be constituted out of the proper business strategies, and that there exists the potential of connecting immediate business actions in such a way as to evoke and engage this global scale. In this regard, the totality of the global is never fully apprehended; it is always displaced to the future edge of immediate action, continuously realized in practice, always at once a context and a product.

Global business is an iterative bet on the inevitability of this spacetime. The plausibility of this rests upon cultural work: routinizing our abilities to persuasively render the global from the shreds and patches of immediate experience that we learn to see as its symptoms. As an ethnography of MBA programs, this book is aimed at some of the more influential sites in which and on which this conjuring and scaling work is done.

Other scholars have called attention to the correlation between changing business strategies and changing conceptualizations of globalization around the turn of the twenty-first century (Applbaum 2003; Foster 2008; Miller 1995; Wilk 1995). Sometimes dubbed "strong" and "weak" globalization (Foster 2008 after Friedman 1995), these discussions trace the shift from a vision of homogenizing globalization (à la Levitt) dominant across the 1970s and 1980s, to an understanding of globalization predicated on irreducible difference. As anthropologist Robert Foster (2008) tells the story through the case of Coca-Cola, the twentieth century saw the emergence of Coke as a global brand, intensified by the reach of the US military during the Second World War and its Cold War aftermath, and facilitated by a franchise system that allowed local bottlers a degree of independence. Beginning in the 1980s, however, and directly citing Professor Levitt's work (2008, 63f.), Coca-Cola sought to consolidate their franchise arrangements and standardize the production and marketing of their product for a newly apprehended global market. So far, so flat. By 2000, however, "this impulse yielded, in turn, to a rediscovery of the local" (2008, xx). Under the leadership of a new CEO, "the company announced a renewed concern with the local, a withdrawal from an aggressively singular global strategy of marketing and a heightened sensitivity to multiple local differences in tastes and preferences" (35). Among the results were the development of some locally specific fruit flavored variants of the Fanta line of Coke products, and corporate reorganizations giving greater autonomy to local and regional managers (67ff.).

This sense of a pendulum swing between different voicings of globalization tells only part of the story. Another crucial factor over this time period, noted in passing a few times already, is the global rise of neoliberalism. I have in mind specifically the working out of neoliberal tensions between a set of policies lubricating the operations of markets at increasingly global scales (by promoting, for instance, deregulation, privatization, and free trade), and a philosophy of decentralized governance and politics that prioritizes local scales of sociality among freely interactive economic individuals (Hayek [1944] 2007, 85ff., Gershon 2016, Grindle 2007, Mirowski 2014).

Economic ideas always rest upon claims, implicit or explicit, about human nature and the relationship between the individual and society. Neoliberalism, politically ascendant since the governments of Reagan and Thatcher and the adoption by multinational lenders of a slate of economic and political policy prescriptions for the developing world, has helped to routinize particular understandings of a capable entrepreneurial subject (Harvey 2005, Ong

2006, Urciouli 2008).[6] At the fulcrum of the pendulum swing, in other words, is a tense balancing of a model of frictionless global capital and techniques of flexible decentralized governance accountable to, and bound to the production of, such subjects. Of particular relevance to my discussion is the way neoliberal globalization has been increasingly premised on the production and the alignment of local sites and situated selves through market and market-like frameworks.

The resulting shift in conventional corporate wisdom regarding the texture of globalization and the nature of its agents exists in a complex push-pull relationship with the curricula of MBA programs, which, as I have suggested, at once chase and make the trends in business. The past two decades have been a boom time for the production of spatialized difference in the training of US business adepts in MBA programs. These years mark a repositioning of international business (IB) studies in MBA curricula. Once packaged as a distinct subfield of business studies—a relatively marginal specialization catering to the intrepid international business traveler—international business is now seen as a curricular component best "infused" across all functional areas of business training (Buckley 2005; Daniels 2003; Robock 2003).[7] This has been a moment, then, of profound routinization of a particular construction of global space as shaped by differences that are relatively enduring, potentially generative of (or threatening to) value, and *unavoidable*. In this regard, MBA programs reflect and authoritatively enact key qualities of contemporary capitalism, requiring the productive engagement with difference and its (always partial) assimilation.

And this refocusing on difference within capitalism has gone hand in hand with the emergence of new business subjectivities required of managers in the "new economy" (Downey and Fisher 2006). Cast as a state of permanent emergency, the new economy compels the production of "fast" managerial subjects and spaces of particular intensity that serve in their production (Thrift 2000, 675). MBA programs are incubators of such subjects, and an integral part of their formation is their orientation to a global field of difference as an arena of business potential for the properly calibrated manager.

The new business subjectivities of the neoliberal economy eclipse certain attributes of managerial capitalism that were central to the ascendant ideal of the MBA over the mid-twentieth century. These involved the framework of the large, often multinational, corporation understood as a nexus of technical, financial, and social processes, all requiring managerial coordination (see chapter 3). Among the consequences of neoliberalism was the erosion of the social contracts of mid-century capitalism, including the model of the firm, through speculative mergers and acquisitions, corporate downsizing, off-shoring of production … all features of a flattening, globalized world united through deregulation and free market orthodoxy. And this trend was enabled by the rise of financialization, fueled by the sway of new models of managerial practice emphasizing the importance of increasing shareholder value as primary managerial objective.

Anthropologist Anna Tsing describes another facet of this moment, linked to what she dubs "supply chain capitalism." "Since the late twentieth century, business elite have stopped imagining the control of workers, and the corporate expansion that follows as the key to success. Instead, powerful firms try to get rid of workers entirely through contracting and putting out. Supply chains rather than vertically integrated corporations are the rage" (2013, 25). A supply chain, like the related concept of a "value chain," is a metaphor for managing business activities across space, and frequently across international space. They recast the sociality of capitalism away from a unitary corporate frame, and toward a sequence of explicitly relational nodes. And, as chains so often do, they assert a hierarchizing and organizing pull in a certain direction (see chapters 2 and 5).

This view gripped the leading MBA programs of the 1980s and 1990s, with the result that the exemplary MBA Masters of the Universe were, perversely, *anti*-managers in their unwinding of the social institutions that once gave rise to their role and in their championing of the short-term, nomadic, gun-for-hire entrepreneurial career path that has become emblematic of the new economy (although, in trickle-down forms such as contracting, putting out, or even the "gig economy," it is not so lucrative). A full consideration of that twist in the MBA story is beyond the scope of this book (but see McDonald 2017). For my purposes here, though, this story is significant because it announces a repurposing of the MBA as an adept of social management, away from intrafirm space and toward an international field of business practice fraught anew with difference, uncertainty, and risk.

ANTHROPOLOGY AND CAPITALISM

Anthropology over the past few decades has seen a growth in research focused on business. In part, this might be seen in connection with a longer disciplinary arc of "studying up": examining sites of power and the constitutive institutions of Western modernity as at once a critical interrogation of modernity and a self-conscious realignment of anthropology's classical preoccupation with non-Western others (Nader 1972; cf. Boyer 2008; Holmes and Marcus 2008). The trend in business studies also reflects a concern among some scholars to bring ethnographic attention to the situated phenomena of globalization. Additionally, the consolidation of neoliberalism and the saturation of economistic rationality across multiple cultural institutions has surely helped to spur an empirical interest in documenting key sites of business practice. And, of course, the 2008 financial crisis triggered further scrutiny of things economic.

One takeaway of much of this recent scholarship is that capitalism as practiced is a complexly social form: culturally and historically sensitive. This is not a new lesson. It follows from more classic anthropological discussion of economic practices (Western and non-Western), which have troubled the taken-for-grantedness of basic assumptions (by classical political economists and their descendants) of a rational, selfish, and singular *homo economicus*, and approached Western economic "truths" as contingent cultural forms (e.g., Dumont 1977; Malinowski 1922; Sahlins 1974, 1988). A related line of analysis has keyed on economic practices as they are "embedded" in other institutions (e.g., Granovetter 1985). The focus here is on the ways market practices may be shaped by cultural norms, repertoires of courtesy or politeness, social roles and statuses, and so forth.

Informed by this work, my approach here is to treat economic practices as wholly cultural. They are culturally constituted and culturally constitutive. They are shaped by a wider cultural milieu and they participate in the shaping of particular kinds of subjects. In Western capitalist contexts, moreover, economic practices are *doubly* cultural. Like all cultural practices, economic practices such as trade serve to make the world. In the (anthropologically) classic example of the Trobriand Kula, made famous by Bronislaw Malinowski's pioneering ethnography of the Pacific Islanders, the prosaic exchange of necessities was inseparable from the context of ceremonial exchange that served to establish and perpetuate connections among trade partners, enact mythic understandings of the foundations of the Trobriand world, and sustain political hierarchies within and among island communities (Malinowski 1922). In my own ethnographic work with Aymara communities of the Bolivian highlands, I have discussed the ways acts of exchange are valued for their ability to create profound alignments between interacting subjects or, in the case of sacrificial offerings, between sacrificer and the intended recipient of the offering. Similarly, networks of exchange partners radiate out from households to constitute communities of kin and kin-like relations connected through trading ties (e.g., Orta 2004a). The ethnographic literature is replete with analogous examples of the dense cultural significance and world-making potency of economic practices.

But as a metapragmatic system—a genre of activity that references and analyzes itself through everyday talk about "the economy," and through more formal channels like, say, MBA programs—the capitalist economy is itself a cultural formation. It is a model of the world that compels approximation to its own vision. Here, the issue is not that economic practices do cultural work but rather that practices marked as "economic" are inevitably attached to a more systematic and authoritative (and cultural) claim about the world. As such, economic practices are complicit in the production of the world in ways that appear to match those claims. The economic sociologist Alex Preda illuminates this in his study of the institutionalization of finance as this required the elaboration of all sorts of institutional boundary markers to delineate, authorize, and order a space of activity comprehensible as finance (Preda 2009). Geographer Nigel Thrift makes a related point when he discusses the routines of business as well as a repertoire of media and other technologies for the production of particular kinds of "fast" business subjects required to enact current conceptions of contemporary capitalism (Thrift 2000). And a stream of other work on contemporary capitalism has called attention to the performative force of economic theory, as authorized reflections about the workings of capitalism are institutionalized as effective blueprints for the production of capitalism (Callon 2007; MacKenzie and Millo 2003). In Donald MacKenzie's apt phrase, economic theory is "an engine, not a camera," constitutive rather than descriptive of the world (MacKenzie 2006).

Capitalism and Anthropology

Anthropology engages with capitalism in another way: as a multipurpose tool of the trade. MBA programs have long incorporated select concepts and methods from the social sciences as part of the technical base of a professionalized approach to management. Not surprisingly, anthropology has typically been seen as a tool for making managerial sense of the exotic and bizarre. But in the context of some business functions such as marketing, close attention to the functions of language, ritual, and the meanings of objects in social contexts have been central to professional practice. Many companies, including Intel and Microsoft, keep anthropologists or other social scientists on staff and make use of ethnographic and other research methods in connection with product development or marketing strategies. Many more contract a growing number of anthropologically focused consulting groups to gain ethnographic insight into business problems (e.g., Denny and Sunderland 2015; Madsbjerg and Rasmussen 2014).

Corporations have also recognized that the object of anthropological knowledge is not only "them" (consumers or exotic business partners) but equally "us." "Culture" figures prominently among the buzzwords in the business literature of recent decades. Corporations, it turns out, each have their own culture. During periods of intensified merger and acquisition activity, commentaries on management challenges might focus as much on integrating cultures as on integrating assets. The 2002 merger of Hewlett-Packard and Compaq, for instance, inspired multiple case studies on the challenges of integrating corporate cultures and prompted a call for "cultural diligence" as part of the standard due diligence undertaken in evaluating the risks and benefits of any potential business merger (e.g., Stachowicz-Stanusch 2009). More recently, the 2017 scandals rocking Uber prompted calls to redesign and reform its corporate culture, understood as a set of routinized bad habits that led to the pattern of harassment and abuses plaguing the organization. There is a double edge to such culture-talk in business. On the one hand, there is a whiff of culture as obstacle: an assemblage of backward traditions that prevent efficiency and progress. "Culture eats strategy" in a slogan ascribed to business "guru" Peter Drucker. On the other hand, culture is a resource for engineering corporations as high functioning social groups. It is in this capacity that many corporations have brought anthropologists on board "as part of their strategic and operational efforts" (Cefkin 2010, 2).

Business schools are in on the trend as well. A number of leading programs employ anthropologists among their faculty. More still include discussions of ethnography and ethnographic methods—particularly in their marketing courses. And it would be difficult to find a program today that does not invoke the idea of "culture" as a concept necessary for professional managerial practice (see chapter 4). To close the loop, leading MBA programs strive to distinguish themselves from their elite brethren by pointing to their own unique culture. "Culture drives innovation," declares the website of the Haas School of Business at the University of California, Berkeley. "At Berkeley-Haas, we believe that a fundamental step in redefining the business leader is to get the culture right because the culture can encourage and develop the attitudes and behaviors of innovative leadership in our students."[8] MBA applicants are advised to pay attention to the culture of each school as a factor guiding their decision of where to apply or attend; the MBA-focused online publication "Poets and Quants" adds to a welter of program rankings with an assessment of "Business Schools with the Best MBA Culture" (Schmitt 2017).

This book examines such culture-talk in contemporary business training and business practice, with an emphasis on the ways concepts of culture are explicitly mobilized as essential to effective business management. At the same time, this discussion is deeply attentive to the more implicit cultural dimensions of capitalism: the naturalized, but by no means natural, habits and sensibilities that underlie contemporary business. Business schools and particularly MBA programs are sites par excellence for examining these features of capitalism insofar as they at once self-consciously distill and crystallize the dominant trends and herald new directions in the field, and, at the same time, reproduce in a less self-conscious way these more silent dimensions of capitalism as culture.

CAPITALISM, DIFFERENCE, AND THE EXCESS OF CULTURE

Threaded across this book is a consideration of difference, and especially difference verging on excess, as a quality integral to capitalism, with particular implications for global capitalism. This cusp of excess is relevant to any consideration of the anthropology of capitalism and of the relationship between capitalism and anthropology. For the robust understanding of culture that has long been the purview of anthropology implies an attention to incommensurability and excess beyond the integrative forces of capitalism.

To some extent, this is an old story. As Marshall Sahlins (1988, 7) has put it in his anthropological history of the capitalist world system in the Pacific, "modern world history since *c.* 1860 has been marked by the simultaneous development of global integration and local differentiation." Writing against conventional narratives of the destruction of local cultural orders by the juggernaut of capitalism, Sahlins calls attention to the ways capitalism—its products, people, social processes—is taken up within local cultural orders, even as different products from around the world, like tea, become indispensable to the production of modern Western selves (cf. Bright and Geyer 1987; Mintz 1985).

As it was for nineteenth-century liberalism, local difference remains a resource for the global under contemporary neoliberal capitalism. However, the conditions of its production and consumption have shifted. The integration of difference under neoliberalism is increasingly predicated on the production of its putatively "continued" qualitative distinctiveness. Richard Wilk (1995) has nicely captured this paradoxical process of serializing and standardizing difference under neoliberalism in his observation that local places are becoming "different in uniform ways." Similar effects have been identified in official multiculturalisms embraced by neoliberal modes of governance as these render specific cultural identities as so many tokens of a generic "other" type—at once uniquely indispensable and all but interchangeable (e.g., Hale 2006; Rivera Cusiqanqui 2012). The alchemy of contemporary capitalism is this functional assimilation of difference explicitly without its complete obliteration. And this rests on the cultural work of reframing difference to the manageable ends of relative legibility and commensurability (e.g., Miller 1997; Shankar 2015). MBA programs are important sites of this work.

But there is another part to the story I aim to tell here concerning the stubborn remainder or excess after all of this commensurating, serializing work. In part, this is the real world talking back: the intransigent messiness that always exceeds the categorical systems for its cultural ordering. In part, this is the outcome of ceaseless processes of cultural production. These include the local cultural ordering of the phenomena of capitalism to which Sahlins has called attention as well as newly emergent local spaces of cultural production at the interstices or friction points of local and global processes of the sort Tsing (2005) has discussed. As I show throughout this book, this excess itself has become an object of metacultural capitalist reflection, part of a routinized recognition of cultural difference as a challenge and resource for capitalism. This apprehension of difference points to the limits of capitalist control and understanding of the social world—an unease that courses throughout the history of managerial capitalism. And, under the current moment of capitalism examined here, excess and the unease it provokes become assimilated as integral features of the cultural production of the authoritative agents of neoliberal capitalism: MBAs.

AN ANTHROPOLOGIST AMONG THE MBAS

This book is an ethnography of the production of the managerial subjects of contemporary capitalism. MBA programs play a key role in credentialing and in building professional networks that many managers rely on in the course of their professional lives. Many commentators, even MBA graduates and the business recruiters who hire them, will tell you that this is all you get from an MBA program. Corporate recruiters insist that they are hiring potential and expect to train MBAs in their own corporate systems. MBA programs cultivate a good-natured contempt for academic faculty who overthink and over-analyze, and who are devoted to teaching in contrast to the doing to which the MBAs aspire. The "value added," it would seem, is not to be found in the syllabi. For their part, MBA faculty chafe at the limitations of their teaching in the compressed two-year setting of an MBA curriculum. Some suggest that they teach more rigorous content to their undergraduate students than to their MBAs.

In this regard, MBA programs are classic boundary-marking institutions (cf. Preda 2009). However, a structural view of the programs—as a gateway demarcating the world of business, a rite of passage for budding Masters of the Universe—risks overlooking the subject-making work done along the way (see chapter 2). The research for this book draws on mixed ethnographic methods to examine this work, centered on periods of participant observation among cohorts of MBA students and faculty.

The "field" for this study involved a set of broadly connected institutional contexts selected as representative of contemporary MBA education, and particularly representative of internationalizing initiatives among MBA programs in the United States. Research sites included a dozen institutions, all falling among the fifty "top ranked" programs surveyed by Peter Navarro in his 2008 study of US MBA curricula (Navarro 2008). These sites included seven MBA programs where I was able to spend time in classrooms, participate in extracurricular activities, or conduct more structured interviews with students, faculty, and administrators. My level of involvement in these programs varied. In one program I was able to shadow a cohort of MBA students for a complete academic year; in others I was a regular visitor to campus: sitting in on classes, hanging out in student lounges, and joining in program events. Alongside these more immersive experiences, I conducted interviews with students, faculty, and administrators from five additional MBA programs, all of these experiences contributing to a broad sense of contemporary MBA training in the United States.

Additionally, my research took me to a variety of professional conferences and workshops for MBA program administrators and staff. These focused on international business themes, the internationalization of business school curricula, and best practices in the design of short-term study abroad classes for MBA programs. These were opportunities to calibrate my impressions from the programs with which I had research contact in the light of national trends in MBA education and business scholarship, as well as to expand my network of contacts to a broader range of faculty and administrators.[9] Finally, my research included close investigation of a range of published materials: syllabi, course packets, case studies, and other scholarly work by MBA faculty, as well as other discussions of MBA education and international business from a range of online and print media.

I approached my time as an MBA student as an immersion in a different culture, requiring a growing fluency with a new vocabulary and new conceptual categories. The simulated corporate energy and self-aware professionalism that suffuses the corridors and classrooms of the well-appointed business schools I studied contributed to an aura of difference that was palpable to me. In other ways, however, my MBA consultants and I were already familiar to one another: as a type of student I had encountered before; as a shaggier version of the faculty they saw at the front of their classes; as a colleague from another discipline engaged in research of interest to them.

Some program administrators sought to limit my access to students and faculty. They were far "too busy" to talk with me, one dean told me. I was not assigned to MBA project teams in the cohort I shadowed because I was not "competing" for a grade. Yet, this has felt in many ways like a collaborative project shaped by converging research interests. My curiosity about international content was legible to students and faculty, for all of whom this was a salient facet of their program experience. As an anthropologist and Latin Americanist, I was an authorized interlocutor on these themes.

Yet in other respects, as a participant observer of MBA programs as sites of cultural production, I was not fully on their radar; for, like "natives" the world over, they were not fully self-aware of all of the features of their daily lives that were of interest to me. The concerns about me not "competing," like the insistence on the unrelenting "busyness" of MBA students and faculty, were data. My participation in orientation activities for new MBAs, or my immersion in daily MBA life through class observations, time in business school cafeterias and lounges, participation in extracurricular events, and time spent with project teams (the students let me tag along) all inform an ethnographic analysis of MBA education. In classic fieldwork style, these helped build rapport and access that have enriched my study. I have also relied on another page from the methods of anthropological analysis by historicizing my object of study (see chapters 3 and 4). For an endeavor presenting itself as the essence of instrumentality, distilling state-of-the-art techniques for managing the world of capitalism, historicizing the MBA project helps illuminate the position of MBA programs as entangled in the production of the world they mean to manage.

Historicizing my object of study also requires reckoning with two historic convulsions that have impacted global capitalism over the course of my study. The first is the global financial crisis of 2008–9, which came to a head just after my primary period of immersive field research. The second is the rise of xenophobic, antiglobalist, protectionist movements reflected in Brexit in the United Kingdom and in the election of Donald Trump in the United States, both occurring as I finalized work on this manuscript. On the face of it, the timing of these events was not kind to this project, which draws on interviews and observations conducted between August 2006 and January 2017.

While I make reference in the following chapters to the impact of these developments on MBA education, on balance, that impact has been relatively limited and more in keeping with longer trends in the reproduction of managerial capitalism than disruptive (Mirowski 2014). Finance capitalism seems to have survived the crisis of 2008; it seems unlikely that globalization will be undone by the current wave of protectionism, nor by the longer arc of antiglobalization movements from the right and the left over recent decades. Of course, the radical upending of capitalism or globalization is something of a straw man for diagnosing the current situation. And identifying core continuities need not ignore changes. As I complete this manuscript around the tenth anniversary of the financial crisis, reckonings of the aftermath point to a down-shifting of global capitalism—evocatively dubbed "slowbalisation" in a January 2019 issue of *The Economist*. Symptoms here include lower rates of growth, decreases in foreign direct investment, and the rise of tariffs and regulations at the levels of nations and regional blocs such as the European Union. While these changes are significant, they remain assimilable to trends in MBA education that frame global capitalism as field of difference to be managed. One of the goals of the book will be to contextualize post-2008 MBA education within a longer set of turn-of-the-twenty-first-century developments, which, in my view, remains the salient historical unit of analysis. One goal of this introduction is to address the matter directly.

The economic crisis of 2008 provoked a torrent of critical assessments of MBA training and the adequacy of the curriculum and the managers it produces for the realities of contemporary capitalist practice.[10] These have set the internationalization of MBA curricula in instructive relief. As I detail in chapter 3, MBA curricula have always been part of a highly reflexive process, linking an anxious self-awareness suffusing capitalist practices with the standardized production of the agents of capitalism's future. The development of the international business curricula reflects one strand of an iterative process of self-examination and reinvention in the face of the perceived new realities of capitalism.

While the resulting changes have been far from fundamental, a couple of trends appear to be emerging. On the one hand are the "if only they had listened to us" reforms: redoubling initiatives already under way in the wake of the Enron and WorldCom scandals to increase ethics education and infuse ethics training across all functional areas of the curriculum. A similar effort applies to the MBA message, examined in chapter 2, that management is part science and part art, with an increasing emphasis on cultivating the "soft skills" and awareness of social and historical contexts necessary for responsible management decisions. The value of international experience (see chapter 5) is highlighted here as one opportunity in the business curriculum for students to link classroom experiences with the real world (Riaz 2009). The focus on case studies (chapter 6) is flagged as another best practice in this regard. Alongside these efforts are trends in some MBA programs toward MBA degrees focused on "green" or sustainable business, social entrepreneurship, or blended with other professional training, such as engineering, as well as a growing emphasis on one-year MBA programs, online programs, and efforts to recruit applicants who do not fit the traditional business school mold. While these developments are no doubt responses to a variety of substantive challenges to the MBA curriculum, they should also be seen as a savvy repositioning of the brand at a time when applications from US students are down, and increasing numbers of MBA students indicate career goals outside of the structured corporate paths of finance and banking, planning instead to start their own businesses.

In this environment, some of the discussion of the post-2008 MBA suggests a shift away from technical competencies and a doubling down on the cultivation of leadership talents. In the findings of one such study, in a world where "nomadic" managers may never be tightly linked to a single corporate community, the MBA programs must embrace their role as "rites of passage—shaping the values, commitments, habits and mores of aspiring leaders" (Petriglieri 2012; cf. Gershon 2016, 2017).

My position on Brexit and Trump is more unsettled, primarily because they are unfolding as I write this. While they are part of a swing toward nationalist protectionism, we know little as yet of what they may mean in practice. In the case of the United States under Trump, the enactment of apparently protectionist policies (unwinding and renegotiating trade pacts, implementing tariffs) has been uneven. I touch on these developments in my concluding chapter, primarily to argue that the move away from regional trading alliances and the amplifying of cultural difference can be located as a marginal extreme within the localizing, particularizing logic of early twenty-first-century global capitalism that is the underlying subject of this book. In this regard, these "slowbalising" shifts in global and neoliberal capitalism are continuous (rather than in tension) with the trends that are the focus of this book.[11]

A final introductory note: I use the terms "international" and "global" almost interchangeably throughout the text. As someone who has joined in lively faculty discussions regarding the naming of a program in "international" or "global" studies, I appreciate that this will trouble some readers. International, after all, refers to relationships between and among nations; global refers to a more inclusive totalizing order.

I plead a mix of sloppiness and insight. "Sloppiness," because these are emic terms used simultaneously and often in different ways by different programs and at different times. I have not rendered this precisely and I do not believe excessive attention to this hairsplitting would advance the discussion here. "Insight," because part of the story being told here concerns the shifting purchase of the "global" label on the phenomena of capitalism. Some of the leading voices in the field of global management are also among the most influential arguing for the salience of regional and national differences.[12] And, as I show below, whether their strategy course is titled "international" or "global," MBAs are schooled in a view of the world premised on the decomposition of global or international complexity to the end of a manageable scalar connection. As theoretical claims about the world, global and international are endlessly rediscovering each other.

ORGANIZATION OF THE BOOK

The chapters of this book twine together discussions of capitalism as a cultural form and of MBA programs as sites of the production of capitalist managerial subjects, all refracted through the ascendant frame of international and cultural differences as a challenge and a resource for business. Here is a brief overview of the organization of the book.

Chapter 2, *Fast Subjects: The Rituals of MBA Training*, provides an ethnographic introduction to the practices of MBA training and the experiences of MBA students. This chapter constitutes a thick description of the MBA routine. It examines the hyperscheduled rhythm of an MBA career and the ways that common MBA program devices such as team projects, compressed deadlines, and simulations of professional life, dovetail with a set of analytic habits modeled in the more conventional curricular content presented in "core" functional courses in accounting, strategy, finance, etc. The chapter also examines the cultivation of risk in MBA training, as a necessary state of capitalist practice and as a condition of possibility for managerial actions.

Chapter 3, *Accounting for Business*, sets contemporary MBA training in historical context, examining a series of critical moments in the formalization of collegiate business education and the development of MBA training in the United States from the turn of the twentieth century. The discussion details the historical responsiveness of MBA curricula to broader developments in US society and the position of the United States globally, as MBA programs emerged as the authoritative incubators and disseminators of persuasive truths about the world of business.

Chapter 4, *The Currency of Culture*, examines the development of the culture concept within business studies. The chapter reviews the influential work of anthropologists and organizational psychologists, and details the influence of the culture concept in business as it was increasingly understood as a dimension of risk that can be measured and managed by appropriately trained MBAs. How MBAs are taught to think about culture is a powerful model of and model for the production of and assimilation of difference within the logics of contemporary capitalism. A crucial quality of culture, as taken up by MBAs, is its near-commensurability as a dimension of difference and risk that can be measured and referenced while still retaining an aura of singular excess.

Chapter 5, *Managing the Margins*, examines a key feature of the internationalization of MBA training: short-term study abroad experiences. Most MBA programs of note offer a set of study abroad opportunities to their students. Drawing upon participant observation as a member of a study abroad cohort, as well as interviews with faculty and students about study abroad experiences, the chapter details the ways these carefully staged international experiences become a constitutive part of the managerial selves MBA students aspire to become. The discussion follows the design and development of a study abroad course, the sort of nation-specific information conveyed as relevant in preparatory classwork prior to the trip, student experiences selecting a study abroad option, the trip itself, and their return.

Chapter 6, *Partial Answers: The Uses of Ethnographic Capitalist Realism*, examines the case study teaching method. If the short-term study abroad experience reflects recent developments in MBA education, the case study teaching method, pioneered by Harvard Business School in the early twentieth century, stands as the enduring signature component of traditional MBA training. Business case studies are short narratives, usually based upon a real-world business situation, detailing a problem faced by one or more of the managers in the case. Students are challenged to develop and defend a variety of recommendations to resolve the problem. This chapter examines the case study method as a quasi-ethnographic simulation of the world and the managerial engagement with uncertainty and risk, focusing particularly on the implications of these features for the presentation of international and cross-cultural business cases.

Chapter 7, *Frontiers of Capitalism*, presents a concluding discussion focused on the turn to social entrepreneurship and so-called "bottom of the pyramid" business strategies aimed at the global poor. These cases draw together a set of core arguments in the book concerning the ceaseless production of manageable difference and correlated risk at the heart of contemporary global capitalism, and the coproduction of local business sites and globally adept MBA subjects in the engineering of the scalar articulations of global business.

TWO

Fast Subjects

THE RITUALS OF MBA TRAINING

A COMMON REFRAIN AMONG FORMER MBA STUDENTS and the executives who hire them holds that they learn nothing in business school. Rather, conventional insider wisdom has it that they attend MBA programs to build a network and be credentialed for lucrative employment, and that they really learn their profession on the job. Such claims often come wrapped with disdain for the classroom and the insulated eggheads who teach there, burdening budding entrepreneurs with their abstract theoretical views of the world. There is some truth to this. The MBA as a professional degree is somewhat siloed from the research of PhD-trained business faculty. For their part, academic business faculty confirm the divide; one professor I spoke with ruefully observed that in her courses on international finance the level of "theory" is reduced in turn as she teaches classes of doctoral students, undergraduates, and, lastly, MBAs.

This chapter begins from the double-edged ethnographic premise that (a) in business education, "theory" isn't everything; there are deep ontological premises, and framings of the world and of capitalism conveyed through multiple channels in the MBA curriculum, and, therefore, (b) "everything" may well be theory. Taking an ethnographic approach to the MBA experience as an emergent ritual of professional socialization, one that makes explicit, in participants' experiences, claims about capitalism that typically operate more implicitly, this chapter proposes that MBA students get much more than they bargained for during their two years of training.

This disdain for the academic aspects of MBA education is itself part of a ritual of emerging MBA subjectivity. Much as law schools steep students in legal epistemology, MBA programs are initiations in thinking (and acting) like a manager (see Lezaun and Muniesa 2017, cf. Mertz 2007 for law schools).

MBAs are trained to be impatient with theory, rarely interested in contextual details of a case, and eager to pounce on the key facts, the nub of a problem that will inform and enable a business decision. The patience of scholarship, the exhaustive search for missing information, is the inverse of real-time business practice (at least as it is conjured in MBA programs), which, MBAs are frequently reminded, requires decisions that risk resources on the basis of always partial and imperfect information. Nigel Thrift (1999) has written perceptively about this bent toward "practical theory" and the conceptualization of "problem spaces" requiring prompt action. MBA curricula require and encourage students to develop precisely these skills (see also Urciuoli 2008).

"Students want to use common sense ... or they want a clear answer," reflected Kevin as we chatted after a meeting of his International Strategy course. "I try to give them ways of organizing a vast amount of information according to the issue at hand." He went on to describe his aims in MBA classes as "teaching decision-making techniques." These techniques, which he cast as "a managerial process," involve a compression of complexity rendering it susceptible to common sense. Our conversation, though, was about his course as an "international" course. In this regard, he moved to his key point: "As we take international, [we start] realizing where those [decision-making processes] may break down, and realizing that in the international context there is a lot more that one has to look at." I'll return below and in subsequent chapters to the MBA framing of the particular challenges posed, and managerial talents required, by international business environments. The task for the moment is to examine the supposedly more straightforward process of applying managerial common sense.

The goal of this chapter is to evoke ethnographically the curricular and paracurricular experiences of MBA students to show how these instill specific sensibilities and orientations to learning and making decisions about the world. To that end, I focus first on correlated processes of compression: time compression and preparation for the fast-paced milieu of business, and the compression of complexity to render the world tractable to business logic. I then turn to counterbalancing claims about managerial action: that it is grounded as much in competent application of technical business knowledge as it is in the realization of qualities of the self. These qualities—talent, leadership, insight—supplement the managerial capacity to rise to the challenge of managing under conditions of incomplete information, with regard to a world that is always more complicated than we can know, and under relentlessly pressing deadlines for decisions and actions. Lurking just beyond all of this, at the edges of managerial decisions configuring information to shape a course of action, is the prospect of risk: a framing of the unknown future that is inevitable and essential to the value proposition of the international MBA.

COMPRESSION AND THE PARACURRICULUM

MBA programs do more than provide technical information (or entrée to elite networks). They instill habits that shape the ways future managers assimilate and act on that information. Indeed, they constitute the very idea of a manager as a particular orientation, enabling a practical engagement with fast-paced complexity. This is a claim about the world and how best to manage it; the fluent embodiment of this worldview is a key emic marker of the MBA "culture of expertise" (Holmes and Marcus 2008).[1]

The sense of "compression" as a key characteristic of late capitalist conditions of globalization was stressed by the geographer David Harvey (1989). Technological changes facilitating communication and transportation around the globe and speeding up decision processes to keep pace with an accelerating flow of information and rapidly changing tastes and consumption patterns all amounted to what Harvey dubbed "time-space compression." Nigel Thrift (2000) has underscored a corollary need for managerial "fast subjects" adequate to the pace of the "new economy." These (critical) analyses converge with contemporary capitalism's sense of itself—at least as reflected in business schools. MBA curricula are designed to produce these fast subjects, confirming a native ideology of capitalism in the training of the managers destined to reproduce it.

In preparing managers for what they cast as the fast-paced life of the executive, MBA programs promise a "boot camp"–like intensity, and a 24/7 learning environment.[2] MBA administrators and lead faculty revel in this; in orientation sessions, new MBA students are challenged to prepare themselves to "drink from a fire hose": assimilating an overwhelming flow of information. Assignments come quickly and MBAs are soon counseled to avoid the "paralysis of analysis" to be able to select only the details relevant to decision and action. During Kevin's class on International Strategy, he called attention to an apt quote from the reading, "It's on page 90, toward the end, so maybe you were skimming at that point." The comment elicited rueful chuckles; rather than a scolding of students for not applying themselves, it came across as wry affirmation of the MBA/managerial orientation:

skimming for key information in a world filled with too much reading and providing too little time to prepare for effective action. This has particular implications for the engagement with international difference and the routinized discernment of which differences make a difference.

One inheritance of the late twentieth-century development of MBA curricula is the idea of the MBA "core": a compressed summary of standard functional business knowledge. As initially conceived, this rendition of core content filled much of the first two semesters and part of the third as MBA students were expected to develop specializations over their second year in the program (see chapter 3). Increasingly, however, there has been a compression of the compression, as MBA programs have found ways to deliver the core in an ever more abbreviated fashion. Stories from MBA faculty about their experiences teaching core courses were often punctuated by asides, "this was when our core was for the full first year. Now it's just one semester." MBA programs deliver this compressed content in a range of ways—sometimes breaking down the university semester or trimester into shorter modules within which a coordinated set of basic functional courses (say, accounting, finance, economics, professional communication, marketing, data analysis) is taught. The fast pace, hyperstructured delivery, and the clear sense of being in a different institutional time than the typical semester rhythm, all contribute to a liminal, hazing quality of the self-consciously intense MBA experience.

This is compounded by a set of other obligatory activities. For instance, MBAs are typically assigned to small teams of four or five students, who share responsibilities for project assignments in the core classes, and also work together on other curricular activities such as case study competitions or simulation games. In addition, the MBA calendar is filled with visits from recruiters and talks from invited executives (often alumni), and MBA students are strongly encouraged to attend and to network.[3] All of these events are directly connected to the cultivation of MBA professional selves. At one program, for instance, one of my research visits coincided with a visit by CNBC's Jim Cramer, who was there as part of his (then) yearly Mad Money college tour. As I observed an MBA class later that day, the professor started with a clip from local news coverage of the Mad Money visit. Although he was dismissive of Cramer's antics, he offered the clip as a point of reference for the MBAs who, he knew, were always thinking about how to present their "story" to a recruiter or to the media.

Finally, the MBA experience is further shaped by a set of other extracurricular activities involving business school student-government organizations and a host of clubs and student societies. These range from some tongue-in-cheek clubs designed for socializing and networking among students (as in the "Mug Club" that meets weekly at a local bar near one school), to clubs intended to enhance the curriculum through topics of interest to students (as in the Global Business Society, or the Latin American Business Society), to clubs devoted to activities like golfing or wine-tasting, which seem to be more about rounding out the professional selves of the MBAs by cultivating more executive-appropriate aptitudes.

This hazing of excessive curricular content, one-hundred-hour work-weeks, and hyper-scheduled days of classes, team projects, meetings with recruiters, and obligatory extracurricular activities, aptly marks this liminal moment in budding managerial lives. Together they constitute a paracurriculum, a layering of experiences by which MBA programs promise to simulate the truths of managerial business practices. This is the mold for MBA subjects, who emerge as the authorized agents of the production of the world the programs aim to approximate.

Of course, MBA programs are not accurate reflections of the real world of business; they are motivated claims about that world. Notwithstanding their reputations as theory-free zones, then, MBA students come to embody a theoretical representation of contemporary capitalism through a set of ritualized performances over the course of their training. Much like other rituals, the MBA programs convert theory into flesh. This is not to suggest that there is a unidirectional process of MBA faculty imposing their claims about the world upon their students. Faculty are acutely aware of the demands of their students and some described adapting their courses to better match the expectations of their tuition-paying customers. In one case, for instance, a faculty member described pressure to continually update the teaching cases he used to accommodate MBA student complaints that cases from more than a few years ago were irrelevant.

> These guys are brutal at looking at dates. And sometimes I get frustrated with them. They'll see a date like 2002 and they'll say "yea, well, it probably doesn't hold today." Well, it DOES hold today. What we're looking at is much more, uh, it travels very well across time if you really understand the underlying issues: the government policy, the local environment.

And the MBA programs are also performing for corporate recruiters who validate the training imparted by the programs even as they also maneuver to attach themselves to the excellence of leading business schools (cf. Ho 2009).

In this regard, the theory-rich environment of MBA training is coproduced out of a synergy of faculty and administrators, student demands, and the expectations of industry. The contours of that theory distill the current state of the push-pull relationship between MBA education and the amorphous field of "business" they claim to be: the professional gateway for—a market they simultaneously chase and make, often in sharply hierarchized competition with other ranked programs.

Simulacra of the World

The pace and burden of MBA education are presented as a taste of real-world business. Students are put on notice that they are accountable to professional-level expectations of the sort they will encounter in their "real" jobs. Faculty and staff strive to embody and enforce these expectations, and the students police themselves. A memo from the first-year academic council at one program reminds their classmates to arrive in class on time, scolding "Remember, this is a professional school. You would not arrive late to a meeting with your employer." A professor of strategy begins the course with a survey of students asking about their work experience as well as their aspirations ("Have you owned or are you interested in owning your own firm or being self-employed? In what size company and in what industry do you think you will work after your MBA?").

And, as the academic council behind the memo and the host of MBA student organizations make clear, the program itself is a quasi-professional space, filling MBA calendars and requiring performances of professionalism. Many programs issue MBAs lapel pins or name badges with the business school logo. These and other branded accoutrements of professional belonging, such as notebooks, portfolios, or distinct online spaces for accessing readings, submitting coursework, or networking with teammates, all fashion an "in group" exclusivity that evokes a corporate world. Recruiter swag—say, water bottles with names of prominent consulting firms—provide additional tokens of corporate aspirations.

The simulation of corporate life extends to the physical spaces of most business schools. Some boast recently designed buildings with opulent atria, security guards, and swiped electronic passkeys required for entrance, much like the more exclusive banks and corporate headquarters MBAs are being groomed to join. Sleek meeting rooms await MBA teams working on a presentation; in-house coffee shops and cafeterias include common areas with flat screen TVs broadcasting financial news and stock tickers tracking the markets. In many of these areas, MBA students enacting corporate life are also on display to their cohorts in a cycle of reinforcing simulation.

Faculty promise students that they will keep them in touch with the reality of business. A managerial economist tells us that we will get our "hands dirty with data." Business case studies evoke a magical capitalist realism as docudramas of business challenges. Some programs offer MBAs opportunities to manage investment funds or to provide consulting services to local businesses or proposed start-ups. Industry leaders visiting classes serve as walking cases, telling their stories to the MBAs who aspire to similar careers. Indeed, the role-playing of senior management—challenging students to make (hypothetically) consequential business decisions—has long been a hallmark of MBA coursework (Drucker 1950; see chapter 3). When MBAs are tasked with an exercise more appropriate to lower or middle management, the assignment will often ask them to deliver their work as a recommendation to senior managers. (This is often in the abbreviated format of an executive summary, which further performs the compression of complexity habituated in the MBA curriculum.)

In all of these rituals of simulation, the enactment of capitalist authority is tightly bound to the reproduction of dispositions to the world thought to be essential to successful contemporary business management. Kevin begins a meeting of his International Strategy course with a quote projected on a PowerPoint slide: "The beast lumbers on painfully aware of small insect bites and nearby shrubbery without ever noticing whether it is walking toward a cliff or to a grazing site in the distance." He tells the class that it was shared with him "by a financial analyst at a Fortune 100 company," and then uses the quote as a springboard to the topic of the day, which involved the balancing of details and big-picture information in international business. The caution to not get lost in the details frames the class discussion and also indexically authorizes Kevin through his links to active business elite. (As we shall see below, international business analysis rests on an assertive scaling and commensuration of complexity to take in the big picture, while at the same time requiring the excess and abundance of detail as part of the qualitative value potential of international business space.)

The class session also included a visitor: a manager from a US manufacturing firm recently acquired by a European company and with international assignments dating from the early 1990s in Singapore, Mexico, Cairo, and India. He discusses his experiences and missteps in international strategy. He starts with a plug for the class.

This dialogue in class reflects what our company has been through in the last 10 years that I've been with them. Things are changing rapidly. We would have done things differently if we had a brainstorming session like this a few years ago. Good to know there are classes preparing people for the international arena. A few years back, certainly in my area, it was one of those things that maybe you got involved in and maybe you didn't.

Along with the legitimacy of real business experience that his presence brings to the classroom, his comments suggest that the classroom discussions are of a kind with the sort that happen (or should be happening) in corporate meetings.

MBA programs are positioned as rituals of simulation in a host of other ways. Class presentations are staged as presentations to a board of directors or stockholders; team assignments claim to replicate the fast pace and high pressure of a business environment. Some programs make use of exercises in which MBA teams manage computer-simulated firms, taking them through a set of decisions linked to quarterly reports that convey the results of previous decisions. Over the week of the simulation, the intensity of the quarterly decision cycle is stepped up: the three-hour window for the earliest team decision is gradually reduced until the teams have only an hour and thirty minutes.

These are the training grounds for the managerial distillation of complexity. MBA programs cultivate a communicative habitus emphasizing brevity and the controlled compression of key points to motivate sufficiently informed action. Through one-page "executive summaries" or thirty-second "elevator pitches," aspiring capitalists are encouraged to create an optic of cut-and-dried essentiality. These exercises in brevity conjure a professional setting: you have been asked by your boss for your opinion and you have the duration of the elevator ride to present your case; you have prepared a detailed report and now must convey your findings in the one page a busy CEO will have time and patience to read.

Such brevity and compression, we will see, is only half the story. Alongside the routinized commensuration of complexity is an acknowledgment of irreducible singularity, requiring MBAs to draw on a distinct repertoire of managerial talents. The following sections focus on the presentation of the more technical skills and concepts in the MBA core curriculum. Later in the chapter, I turn to the framing of the complementary "art" of management, cast as crucial to doing business in a world that exceeds its models. Managing this excess of the world is particularly relevant to international business contexts.

Of course, MBA curricula are also about the teaching in condensed form of basic functional areas of business: typically some combination of accounting, economics, finance, marketing, organizational theory, statistics or data analysis, professional communication, and ethics.[4] The language of function, however, masks the ways these courses—perhaps particularly in their heavily distilled form—rest upon a set of mutually reinforcing assumptions about the world and the aims of business. Many of these assumptions are so ubiquitous and commonsensical—particularly as they have been routinized across so many domains of life under neoliberalism—that rehearsing them here may seem unnecessary. There is analytic value, and anthropological pedigree, however, in calling attention to such hegemonic assumptions that go without saying because they come without saying (Bourdieu 1977, 167). Business schools, like other institutions of explicit social reproduction, are places where the unsaid, and seemingly unremarkable, comes closest to the surface.

But something more is happening here. Business schools weave these axioms into a dense, self-contained worldview that shapes, because it is held to require, a specific MBA subjectivity. As it is presented in MBA programs, international cross-cultural business scaffolds upon this naturalized understanding of (compelled) managerial qualities with specific implications for what is announced as the requisite twenty-first-century global manager. There is something of a corollary cultural circuit of capitalism (cf. Thrift 2005) at play here, as business schools produce the world that embodies the demand for the managerial talent only business schools can provide. In this regard, international space is not an exception to the general capitalist rule; rather, global business contexts are presented as the cask-strength world of business, an especially dense embodiment of the sort of challenges, risks, and potential that are the core rationale for the application of managerial capitalism as taught in contemporary MBA programs.

Kevin's class had previously examined the case of Royal Dutch Shell—a popular business school case study that examines Shell's strategy with respect to oil and gas reserves on Russia's Sakhalin Island (e.g., Abdelal 2006). The case rests on Shell's decisions to tolerate and mitigate risks as part of a tenuously structured joint venture in Russia. Among the challenges facing Shell in the 2007 case are: changing internal politics in Russia, particularly as Vladimir Putin consolidated power and sought to renationalize control of Russian oil production through the national company Gazprom; the differing mechanics of extraction, production, and distribution for oil and liquefied natural gas; and the complexities of a variety of legal and quasi-legal instruments involving joint ventures, production-sharing agreements, and other arrangements designed to increase the likelihood that Shell would recover its initial investment in the venture and have legal recourse outside of the opaque Russian legal system in the event of any disputes. Teaching notes[5] for the case advise instructors to subordinate details of the Russian political situation and encourage students to think about the physical realities of Sakhalin's location and related challenges of infrastructure and transportation, as well as the fundamentals of producing oil and gas as commodities. The upshot of this is that, given the unquestioned orientation of Shell as a global oil company, the risks posed by the Russian case are presented as normal "costs of doing business." Shell's experiences with production-sharing agreements, and the structure of joint venture arrangements can help students think about ways of mitigating risk factors. But among the takeaways of the case is that Shell's decision to face these risks was an expression of a business model that all but requires doing business in what is referred to delicately in the case as "difficult places." MBAs are asked to consider how Shell's "bottom line" performance would be impacted if they refused to do business in countries characterized by this sort of political and economic risk and instability.

The parable of the lumbering beast captures this dimension of the case analysis, as the MBAs are cautioned against getting lost in the specifics of Russian political economy. As Kevin noted, updating the case with some more current news stories about the Sakhalin project, Shell's alternatives to production in Russia include projects in Nigeria, Venezuela, or Iran. These are quickly deemed commensurate along the dimension of risk, and those country-level details drop out of the decision, leaving only the residue of risk that will shape a firm's expected return from a project undertaken in such "difficult places." This conjuring of pure risk, distilled from the particularities of context is a key by-product of MBA habits of commensuration and compression.

Kevin's strategy class that day was focused on Michael Porter's classic work of international business: "The Competitive Advantage of Nations" (Porter 1990). In contrast with David Ricardo's (1817) discussion of the *comparative* advantage of nations, Porter argues that a nation's competitiveness in international business is made rather than found—a function of policy environments, education of a labor force, and innovative strategy implemented by managers. Reviewing a series of national success stories, Porter distills the lessons learned into a set of four factors determining national competitiveness: Firm Strategy, Structure, and Rivalry; Demand Conditions; Related and Supporting Industries; Factor Conditions. The four factors[6] are themselves further distilled through their graphical rendering as a "diamond," with a box for each factor at each of the corners, and arrows indicating the interactions between each pair of factors. Later in the class, Kevin would ask the MBAs how they might update "Porter's diamond" to better reflect contemporary international business. But there was little question that some sort of dimensional rendering of distilled features could provide a crystalline and powerful tool for commensurating and comparing diverse national business contexts. This is the big-picture view of strategy, ensuring that the lumbering beast is not heading for a cliff.

As Peter Navarro (2008) has noted in his survey of MBA curricula, "strategy" courses have often served as something of a "capstone" for MBA programs. This is because they draw on knowledge and skills rooted in functional courses in the curriculum and, in scaling from details and data to big-picture considerations, they enact the apotheosis of the managerial vantage. In this regard, the various functional courses focused on accounting, marketing, and so forth provide the MBAs with a basic grammar of compression and commensuration. It is to the teaching of those more elemental skills and habits in MBA curricula that I now turn.

Modules, Markets, and Graphs

Economics, Data Analysis, and Finance. These were part of a first-year module that also included courses in Marketing, Accounting, and Professional Communication. These first-term courses provide a basic competency in the language and techniques of business. And they do so through a cascade of mutually reinforcing representations that make presupposable a characterization of the world as a specific sort of problem space requiring specific managerial orientations.

These three classes reinforce an aggressive simplification of complexity, adequate to the sort of fast-paced decision-making that MBAs are told is the characteristic of a successful manager. These classes routinize the reduction of complexity to actionable elements through a series of articulating "just so" stories about the world. This is, perhaps, most evident in Economics, where so many axiomatic claims turn on a rendering of the world as a two-dimensional matrix. Consider, for instance, the classic graph space of economists illustrating the relationship between supply and demand or plotting, say, the relationship between the price of a cup of coffee and the supply of coffee beans, or drawing an indifference curve to plot consumer choices between purchasing milk or Mountain Dew.

These renderings are claims about the representability of the world and a good deal of work goes into defending these two-dimensional graphical representations. An economics professor pauses during our second class meeting to acknowledge that the demand curves he has been drawing assume linearity. "The real world is more complex," he says, "but adding complexity doesn't give us more answers." Similarly, in our first Data Analysis class, as we work through a case involving a decision concerning whether to produce road bikes or mountain bikes, the professor develops a model to assess the probability of sales of the two different bikes, stressing the need for models that "simplify a complex reality." He said our "initial reactions may be, 'that's not how the world really works.'" But, he added,

> Compare high school Newtonian physics; [it's] not about whether it is real or not, it is whether it is useful or not. . . . Don't prejudge about whether it seems realistic to you. The models we'll be showing you have proved to be useful many, many times.

In an interview with a professor of International Finance, I respond to her extensive comments about exchange rates by asking whether it is only exchange rates that matter. What are some other factors? She responds that it is not only exchange rates,

> in finance there are a whole host of things we tend to extract from. . . . One of our behavioral assumptions is that what matters to investors are the expected return they might get and the risks associated with that. So we take all of the stuff out there and basically map it into those two dimensions.

And in a core Finance course (with a different professor), the class begins with a series of exercises aimed at a binary "deal or no-deal" decision based upon a comparison of value across two different states of the world. After working through the calculation of future values of investments at known interest rates ($2,000 invested at 10% per year for one year is $2,200; conversely, if you had agreed to pay me $2,200 next year, I would also accept a payment of $2,000 today), we consider some scenarios. A land deal promising a return in two years of $12,000 on $80,000 invested is a bad deal if financial markets are returning 8%, but an attractive alternative if prevailing rates are 7%.

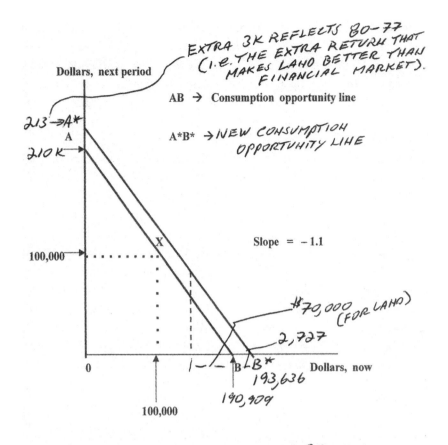

Dollars, next period

EXTRA 3K REFLECTS 80-77 (I.e. THE EXTRA RETURN THAT MAKES LAND BETTER THAN FINANCIAL MARKET).

AB → Consumption opportunity line

A*B* → *NEW CONSUMPTION OPPORTUNITY LINE*

213 →A*
A
210K

Slope = − 1.1

100,000

X

$70,000 (FOR LAND)

2,727

0   B *B**   Dollars, now
193,636
190,909

100,000

Land cost = 70,000   [can be sold next period for *80,000*

FIGURE I. Consumption choices revealed in black and white (source: author's notes).

We return to a two-dimensional graphical representation, familiar from Economics, to clarify the comparison by mapping investment decisions as "consumption opportunities" (see figure 1). I have an annual income of $100,000. We draw a graph for a two-year period depicting the money I might have available to invest now along the horizontal axis, and the dollars I might have available in the "next period" (i.e., next year). A line with a slope reflecting the prevailing interest rate (10%) connects the axes: reflecting up to $190,909 available for present use (this includes my $100,000 as well as the present value of next year's $100,000 discounted by the 10% interest rate [$90,909]), and up to $210,000 potentially available next year ($100,000 invested at 10% [= $110,000] plus the $100,000 I expect next year). The space under the line (A—B), we are told, reflects the various ways I might consume or invest my money and the implications for the amount I would have available in the next period under the prevailing rate of interest. An alternative investment opportunity is depicted by a new line on the graph: an investment of $70,000 in land will yield $80,000 next year. That opportunity displaces my line of consumption choices revealing in black and white (and x and y) whether and to what degree the investment option improves or diminishes my position. (It shows that any consumption choice in the present period leaves me better off, as reflected by the vertical axis values along the line A^*—B^*, than under the original range of opportunities.)

These two-dimensional simplifications and the hypothetical decisions connected to them are further routinized by repetitive classroom and homework exercises. That these seem geared as much to having us develop a facility with our business calculators and relevant Excel functions further dissociates the comparison of calculated future values (Did I get it right?) from any reflection on the business principles at stake, the simplifying assumptions about interest rates or potential risks, or the autonomy of the "investor."

MBA life is saturated with these graphs, charts, and curves, and one takeaway, of course, is that the world is knowable in this two-dimensional format. One significant outcome of this habit of simplification is the immediate commensuration of alternative states of the world. Choices are clear.

Marketness

One thing that makes these graphical representations of the world compelling is that they are cast as distillations of a more perfect truth: the market. The market emerges across the MBA curriculum as an abstract aggregator of individual human behavior that perfectly condenses and enables a more collective social state. The market, MBAs are taught, is an allocation mechanism that enables the distribution of resources that are always limited and scarce. A central planner or king (these are the "central casting" alternatives to the market in MBA programs)[7] could do a good job allocating resources. But as social complexity increases, the job becomes humanly impossible. "In a big economy the number of decisions to be made is very, very high." So, there is a whiff of the Durkheimian about the market, which, in a way that is greater than the sum of its individually trading parts, comes to shape collective behavior.

Now, there is a curious temporal sleight of hand here. By one reckoning the market is a lagging indicator. It comes into view always at the trailing edge of action in the world, the precipitate of a state of supply, demand, and the pecuniary decision of buyers and sellers. At the same time, however, as a synoptic rendering of the immediate past, the market is celebrated as a powerful indicator of the future. MBAs learn this through anecdotal examples like the political futures market, where traders can buy and sell futures contracts linked to the predicted success of candidates for office, or accounts of experiments in behavioral economics that look at the ways information available to only a few participants becomes generalized across the market. The takeaway for MBAs is that (experts agree!) markets are efficient information aggregators and that the nature of market engagement (investment, or "skin in the game") endows market information with a purity of truth that confers significant predictive powers. As one MBA economics faculty rhapsodized: "[The] market is extracting information from the heads of all participants and the market somehow knows what information is good and what is bad. We don't know how this process works."

The conceptual power of the market idea stems from its range of flexibility. Markets are ontologically "shifty," signifying differently across a variety of domains of business. This is not to suggest that the market idea is semantically empty, but, much like indexical shifters (words like "you," "here," or "now"), the market takes its meaning from an interactional context. That such a load-bearing concept of capitalism operates in such a flexible and contingent way should make us alert to the supporting cultural work necessary to sustain the world of capitalism.

Market is a strongly spatial concept, grounded in the classic referent of a physical marketplace where buyers and sellers interact. However, the term is serial and scalable, aligning national, regional, and global frames. One market may be interchangeable with another. A professor of international management points out that managers with successful international postings on their resume, who have proved themselves to be "good in a number of markets," are assumed to be a good fit for any other foreign assignment, "because of what they know about the business and doing business worldwide."

In other conversations, firms operating internationally are cast as needing to assess and manage their relative orientation to "home" or other markets. Here, markets are aligned through scalar or relational arrows and "market" provides a shorthand for referencing a place through its business connections with other places. A case in an Operations Management course takes up a decision by a joint venture involving Hewlett Packard to enter "the Japanese market." Another discussion looks at manufacturing processes in Europe and the tension between factories making distinct product lines tailored to the demands of separate national markets and the emergence of a more unified European market. In the catechism of operations management, the single market allows a single factory to produce a larger volume of a product with a greater geographical spread and allows what would have been other factories producing nation-specific variations of a single product to instead make distinct products of their own. This is cast as a struggle between the end-user-focused marketing specialists and the factory-focused operations management people, but the scalable presupposability of the market—national or regional—serves each of their causes. The extension of the term gives a spatial solidity and bundleability to things of varying scale.

A similar effect is achieved by the use of "market" to frame an industry, a product, or a service. Thus, the visiting executive in Kevin's strategy class discussed a decision he faced as an executive for a US company that manufactures transmission components and gears whether to "pull the plug" on an investment in a factory in India. "I understood the market," he told the MBAs, "and put together a business plan projecting success based on market changes in the United States and opportunities in India." A finance professor, Natalie, illustrates the focus on exchange rates (rather than cultural factors) in international finance, and ends up illuminating the scalability of country-level and global financial markets:

> From the perspective of finance, we kind of neglect these cultural differences. And we look at it from a perspective of, you know, "here you've got one economy, here you've got another and the only thing different is an exchange rate between these two. Once you deal with the exchange rate, then it's all one market." I think there's a tendency to view the world along those lines. And I think the world is moving in that direction. Are you familiar with statistical correlations? If two markets are segmented, driven by different factors, returns from those markets will be relatively uncorrelated, close to zero. If they're driven by similar factors, that correlation will start to rise. And what we're seeing in a lot of these markets is that the correlation seems to be drifting upwards over time.

I asked her if that correlation was an index of globalization.

> I think it's one measure, and it is in part because you have larger investors—mutual funds, hedge funds—trying to get the best return and increasingly looking to markets that people haven't really paid attention to as much in hopes of finding something better. Like looking for a new fishing hole.

Finally, consider David: an MBA student talking the talk as he described his interest in international business in terms of his background in the "tech" field. "The market here is tapped out," he told me. Instead, he saw his opportunity as an MBA to learn about emerging markets—particularly in South America—"as an opportunity to jump in and see where the market was going to be . . . maybe not in 5 years, but 10 years down the line."

As these last comments illustrate, while the use of market to describe a business sector is not strictly spatial, the solidity conveyed by the market metaphor can be attached to a space—the tech market in Latin America. So there is some ontological resonance and feedback whereby geographical/political/cultural/spatial buckets give shape to markets and markets become a shorthand for gesturing to a sort of boundedness roughly equivalent to—because it is indexically associated with—national, regional, and global frameworks. One upshot of this effect is that the use of the market frame helps establish a serialized commensuration as any referent "market" *as a market* becomes locatable as one among a set of relatively like units varying by geographical coordinates (Japanese vs. "home" [United States]), by industry (tech vs. healthcare), or by scale (nation vs. region vs. global), but similar enough to make self-evident the utter comparability of the units for the purposes of the extension or transfer of action from one frame to another. Talking about the "market" is thus a discursive achievement with specific consequences for a managerial framing of the world. In the context of international business, the market idea is an engine of commensuration that frames specific paths of capitalist action.

At stake here (and with apologies to linguists everywhere) is a quality of "marketness:" a condition of relative coherence vis-à-vis some channel of capitalist practice.[8] In linguistics, *markedness* indicates a subordinate term in a semantic pair or set, such that the subordinate term is marked while the unmarked dominant term is otherwise presupposed and may even stand for the entire domain.[9] I intend marketness to evoke a relational condition created by the market frame. That is, with an entire world available to capitalism, claims of marketness denote and define operable parts of the global whole. Marketness brings capitalist potential into actionable focus.

A correlated implication of marketness, then, is that it opens up a specific sort of agentive space for the business actor. As spaces of action, markets are produced by capitalist agency. That is to say, a space (physical or virtual) is realized as a market from the vantage of, and as a condition of, a specific business action or intent. In this sense, markets are a pragmatic result of capitalist consideration, called into being by a specific sort of comparative, commensurative evaluation of some part of the world.

This last point is close to the sort of argument made by some scholars regarding the performativity of markets. A number of these discussions have focused on markets as social collectivities to underscore that market functions emerge as much from social relations among participants as from the supply and demand drivers of market relations (Ortiz 2014, Preda 2009; cf. White 1981). Others key on the impact of influential theories about market behavior to argue that markets effectively perform theory (Callon 2007; MacKenzie 2006). These discussions share with my argument here a commitment to the proposition that markets are made rather than found, embedded as they always are in a host of social and cultural contexts (cf. Granovetter 1985). But a more precise point to be made in the present case concerns the ways the subjective capitalist orientation effects the attachment of the market metaphor (i.e., marketness)—with all of its shorthand, naturalizing, commensurating entailments—to spatialized units. Marketness entails the culturally motivated capitalist bundling of spatialized phenomena.

Made though they may be, markets are not created ex nihilo from the vantage of each agent. Markets that are called into being by capitalist inclinations at the same time appear or are figured as collective agentive forces compelling new actions by managers. Recall the student's comment above about a "tapped out" tech market. Or consider the comments of an industry visitor discussing three typical reasons for going global. One involves a desire for growth. Another has to do with international acquisitions. The third was cast as a response to (fetishized) market forces: "Market came in and said, 'if you don't do this, I'm going to do that to you.'"

Although the sources of the market's powers remain mysterious, the aspiring MBAs are compelled through an interlocked set of course lectures, assignments, and team exercises to base managerial action with respect to established claims about the market. They are taught that managerial action requires tapping the wisdom of the market and extrapolating from the two-dimensional renderings of market space to learn what the market may have to tell us about the future.

Futures

The Economics module pivots about halfway through the course from the axiomatic truths of consumer theory to a focus on the theory of the firm, introduced as an "entity that bears risk, brings in inputs and makes outputs that it hopes to sell in such a way that it has positive residuals [i.e., profits]." The framing recasts the apparently natural behavior reflected in consumer theory into a temporal framework marked by the future-reaching sequence of inputs and outputs, directed by hope, and negotiating the risk of uncertainty. The turn to the firm sets up the explicit space of managerial subjectivity for which MBAs are being groomed, in the process naturalizing a very specific compulsion to the future. With the future comes risk; like the future, risk is inevitable.

MBA students quickly learn that they are being schooled to be time travelers—adepts of the future. This is nowhere more apparent than in their introductory Finance course. The course turns around a core concept—the time value of money—and, as we have seen, routinizes an assessment of capital as always accountable to potential future increases. The time value of money sets up a ceaseless compulsion to move money into the future by introducing the only certainty: that money not circulating is degrading in value—at least as compared with the forgone possibilities of increase.

The Finance course begins in sync with the consumer theory section of the Economics course: my first notes report that "money is worthless unless you consume," to which was added "financial markets help us choose consumption patterns." Scaffolding on the truths of economics, our Finance professor told us that financial markets facilitate the efficient transfer of funds from savers to borrowers and that the market thus establishes an equilibrium rate of interest reflecting the balance of the supply of capital and the demand for capital. This benchmark equilibrium rate poses a double bind for capital. On the one hand, capital not moving is degrading. On the other, moving capital not surpassing the equilibrium rate is falling short.

As "colonists of the future" (cf. Zaloom 2004), managers are compelled to push beyond the boundaries of certainty. The firm, introduced in Economics as "an entity that bears risk ... [hoping for] positive residuals" is here described as "a bundle of cash flows."[10] The objective of the financial manager is to "maximize shareholder value" by accepting investment opportunities for those cash flows that surpass the benchmark interest rate.

Put differently, this is about moving into a space not fully captured by the models. This is not the cliché of staying ahead of the (graphed) curve; this is about being *off* of the curve. The curve traces the boundary of certainty through a modeling of the past. As a claim about the world, it sets a putatively risk-free standard. Compelled to go beyond the benchmark, MBAs are told they must evaluate future states of the world to assess their desirability. This is, unsurprisingly, difficult to do. In the Finance course, this is when the concept of risk is formally introduced. Indeed, "risk" becomes a shorthand for the possible qualitative states of the world that cannot yet be distilled into the reduced dimensions of the graphical and formulaic representations—a bundling of complex excess and uncertainty.

The narrative arc of these courses moves from the foundational simplicity of the two-dimensional graphs and binary state comparisons to representations of an admittedly more complicated world. That is not remarkable. More significant is that the complexity remains ultimately reducible to the foundational principles. They weren't kidding when they said "adding complexity doesn't give us more answers." Rather, the complexity of additional unknowns is bundled as a single measurable supplement to the formula: an additional variable. Indeed, in many models for evaluating risk, analysts lean on the mystical power of the market to render complexity by sampling market data from different points in history and using past variation as an indication of the range of possible uncertainty in the future.

This is the basis of a "risk premium"; that is, the increment above the benchmark rate of interest that reflects the extra rate of return investors should reasonably expect for assuming the risk entailed by the investment. Risk is a supplement and quality, characterizing and bundling the excess of the world—an excess MBAs learn to see in especially potent form in international settings. The concept of risk thus manages a messy world, preserving the plausibility of the sleek certainties of business logic otherwise conveyed in MBA programs. This is nicely captured in a performative preference for pithy turns of phrases and authoritative aphorisms.

Aphorisms

> Eye level is buy level.
> If you can measure it, you can manage it.
> If it's cold, it's sold.
> Capital is a coward.
> Clicks not bricks.
> The paralysis of analysis.
> You have to risk it for the biscuit.
> Culture eats strategy.

MBA education, and business culture more generally, is saturated with aphorisms. These pithy turns of phrase are dropped into MBA class discussions and repeated by students in their classroom presentations. They perform a style of swaggering fast-paced certainty as they embody distilled truths from the front lines of managerial capitalism. They also serve as alibis for commensuration and standardization; explicitly in the "if you can measure it, you can manage it" example, but equally for the others insofar as they come across as natural law. These aphorisms are part of a broader set of stylistic tropes of management speak that stand as qualisigns of a managerial subjectivity: they embody a quality or style that has come to signify capitalist expertise (cf. Peirce 1955).

Other examples include mnemonic procedures such as the marketing catechisms of "Four Ps" (Product/Promotion/Price/Place) and "Three Cs" (Customers/Competitors/Collaborators). These function as a checklist of thinking through the details of a given case, thus rendering specific details commensurable through a routinized set of analytic categories. Euphony and alliteration contribute to the mnemonic convenience of these checklists, but they also give weight and elegance to this as a compelling claim about the manageability of the world. A quick turn to the internet will reveal alternative Ps and Cs and even (radical!) claims that there might be Five Ps and as many as Four Cs. That variation underscores my point that the key feature here is not the conceptual details of the mnemonic but the quality of sleek managerial certainty conveyed by the shorthand. This business aesthetic of compression is applied most directly to global business practices through the tendency in recent decades to denote clusters of favored emerging economies with acronyms like BRICS, MINTs, and CIVETS (see chapter 5).

And all of this is of a piece with a broader stylistic habit in business publication like the *Harvard Business Review* or *McKinsey Quarterly* to stud longer articles with pull quotes and pithy graphics delivering key takeaways in parallel with the main text. This is a graphical rendering of an executive summary, and it sets up a surface-level payoff, which may be reward enough for a busy manager. Of course, if a manager decides to learn more, she can always examine the article at a more "granular level" through a "deep dive" into the issue. I write this with my tongue in cheek, but the metaphorical richness of these terms (not limited to business, but cultivated there) discloses a play between an acknowledged and presupposed three-dimensional problem space, for the reckoning of which a well-crafted two-dimensional mnemonic insight may be good enough. In this sense, MBAs learn to do things with words in ways comparable to how they do things with graphs.

Perhaps the most familiar sense of "margin" has to do with the edges of legibility and convention: the unknowable, the unusual, the foreign. Think of marginalia, the emendations at the edges of a text or a ledger book that point to meanings that escape the systematicity of the main body of writing, or an area that reflects the notes and calculations that transform the raw data into entries in the ledger. In all of these senses, margins mark and manage the space between incommensurable singularity and the serial commensurations of ordered information.

Margin[11] is a multiply resonant term in "business speak." For traders, the margin can refer to borrowed capital used in an investment or an account of personal funds deposited as a guarantee of a percentage of the value being traded through securities. Margin is also a synonym for profit—the space between a selling price and the cost of production. In all of these cases, the margin is a space of pure risk and potential—it is a measure of "skin in the game," while it also points to the anticipated, but unknowable, future state of a market transaction.

In this regard, consider "marginal analysis." A fundamental calculus of capitalist thought, marginal analysis presumes to calculate the cost and profit potential of the $n + 1$ item in a series of actions currently containing n moves. It is a way of reckoning incremental change and it is grounded in the premise that additional effort will eventually yield diminishing returns. An economics professor, Dennis, introduces this with the concept of diminishing marginal production, illustrated with a graph tracking changes in a factory's output (see figure 2). Under a "short run" (SR) scenario, which is premised on holding certain variables such as capital expenditures (K) constant, the y-axis tracks output quantity and the x-axis labor inputs. Although adding labor through second or third shifts will increase the output quantity, at a certain point additional labor will not increase output beyond the physical capacity of the production line. This is presented to the class as "a grim law handed to us by nature that we can't get around," reflected in the changing slope of the curve.

Given this natural law (which only applies in the unnatural environment of a single-variable economic thought experiment), the MBAs are next invited to consider "marginal cost" and "marginal revenue." Here, the MBAs work with the graph of diminishing returns to track the relationship between total cost and output quantity. Labor is taken out of the equation (except implicitly as a driver of cost and a factor in output quantity) and the managers in training

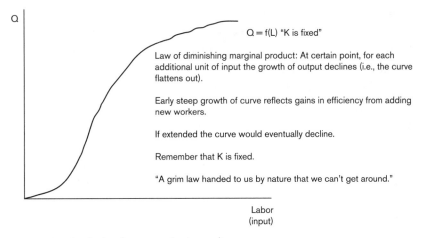

Q

Q = f(L) "K is fixed"

Law of diminishing marginal product: At certain point, for each additional unit of input the growth of output declines (i.e., the curve flattens out).

Early steep growth of curve reflects gains in efficiency from adding new workers.

If extended the curve would eventually decline.

Remember that K is fixed.

"A grim law handed to us by nature that we can't get around."

Labor
(input)

FIGURE 2. A grim law (source: author's notes).

see that the slope of the graph of total cost (TC)—the rate of increase in cost— changes at different points along the axis of output quantity. This changing rate of change of total cost—a derivative dTC/dO—is the marginal cost (MC). It can itself be graphed, and the resulting graph is a U-shape showing that the rate of increase in cost for increased production is relatively high at low output quantities, declines to a relatively efficient sweet spot, and then rises again in obedience to the grim law that after a certain point, more labor does not generate significantly more output (see figure 3).

Marginal revenue (MR) is obtained through a similar graphing process— now mapping the change in total revenue (TR) against the change in quantity. (Labor remains in the background; an explicitly changing variable that never stands for itself.) But here, Dennis introduces a set of other considerations related to the nature of the market and the economist's concept of "perfect competition." Under conditions of perfect competition, a market comprises a large number of small buyers and sellers with no one able to set prices. All products in the market are relatively interchangeable, buyers and sellers can participate or withdraw from the market at will, and all participants have complete information about market choices. This is an economist's just-so story; a theoretical state not likely to be encountered in the world. Dennis tells us that "microeconomists know what happens in competitive economies very, very well." The elegance of a perfectly competitive market is reflected in a graph of marginal revenue, which, we are told, in a competitive economy is a horizontal line as each increase in quantity sold generates the same increase in revenue. Our professor's point is that different industries approximate a competitive economy more or less perfectly. He sketches a continuum from "perfect competition" to "monopoly" with the variation being the number of firms in the market, and this is the entry point to begin to think about the economics of the firm, the impact of different regulatory or tax environments, and the ways various managerial decisions (mergers and acquisitions, predatory pricing, increasing or decreasing production) impact markets.

I review all of this fairly basic economic theory to make two points. The first is that the economists' rendering of axiomatic truths grounded in rarely seen perfect states helps to shape a managerial disposition of navigating through the complexities of the real world according to the compass points of an unattainable condition. This is a commensurating and simplifying move. Moreover, it creates a recursive dichotomization of knowability. Thus, "microeconomists know what happens in competitive economies very, very well," and microeconomists have experience mapping murkier conditions of familiar market contexts according to truths derived from assumptions of perfect competition. This has direct implications for the managerial orientation to international markets, where the deviation from conditions of perfect competition are thought to be greater and less familiar. We will see more of this in chapters 4 and 5, focused on the MBA framing of cultural difference and related dimensions of global and international business contexts.

Given that most market settings deviate from the horizontal-line certainty of a situation of perfect competition and unchanging demand, the graph of marginal revenue will typically be a negative slope rather than a horizontal line, reflecting a decrease in prices as quantity sold increases. This returns us to the classroom and brings up my second point, which is also Dennis's coup: the U-shaped graph of marginal cost can be superimposed on the graph plotting the line of marginal revenue, with the result that the graphs will intersect at two places. The point of intersection farthest from the origin point (i.e., at the greatest quantity sold) is the point at which profits (π) are maximized. This is "a fundamental rule of profit maximization across any kind of market." The point is driven home with an equation—$\pi \max \rightarrow MR = MC$—and further illustrated by shading in the space of the graph bounded by the lower curve of the marginal cost curve and the line of marginal revenue. The result is a sense of profit as a tangible objective fact,

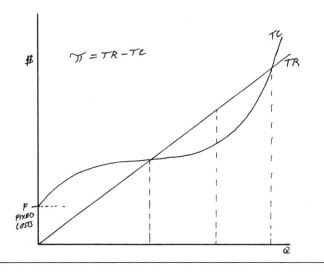

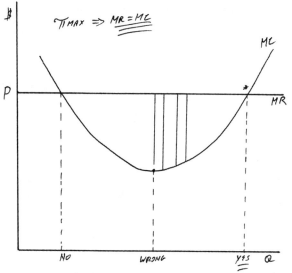

Finding the largest vertical gap at the point where the slopes of two curves are equal (i.e., where they are neither diverging nor converging).

Π = TR−TC

dΠ/dq = 0 = d(TR−TC)/dq = dTR/dq − dTC/dq

   Or, dTR/dq = dTC/dq

| MR | = | MC |

MARGINAL REVENUE = MARGINAL COST. At this point, profits are maximized.

Note that this is derived without reference to kind of market. This is a fundamental rule of profit maximization across any kind of market.

FIGURE 3. Graphing the margins. This composite of hand-drawn graphs and typed notes, from a sequence of a core MBA economics class focused on marginal revenue, reflects both the shorthand rendering of business data and the spatial concreteness and apparent self-evidentness of derivative concepts like marginal cost as they figure in MBA training (source: author's notes).

distilled from the murkier circumstances of imperfect and idiosyncratic markets to clarify a managerial decision.[12] What is the cost or the benefit of producing one more pair of shoes or one more circuit board? As a maximizing decision-making strategy, marginal analysis is a tool for managing the spaces between the singularity of a given moment of production or decision point and the seriality produced by previous moments and decisions, by rendering these all commensurable with respect to grim natural facts and universally applicable laws.

The economics classes I observed reinforced this in a different performative register through the invocation of real-world cases. The marginal analysis material was presented over the course of three class sections, during which Dennis began each session with a presentation of economic themes in the news. This was an effective and engaging strategy to connect with the professional aspirations of the MBA students by tempering the abstract and theoretical tone of introductory economics material. But it also layered in interesting ways with the topical unit and scaffolded on themes from other classes in "the core." Thus, the discussion of marginal analysis was part of a pivot from an introductory section on consumer theory to the economics of the firm. The firm, we were told, was focused on maximizing profit, and a key characteristic of the firm is "the separation of ownership from control" through the device of the stock market (cf. Berle and Means [1932] 1991; Jensen and Meckling 1976; see chapter 3). Dennis added with some gusto that the stock market functions "as enforcer," writing "Mkt will punish you if you fail to max π" on the board. (Recall a similar sense of an animated, and punitive, market in the comments of the visitor to Kevin's strategy class.) Dennis continued to discuss executive compensation in the form of stock options, noting: "Stockholders love this form of compensation . . . [because it serves as] a mechanism to make sure managers have the same incentives stockholders have." He illustrated this somewhat ominously: outside observers might see a "possibility to maximize profit and will take over the firm," firing the current managers. Because the "managers will be worried, they have an incentive to maximize profit."

This grim lesson in economics was underscored during the same week in the first semester module in Finance class, as we started to apply our exercises in the time value of money, calculating the present or future values of investment given certain assumptions of interest rates and other rates of return. We took up examples first of bond and then stock investments, to work through

how bonds and stocks are valued, and how changing interest rates and investment horizons increase or mitigate risk. The wisdom of "the market" was on
display here through discussion of forward rates—interest rates agreed to in
advance of a future bond transaction reflecting "what the market is thinking
about periods in the future." And one of the lessons for future managers,
already nervous about profit maximizing in the interest of shareholders,
was that retained earnings may result in increased dividend payments to
stockowners, but may not increase the value of the stock. The lesson instead
was a ceaseless "need to find projects that give a higher rate of return." Further
reinforcing of the message was available in Accounting class, where the
MBAs were working through cash flow statements to reckon a firm's assets
and liabilities.

In connection with this cascade of reinforcing claims, contemporary news
articles discussed in Economics class included stories about

- a supermarket chain that reported increased earnings for a recent
  quarter, but nonetheless saw their stock price tumble because they missed
  forecast profit margins;
- an investment bank that, despite declining profits, saw their stock price
  surge because their earnings surpassed expectations;
- the ways shoppers in big box stores were hampered by imperfect information about their "bargains";
- the ways new FDA regulations on medical services or new federal
  regulations on corporate accounting practices impose new costs that
  needed to be factored into a firm's cost curve;
- corporate and public pensions severely underfunded because of unrealis-
  tic expectations of growth and beneficiaries' longer life spans.

Through this curated set of hot-off-the-press headlines, Dennis presented the
MBAs with the social lives of margins, much as the other functional core
courses were involved in demonstrating the ways marginal thinking suffused
every dimension of managerial practice.

A final point to be made about the concept of margin is that it is scalable.
This is especially important when we distinguish between margin (revenue
above cost created by each unit sale) and profit (the surplus of total revenue
after costs are deducted). A high margin product may be less profitable than
a low margin product with a high volume of sales. For MBAs being taught to

anticipate international operations—particularly in terms of marketing consumer goods—this is a crucial point. Global marketing courses stress the tremendous opportunities in developing economies where the slightest increase in the purchasing power of the poorest and most numerous sectors of society creates an opportunity for firms with the right low margin product to tap into "the fortune at the bottom of the pyramid" (Prahalad 2005; see chapters 5 and 7).

Decomposing Value

"Value chain analysis" is a comparable technique of decomposing business operations, facilitating the comparison through commensuration of distinct projects by focusing on selected loci of capitalist activity. A value chain is a rendering of a productive activity as a set of potentially discrete processes: for instance, from research and development, through product design and manufacturing, to marketing, distribution, retailing, and after-sales service. The rationale for value chain analysis is that firms should examine which of these activities are points of strength or competitive advantage, assessing as well the marginal benefits of activities at each link of the chain. Few firms do everything well, and few value chains are equally profitable at each step of the way. Value chain analysis enables firms to determine where their competencies fall and where maximizing opportunities lie.

The concept of a value chain analytically breaks down what may be a more integrated productive process. It provokes realignments of business activities such as selling or acquiring part of a business and redirecting efforts away from low-margin areas of the chain (like assembly plants) toward activities that "create more value"—research and development, patenting new technology, etc.—with consequences that may include closing factories or outsourcing activities. Value chain—and correlated tropes such as "supply chain"—opens up spaces for disintegration, facilitating the conceptualization of articulated, but potentially discrete activities, often mapped upon the transnational space of international business practices (Bartlett and Ghoshal 2000). And as we've seen from discussions like Anna Tsing's (2013), the modes of framing, analysis, and action enabled by value (or supply) chain capitalism are especially congenial or native to the conditions of late neoliberal capitalism and its reenchanted global landscape.

As a sequence of activities, a value chain moves across space. In processes that cross borders, the analytic frame of a value chain can be superimposed on national boundaries, distilling the complexities of a national space to a function defined in relation to the larger productive process (a source of particular supplies, a location for low-wage manufacturing, a site of changing risks or costs connected to protectionist trade policies or political instability, a target market of consumers with specific characteristics). In its traversal of space, however, a value chain also navigates scale, moving from manufacturing processes to marketing, sales, and services.

In the MBA worldview, this is cast as a move from global to local, and this can elide the fact that all value chain processes take place some place. Manufacturing operations, for instance, are thought to be relatively standardized and global. In an interview with a professor of Operations Management (focused on factory operations), I was almost laughed out of his office when I asked him about different locally shaped "management models" for factories. "What do you mean 'management models'?" he scoffed. "We just think about things. We're not thinking 'management models.' We're trying to get the factory better, or the service operation better." Although he allowed that "HR" may have to deal with some country-specific nuances, "a bottleneck here is the same as anywhere else in the world. A well-run factory is a well-run factory anywhere."

At the other end of the value chain, the standardization of global production models is tempered by the demands of customers shaped by country- and region-specific contexts. "The farther you go in the value chain," explained Kevin to his International Strategy class, "the closer you get to the customer, [requiring] the greater tailoring to customer needs." In this sense, value chain is a framework to conceptualize the balance between (global) standardization and (local) customization. In fact, it is a conceptual engine to segment this process generating localizations across scale as a discrete value-producing process. In a conversation with Kevin after class, I asked about the balance of standardization and localization. If you're focusing on the firm, he said, "look at the value chain to see how value is created and how this must be adjusted by country according to what customers value. Value chain is a nice way to take a lot of information and standardize it."

Managerial Futures

The MBA curriculum and paracurriculum effect a scaffolding of core capitalist axioms and analytic habits in ways that routinize specific techniques of compressing, commensurating, and decomposing worldly complexities.

These habits have particular implications for international business. And the scaffolding of these habits is crucial to the successful performance of the managerial selves of the MBA. MBA programs cultivate senior managerial perspectives in their junior protégés. Case studies and other class assignments place them in the role of decision-making leaders, or create scenarios where they are presenting recommendations to senior leadership. The cross-functional ferment of strategy courses, like Kevin's, model a managerial fluency in bringing these habits to bear on complex in-the-world challenges.

Faculty and program administrators encourage this; indeed, it is what they are selling. We have already seen the variety of simulacra of executive prestige woven through the MBA experience. MBA faculty speak explicitly about the managerial futures of their students. In a class discussion of Porter's diamond, a professor tells the class it helps address queries he has heard from them, "How can we use this class for investment options?" In a class on international marketing, a professor talks about political pressures linked to growing inequality in emerging economies, adding, "As we become marketing managers and get to the top end of your company—and this won't affect you for 5 or 10 years, but when you get there—these are the issues you're gonna face."[13]

MBAs aspire to the consequential management positions they simulate in their classes. And yet, there is a whiff of panic in this aspiration. For many of the MBAs I worked with, their decision to pursue the degree was also motivated by experiences of precarity. Some described stalled or limited careers: stuck in back office "cost centers," working in markets that they feared had run their course, vulnerable to being displaced by international talent. "I was nonbillable," David, told me, describing his previous career in a technology field. "Not being billable is a second-class citizen. They are the first to get cut." Business school training, he said was a way to be more "client facing," "to attach myself back to revenue."

Another student, Ricardo, told me that he sought his MBA after spending a few years as an engineer with a communications company because he wanted to get away "from the research and development side of the house." He hoped to work for a corporation for a period of time and eventually start his own business. Ricardo expressed some frustration with his first-year core, which he felt was too classroom-based, and did not provide enough opportunities "to lead and take on projects." "Maybe I watched *The Apprentice* too much," he joked to me, "but I thought we would have opportunities to take on interesting projects." Emre described his experiences working for a family business in Turkey and saw his MBA training as a stepping-stone to a position in "a truly global corporation." Denise had worked for a consulting group focused on healthcare. She was seeking an MBA to position herself for a managerial position in international healthcare. Other students had bolder dreams of entrepreneurial freedom—an increasingly common aspiration for MBAs after the financial crisis.

This sense of precarity is very much in line with the sort of managerial unease said to be characteristic of the fast-paced, new economy. In response, some wanted to solidify their corporate bona fides by rounding out their education and cultivating managerial qualities; while some set themselves on a path to a more independent entrepreneurial future, no less anchored in a broader condition of cultivated managerial agility. International students, like Emre, often spoke of a competitive edge gained by learning how business is done by some of their primary trading partners. What is clear from all of this is that the MBAs were looking for some form of excess: a supplement to the experiences and qualities they so far commanded, a marginal difference they could monetize in their careers. As we will see in chapter 5, international exposure and experience confers this excess in especially potent forms.

But there is a more basic quality of excess at the core of the managerial subject produced in MBA programs. This has to do with the acknowledged limits of technical training to represent and manage an always more complicated world. The added value of the contemporary capitalist manager, beyond functional competence in the core areas of business, indeed the art complementing the science of management, is the cultivation of innate talents within the MBAs. MBAs thus learn to embody the excesses and contradictory limits of neoliberal capitalism as a frame for making sense of, and assimilating, the excessive complexities of global business.

SCIENCE AND ART: TALENT AND
THE MANAGEMENT OF EXCESS

The managerial challenge of making decisions in an environment in which there is too much information and no "clear answers" undergirds another key premise of the MBA curriculum: that it merges "science and art"—highly technical competencies along with qualities of leadership and sensitivities to the world that promise to optimize executive insight and action. To some extent, this is a legacy of the long curricular positioning of business education—particularly at the managerial level—as a hybrid of vocational/technical education and broader liberal arts training (see chapter 3). But the referent "liberal arts" and its perceived value are far from stable—shifting according to different readings of the business environment and different tensions and challenges to be managed by the MBA.

In the MBA programs I observed, the key qualities supplementing training in core functional areas of business involve capacities related to living under uncertainty and heightened knowledge of the self. Many programs begin with personality tests and assessments of cultural competency geared to the cultivation at once of forms of subjective self-knowledge and a managerial overview of the connections among diversity. MBAs speak ceaselessly of their personal "stories" as they narrativize their arc of professional and personal development. Go into a bookstore and you are likely to see "business" books (particularly memoirs and distillations of advice for managerial success) shelved in or near the self-help section. There is a self-actualizing quality to managerial culture, and business programs stress the identification and cultivation of qualities of self that supplement the inadequacies of technical and quantitative ways of knowing and measuring.[14]

Alongside this emphasis on core technical competencies and the commensurating impulse in MBA training to measure in order to manage, runs the contrapuntal theme of the "art" of management. For many MBA students, calculating the opportunity costs of two additional years of high-priced schooling, this is the added value they seek. MBA programs market this quite clearly, offering training in the ineffable: the management habitus that routinizes the seizing of singularity at the margins. In this, they enact the cutting edge of management literature, stressing the need to cultivate talent and creativity and capitalize on the intuitive insights of managers (e.g., Kahneman and Klein 2010).

The art of management is the marginal quality of leadership that separates mid-level managers from their superiors: senior managers require an intuitive grasp of problems and solutions that is not reducible to the quantitative "plugging and chugging" of middle management decision-making (Hayashi 2001). In one management course I attended, the professor referenced the sports experience of "being in the zone" to illustrate a sense of unconscious competency: a heightened functional state that transcends rational or reflective knowledge. Some management texts present this as an alternative to a dominant rational mode of thought and action in Western cultures. Embracing your full set of management potential may prepare you to manage in an international business environment. Conversely, getting in touch with business in other cultural contexts may awaken a broader range of management talents than are typically cultivated in Western settings (cf. Dane and Pratt 2007). I take this explicit emphasis upon personal qualities and the need to complement the inevitably inadequate models asserting straightforward commensurability as a reflection of the particular, flexible nature of capitalism today.

This combination of science and art, technique and talent, constituted as essential to managerial competence, is presented as particularly crucial to working internationally and cross-culturally. MBA programs strive to locate in the managing subject a competent nimbleness, enabling capitalist action across a variegated global space. Because there seem to be more unknowns and more variables overall in working internationally, MBAs are taught that international business compels a specific blending of these qualities. The rhetorical space between "science" and "art" marks the margins of commensurability of international experiences. Insofar as managers must embody the blending of the habits of effective commensuration with the artful assimilation of the incommensurable, these margins are realized as a space of potential value for the contemporary manager.

Signs of Risk

Deeply imbricated with the incommensurable excess of international business space is the quality of risk. Intractable, incommensurable, and essential, risk is an unavoidable part of doing business. The production of MBAs is bound up with the production of risk. And the productive engagement with risk is dependent upon the application of managerial intuition and talent.

Economists speak of a perfectly efficient market as one in which all participants have equal and complete information about resources available and all have equal capacity to act. Of course, like other Edenic states, this is unsustainable; the utopian ideal is a terrible sort of perfection. It is "terrible" because it represents the negation, through transcendence, of the potential energy of the system. The lesson of the myth, a subgenre of the broader tragic backstory of Western capitalism, is that imperfect knowledge of the world, unequally distributed, is the glorious potential of the market. In this regard, market participants strive for more perfect knowledge, not as a collective enterprise, but in agonistic competition with others. The attraction of an arbitrage opportunity,[15] for instance, is not that it is risk free, but rather that it presents a different level of risk vis-à-vis other market participants. The objective is the achievement of a marginal difference in risk rather than its amelioration.

In this regard, risk is a necessity.

This is not to claim risk as an objective condition of the world. Although risk may appear to members of the business community as "a natural object," my interest is in risk as a quality performatively evoked in the world and intertwined with the practices of managerial training, analysis, and action (cf. LiPuma and Lee 2004). At issue are practices—ways of being in the world; ways of framing and executing action—that endow the world with risk. MBA programs present an institutionalized practice of performatively evoking risk in the world that, at the same time, compels specifically culti-vated expertise and talent for its management. Managing the risk involves putting a price on its successful negotiation. Risk thus calls value into being. This may be the founding arbitrage opportunity: finding the future uncer-tain and putting a price on moving toward it.

Donald MacKenzie, following Michel Callon, takes up the question of the performative force of economic theory. Focusing on options trading, MacKenzie argues that the success of a key model for pricing futures options—Black–Scholes–Merton (BSM)—derives less from the absolute accuracy of BSM as a model of the world and more from the consistent pro-fessional consensus in applying the formula. This accepted model of how future options work was thus generative of the way future options work (e.g., MacKenzie and Millo 2003).

I think this is helpful for thinking about the case of MBA training—although with an additional twist. The introductory courses present a set of axiomatic claims about the world and about the power of specific profes-sional models to represent the world. While these models are necessarily retrospective, the manager's task is established as necessarily prospective. The courses acknowledge the failure of the foundational models to represent the future in all its uncertainty. Against the backdrop of the elemental and lim-ited models, the excess of the world becomes framed as "risk." Thus framed, "risk" is bundled back into the pricing models as a supplement constituted by the limits of the original models. In the words of one student reflecting on his work in a class on "emerging markets,"

In these countries you face a lot of risk: politically, microeconomically, civil wars. . . . We tried to put all that information in the cash flow, trying to understand the fundamentals of the business, the country, the industry, the project. Or, if you cannot do that, in the interest rate, the discount interest rate.

Risk, as I am casting it, operates like a qualisign: a quality that functions as a sign or signifies potential. Positioned as the remainder of the simplifying commensurating logic of economic and finance theory, risk as an analytic category endows the complexity it contains with a potential to generate supplemental value.

The qualisign of risk is also attached to the MBAs themselves. MBAs I spoke with cast their MBA training explicitly in the language of risk. They are undertaking a costly investment, made more expensive by the opportunity costs of two years away from their careers. The sense of having something at stake—skin in the game, as they like to say—made for a qualitatively distinct experience of the program. This was particularly palpable in frictions I observed between students who had really taken a leap to get their MBA, and students whose training was being sponsored by an employer. This was often the case for international MBA students, and the domestic students' gripe was that, with the security of a job waiting for them, they would not work as hard in the program. They were considered poor MBA team members.

"Capital is a coward" goes the saying. And, to the extent that cowardice is not in the best interest of capital, it requires a managed engagement with risk. "Managers bear risk" might then be the corollary. Many MBAs approach their business training as an opportunity to cultivate an aura of productive risk-taking. This is nowhere more evident than in their relationship to global business, in which the reenchantment of the world with difference is a condition of the possibility of such risk-taking. MBA programs are engaged in the reciprocal production of a complex but manageable world studded with incommensurable excess and risk (and so potentially generative of value), and a cohort of globally adept MBAs prepared to manage these global margins.

MBA programs, then, are engaged in framing the world as requiring the talents the MBAs are best suited to provide. That they do so persuasively, and in the face of a steady stream of crises of more or less historic proportions, is a testament to the authoritative position of collegiate business programs in the United States as well as the increasingly tight interlacing of economistic and business-inflected "truths" and styles of action among the conventional wisdom, the "grooves and rails" of thought and behavior, in neoliberal US society. Before continuing with an ethnographic examination of how they do this, the next chapter presents a cultural history of how this came to be, examining the rise of business education in the United States.

THREE

Accounting for Business

This course focuses on the strategic challenges confronting firms which compete in the global economy. The course requires thinking about multi-country business decisions from a managerial perspective. In taking a top management perspective, our dominant concern is achieving and sustaining competitive advantage. (excerpt from the "Course Objectives" section of an MBA Global Business Strategy syllabus)

At one time scorned by classics and humanities departments, the [MBA] degree has come to be envied and emulated by them. Once derided as narrow and vocational, it has come to be probably the broadest and most interdisciplinary of all graduate degrees. Although ostensibly practical and career-oriented, it is probably more undefined in its nature and more flexible in its applications than a master's degree in English, geology, or math. (Daniel 1998, 16)

THIS CHAPTER TURNS FROM MBA CLASSROOMS to the history of the emergence of MBA and other business programs in the United States. I do so with two goals in mind. One is scene-setting: telling the story of the rise of the MBA within the history of US capitalism provides the context for this ethnographic study of twenty-first-century MBA programs. But the fact that there is a story to tell clues us in to something more. Historicizing something, accounting for how it came to be, can help to illustrate the culturally constituted qualities of institutions that seem otherwise to be naturally given in the world. The idea of the manager or of a "management perspective," the legitimacy of MBA training as the site for the production of such expertise, and, indeed, the very premise of "business" as subject of professional or academic study . . . all of these apparently self-evident truths stem from an oftentimes contentious history through which they were made rather than found. At issue is how "business" has come to stand on its own, and, indeed, how it has come to stand as an exemplar of the neoliberal social whole.

The second goal of this chapter, then, is to denaturalize MBA training, to examine the ways MBA programs have repeatedly and effectively invented themselves as the primary legitimating path to "a top management perspective." Part of that process turns on claims about the world that serve to establish managerial expertise as a national and global strategic necessity. That is to say that MBA programs define and legitimate themselves through calculated framings of the world. This chapter tracks a century-long process of defining the emerging field of professional business training through a reciprocal effort to make sense of the dynamic twentieth-century global order and the place of the United States within it. This is a story, then, about boundary-making: the ways expertise is institutionalized by separating certain knowledge and skills from everyday practices and other domains of specialization, and limiting the ways such expertise is formally conferred and recognized (cf. Preda 2009). At the same time, ironically, this is a story about the remarkably underspecified character of "business." As Daniel's laudatory assessment of the MBA degree reveals, business training is also something of a cypher—broad to the point of being borderless; flexible to the point of shapelessness. The MBA is a specialization that not only seems to be about everything and nothing, but also actively leverages that quality in a constant negotiation of its relevance.

FROM CLERKS TO MANAGERS

Over the course of the twentieth century, collegiate-level business education, including MBA programs, effectively invented and established themselves in academic and professional-commercial landscapes in which they did not previously exist, and in which they were initially scorned and derided. Business programs had to account for themselves. This accounting involved strategic framing of the social, political, and economic conditions of the day and the cultural production of business expertise presented as authoritative and necessary to effective business practice. The rise of the figure of the "manager"—increasingly equated with the MBA over the second half of the twentieth century—reflects the distillation of this process of legitimation and cultural (re)invention, embodied in MBA programs and the cohorts of men and women who have been at once their customers and their products.

Commercial skills—such as bookkeeping and stenography—were part of eighteenth-century high school curricula in the United States, with business-related study increasingly formalized over the nineteenth century. Bookkeeping, for instance, was officially recognized as a high school subject in Massachusetts in 1827, in New York in 1829, and in California in 1851 (Graham 1933, 26). The expansion and formalization of business education attracted the attention of recently established professional organizations like the National Education Association (1870) and the federal Bureau of Education (1867). These in turn produced various reports and conference proceedings focused on the challenges to, and the necessity for, business education in the United States.

These reports, part of a long project of framing business education, signaled the increasing complexity of modern business practices as these required a cohort of clerks, office boys, salesmen, and businessmen prepared to meet the challenge. They also typically invoked the increasing role of commercial enterprise as the core of "American" society, and so connected education in the skills of business with the ongoing development of the United States. Particularly in the wake of the Spanish American War and World War I, commentators connected the growing need for a cohort of modernized business clerks and leaders with the expanding role of the United States in international commercial activities. And, as authors of the reports called for the systematizing, professionalizing reform of business education, they were at pains to defend its legitimacy as something more than merely vocational training and as a morally beneficial practical science to be included as part of the curriculum for an informed modern citizenry.[1]

These framing habits shaped the rise of collegiate business education, spurred in part by a growing demand for trained business educators in high schools and private commercial colleges. By 1871, some two dozen colleges in the United States offered coursework in the field of business (Benson 2004, 18). The earliest collegiate business programs were established around the turn of the twentieth century. The first business school was the Wharton Business School at the University of Pennsylvania, established in 1881. In 1898 the University of Chicago established the College of Commerce and Politics. That same year, the University of California, Berkeley, introduced a business program housed in its Economics Department. By 1900, New York University (NYU), the University of Wisconsin, and Dartmouth had business programs. Harvard's business program was founded in 1908. By 1911 there were twenty-one business programs at US universities; by 1917 there were thirty (Graham 1933, 29). The first graduate school of management was established in 1900 at Dartmouth, which offered a Master of Science in

Commerce. The first MBA degree program was offered by Harvard Business School, beginning in 1908.

The rapidly growing cohort of business programs soon had their own professional association. The Association of Collegiate Schools of Business was founded in 1916, with sixteen founding institutional members.[2] Accreditation standards for business programs were approved in 1919 (United States, Bureau of Education, and National Education Association of the United States 1919). As such associations do, the ACSB (which later became the American Association of Collegiate Schools of Business, and is now called the American Association of Collegiate Schools of Business, International), served as a legitimating and standardizing institution for business education, bounding the field. The AACSB helped establish standardized admission tests for graduate education in business, introducing the ATGSB[3] (precursor of the GMAT)[4] in 1954. And much like the reports and assessments produced at the turn of the twentieth century, the Association has commissioned a set of reports that mark moments of crisis and consolidation in business training—including a 2011 report on "Globalization of Management Education" (AACSB 2011).

Collegiate business training was a child of the dawning twentieth century; part of the fledgling business schools' pitch involved a critical sociology of turn-of-the-century capitalist modernity. In this view, business was cast as at once an engine and moral measure of modernizing US society. Professionalizing business practices would redound to the benefit of society, and the challenges of social change were reflected in the expanding field of "business." In founding the Wharton school, for instance, Joseph Wharton was motivated by a "desire to promote a higher standard of morality in American business than that commonly exhibited in the decades immediately following the civil war" (Abend 2014, 284). In a 1906 *New York Times* column, Joseph French Johnson, dean of the recently established School of Commerce, Accounts, and Finance at NYU, sought to clarify the new need for university-level business schools. He anchored his case in the entwined complexity of modern business and modern society, suggesting that "business" "covers the work of a very large proportion of the population of this country." And the sheer scale of business activity—"this vast army of business," in Johnson's words—entailed a complex set of business roles (Johnson 1906).

The diversification of business education thus matched the need for different skills and levels of responsibility. Johnson resolved the vast army into three classes: "clerks," "semi-independent outside men and office managers," and "managing officials." And he argued that the "qualities that are essential to success in each of these three groups" require at least three kinds of business education: "The private business colleges are adapted to turning out clerks, the commercial high schools to turning out salesmen and office managers, the university schools of commerce to turning out managing officials."

This is what contemporary MBAs learn to call market segmentation. In addition to identifying the niche to which their new product appeals, the analysis connects the need for a new form of business training (producing managerial expertise) with an assessment of the contemporary condition of business cast explicitly as a symptom of modernizing society. Coordinate with the framing of professional business education, business comes to stand as a reflection of the contemporary social whole.

Johnson goes on to note that in recent decades, a growing number of college graduates have gone directly into "business life." This is a progressive development as "old-time prejudice" in favor of professions like law, medicine, and ministry "has been slowly dying out." The "most progressive universities" (he lists "New York, Dartmouth, Pennsylvania, Michigan, Chicago, California, Wisconsin, and Illinois") have recognized that this trend requires some kind of "special training for business." Tellingly, Harvard, Yale, and Columbia—perhaps the embodiment of the "old time prejudice" of classical collegiate training—do not make his list of vanguard progressive institutions, although Johnson notes that they have attempted "practically the same object" through marked increase of their departments of economics (1906). What Johnson dubs "business life" suggests a new mode of engaging with the world. Its increasing popularity stands as a symptom of a modern progressive age and heralds the disruption of traditional professions.

Disruptions

The idea of "disruption"—a rapid unsettling of an established order, creating new business opportunities, sometimes with a sense of a self-correcting marketplace of innovations and ideas—has trended strongly in the business literature of recent years, and quickly achieved the dubious status of a cliché (cf. Christensen, Raynor, and McDonald 2015). Yet it may be helpful for thinking about the convergence of factors in the bounding of the field of professional business training in the United States.

The ascension of business education from the more common public high schools and semireputable business colleges to the university level was met with contempt by many academics. Edmund J. James, the first director of the Wharton School (1883–96), reported that

> other departments in the University and most of the other members of the faculty were bitterly opposed to the whole project. And even if they did not actually interfere to prevent the progress of the work, they stood with watchful, jealous eyes to see that no concession of any sort should be made to these new subjects, which, in their opinion, might in any way lower the level of scholarship as the ideal had been accepted by the upholders of the traditional course. (Daniel 1998, 28)

Similarly, the Harvard Business School (HBS) took shape "under attack from academicians and businessmen alike" (O'Connor 1999, 117).

This sense of early business programs encountering the disdain of more established academic disciplines should probably be taken with a grain of salt, for it fuels accounts of the triumphant rise of business studies in the face of sniffing academic elitists in US colleges that are a stock part of the native cosmology of business schools. And, while I never heard anyone make a direct connection with the history of the field, this founding myth of academic scorn is entirely congenial to the contemporary contempt in US business schools for academic scholarship removed from the fast-paced "real world" of business. That said, like most myths, this one builds on a kernel of truth. The legitimate standing of business education in US colleges and universities was an ongoing project, requiring considerable cultural and political work. The contemporary status of business schools was made rather than found, and made in the face of mistrust from all sides, heightened by a period of institutional disruption.

As Wharton's Edmund James reported, established scholars viewed business education as a vocational field sullying the reputation of classical scholarship and scientific standards. Abraham Flexner, Director of the Institute for Advanced Study in New York, and author of the Flexner Report that helped establish many of the contours of twentieth-century medical training in the United States, was an outspoken critic of business schools, citing them as the source of falling standards of higher education. Wallace Donham, second dean of HBS, reportedly kept notes of a speech delivered by Flexner in Boston in the 1930s, indicating that Flexner made reference to "researches carried on by Harvard Business School, to which no genuine scientist would give the name of 'research'" (O'Connor 1999, 121). The Business School further stained Harvard's reputation by hiring the first professor without a Bachelor's degree and being the first program to issue a degree not conferred in Latin (Cruikshank 1987, 42, 50).

Some attacks on the scholarly legitimacy of university business education came from critics of capitalism. In 1918 Thorsten Veblen published a critique of the encroachment of businessmen in higher education that condemned the focus on "material competency" and "pecuniary standards," which sought to "substitute the pursuit of gain and expenditure in place of the pursuit of knowledge, as the focus of interest and the objective end in the modern intellectual life" (1918, 203). In contrast with the training of physicians, dentists, pharmacists, agriculturalists, engineers, and "perhaps even of journalists," which is beneficial to the community at large, Veblen wrote,

> such is not the case with the training designed to give proficiency in business. No gain comes to the community at large from increasing the business proficiency of any number of its men. There are already much too many of these businessmen, much too astute and proficient in their calling, for the common good. A higher average business efficiency simply raises activity and avidity in business activity to a higher average pitch and fervor, with very little other material result than a redistribution of ownership; since business is occupied with the competitive acquisition of wealth, not with its production. . . . The work of the College of Commerce, accordingly, is a peculiarly futile line of endeavor for any public institution, in that it serves neither the intellectual advancement nor the material welfare of the community. (Cruikshank 1987, 25)

At the same time, the politics of turn-of-the-century higher education in the United States was grappling with critiques of classical scholarship as being out of touch with the demands of the era. The introduction of business education thus crossed a line separating the erudite classical training of universities with the more common vocational education offered by high schools and business colleges precisely as traditional college faculty were already in a defensive position in the face of mounting critiques over the practicality of classical education.

By the mid-nineteenth century, institutions like Harvard were facing criticism "that the institution was teaching little of any practical value. The curriculum was centuries old; learning was by rote; and examinations were largely meaningless" (Cruikshank 1987, 15). This was alongside calls, such as the one in an 1869 *Atlantic* essay by Charles Eliot, for more practical education in applied sciences. Eliot, a professor of chemistry at MIT, would soon be appointed president of Harvard (Cruikshank 1987, 17).

In testimony before the Senate in 1885, Joseph Medill, editor in chief of the *Chicago Tribune* and mayor of Chicago (1871–73), remarked,

> Our college system certainly does not train our youth in habits of useful industry.... On the contrary, college education is conducted with a view to imparting a knowledge of dead languages and the higher mathematics to the pupils, which is all well enough for the wealthy and leisure classes, but is not best suited for bread-winners. These academies attract hundreds of thousands of our youth, whose purpose is to acquire the art of living by their wits and avoiding manual labor; this, too, is the purpose of their parents in sending them to such schools. These academies have flooded the professions with men destitute of natural capacity for them, and have swollen the ranks of office-seekers, gambling speculators, and professional sharps, who subsist by preying upon the rest of the community. This American system of education has destroyed all desire upon the part of the youths to learn trades and become honest artisans, and it has crowded the ranks of the middle-men with searchers after genteel employment at wretched wages. (United States Senate, Committee on Education and Labor 1885, 964)

Medill's contempt for college training was shared by other business leaders of the day. R. T. Crane published a 1901 pamphlet critical of classical education. Andrew Carnegie penned a 1899 *New York Tribune* article decrying college education as "almost fatal to success," critiquing time wasted on the "barbarous and petty squabbles of a far-distant past, or trying to master languages which are dead" (Daniel 1998, 26). Wall Street financier Henry Clews similarly considered "college men ... spoiled for a business life" (Daniel 1998, 26). And Frederick W. Taylor, who, without college education, had developed a career as a machinist and apostle of industrial efficiency, is said to have remarked in 1908 that he had "ceased to hire any young college graduates until they [had] been 'dehorned' by some other employer" (Cruikshank 1987, 53).

Related factors involved the gradual democratization of higher education. As a slowly increasing percentage of the US (male) population enrolled in universities, the role of universities in preparing the elite for the genteel work of ministry, law, or medicine was changing. From slightly more than 1 percent in 1870, the percentage of young adults attending college in the United States had increased to more than 7 percent by 1920 (Daniel 1998, 24). As

Dean Johnson noted in 1906, a growing number of college men were seeking careers in business. Two years later, Harvard's president Eliot introduced the newly established Harvard Business School to a meeting of the Harvard Club of Connecticut, noting two compelling reasons for the new endeavor: "the prodigious development of many corporate businesses in our country" and "the fact that more than half the recent graduates of Harvard College have gone immediately into business" (Cruikshank 1987, 35). With their colleges of business, universities were chasing an emerging and transforming market. Between 1890 and 1910 nearly four dozen US colleges had closed their doors (Daniel 1998, 24). It was, indeed, a time of disruption; the expanding cohort of college men were apparently seeking something new.

Seeking Academic Legitimacy

Although professional programs in law or engineering also served as models for the emergent field of business education, in the context of the academic politics of the time, the canonical disciplines of the liberal arts and sciences were a standard of intellectual legitimacy and moral authority against which business schools (lacking the pedigree of law or the clear-cut triumphant modernist applicability of engineering) were inevitably measured. The predecessor to the Booth School at the University of Chicago was initially established in connection with the Department of Political Science; the business program at the University of California, Berkeley, was housed in the Economics Department until 1940. Over its early decades, Harvard Business School—housed in the College of Arts and Sciences for the first four years of its existence—established itself through two coordinated strategies of institutional positioning. On the one hand, the school established academic legitimacy through funded and published research and through strategic alignment with existing academic disciplines. On the other, as I will discuss in greater detail below, the school sought to establish industry legitimacy through taking on what were cast as the most pressing social and economic issues of the day (O'Connor 1999).

Business schools also invited eminent scholars and accomplished professionals to address their faculty and students. Alfred North Whitehead was invited by Harvard Business School (O'Connor 1999). And despite his contempt for collegiate education, Frederick Taylor presented lectures at the University of Pennsylvania, Harvard Business School, and the Tuck School of Business at Dartmouth in the decade before his death in 1915. These were the years around Taylor's publication of his 1911 work, *Principles of Scientific Management*, and "science" figured as an important trope for the legitimation of business education, which aspired to be, in the words of the first Harvard Business School dean, Edwin Gay, about "the science of business" (Cruikshank 1987, 54).

During his 1908 introduction of the new Harvard Business School to the Harvard Club of Connecticut, President Eliot expanded on his observation that a growing number of Harvard graduates were joining the ranks of corporate businesses in the United States.

> The explanation of that new phenomenon is that business in its upper walks has become a highly intellectual calling, requiring knowledge of languages, economics, industrial organization, and commercial law, and wide reading concerning the resources and habits of the different nations. (Cruikshank 1987, 35)

Eliot's vision may have been imperfectly reflected in the curriculum of the nascent business school.[5] But it captures an effort to align business education with respect to a repertoire of familiar and established fields. It also affords an early glimpse of the flexibly competent businessman—a model for what became the MBA.

Connections to recognized academic disciplines, conformance to established academic standards (degreed faculty, accreditation norms, the pomp and circumstance of academic ceremony) all played a role in the early performances of business school legitimacy. Another consideration is the appearance of business-focused journals and professional societies, which provided the contours for the field of business and its component specializations.[6] An early example here is *System: A Magazine of Business*, which began publication in 1900, offering brief reports detailing cutting-edge business practices, often written by leading figures in industry, and with the aim of systematizing the knowledge necessary for modern business practice. The magazine was purchased by McGraw-Hill in 1927 and became *Business Week* in 1929. Its publisher, Arch Wilkinson Shaw, had participated in the development of the business curriculum at Northwestern. In 1910 he began an affiliation with HBS—studying economics, and later lecturing—that also contributed to the establishment of a research arm of the school: the Bureau of Business Research, which soon began publishing research results in the *Bulletin of the Bureau of Business Research* (1913–63). The establishment of the Research Bureau was followed by the founding of the *Harvard Business*

Review (1922–), and the formal introduction of the case method of business teaching in 1923.[7] The case study method became an additional outlet of academic publication for business faculty, with some of the early studies of the Bureau becoming the earliest published teaching cases. The business case method further branded the discipline of business education as a sui generis academic endeavor (see chapter 6).

MANAGING THE MODERN

Business schools emerged in the context of the rapid expansion of modern capitalism in the United States and they established their legitimacy by casting themselves as the modern solution to a set of correlated changes and challenges. At the core of these were substantial changes to the ways in which business was organized, as the increasing complexity and scale of some industries, as well as changes in the financing and ownership structure of large firms, shaped new types of managerial practices. The business historian Alfred Chandler documented the emergence of "managerial capitalism" beginning in the second half of the nineteenth century. Chandler contrasts the entrepreneurial capitalism of smaller firms operating in immediate contact with market demand with a qualitatively different set of managerial challenges faced by larger corporations taking advantage of expanded scales of operation enabled by technological advances in manufacturing, distribution, and communication. For Chandler, this new repertoire of managerial practices amounted to such an epochal break that a businessman in the 1970s would find much in common with his counterpart from the 1870s, but a businessman in the 1830s might have more in common with a merchant from the sixteenth century than with the more contemporary managers (1977, 1984).

At the heart of this was the "modern corporation," identified as a sign of the times in a 1932 landmark study by Adolf Berle and Gardiner Means, a legal scholar and an economist. Taking as their point of departure a recognition that corporations in the United States were rapidly becoming much more than legal frameworks for doing business, Berle and Means set out to examine the corporation as a method of property tenure and as a means of organizing economic life. They document the emergence of the corporation as a normative framework for business and detail the concentration of economic power—the "centripetal attraction of wealth" in corporations—through a table presenting the assets of the largest nonbank corporations in the United States in 1930 (Berle and Means [1932] 1991, 18). At the same time, they note that corporations, which tend to have ownership dispersed across many relatively disorganized stockholders, create a situation in which control of these increasingly powerful institutions is largely in the hands of a small group of corporate managers. Their focus is on the growing distance of (relatively powerless) ownership from (increasingly powerful) managerial control.

The Modern Corporation and Private Property is a foundational study in corporate governance. It reflects a sense—increasingly acute after the Depression—that the institutional contours of twentieth-century American capitalism represented a shift of profound economic and social consequence: the rise of big business and managerial capitalism. The MBA manager through the middle of the twentieth century was closely linked with corporate big business, the management of which was never taken to be purely business. What is more, as Chandler notes, the expansion in business scale was linked to internationalization—seeking new markets and expanding production processes. In this regard, managerial capitalism and the (implicitly American) firm were tightly bound up with a consolidating twentieth-century American position in, and vantage on, the world (Chandler 1984; cf. Hegeman 1999; Pletsch 1981).

The dawn of the MBA and of collegiate-level business training is coordinate with the rise of managerial capitalism; MBA programs were positioned explicitly in terms of these changes in the organization of business. The MBA manager thus develops as an avatar of American modernity: embodying the promises and the perils of a self-consciously modernizing and globalizing US society.

Preparing the Managerial Class

The rapid expansion of commercial and industrial capitalism provoked a sense of crisis deriving from shifting and sharpening social hierarchies. *Chicago Tribune* editor Joseph Medill's comments decrying the inadequacy of college education to prepare young men for useful employment in industry was part of his testimony before a Senate committee on "the relations between labor and capital." Along with NYU Dean Johnson's characterization of the complexity of the world of business comprising multiple classes of men, it reflects the challenging class politics of the time. Johnson's analysis adds another step, though: transposing a social hierarchy to the arena of business education, he introduces the figure of the manager as called forward by the very fact of social hierarchy, and, as a consequence of his new education and training, uniquely prepared to address the pressing social challenges emerging from that hierarchy.

In her historical essay on the Harvard Business School, Ellen O'Connor (1999) details the increasing inclusion of Psychology as a core contributing discipline in the business repertoire. Psychology, she notes, carried at once the credibility of a quasi-medical science, and was also emerging at the time (1910s and 1920s) as a discipline held to be of great promise in some corners of industry for what it might offer by way of engineering better relations between labor and management.

A similar example comes from Harlow Person, the first administrator of the Tuck School at Dartmouth. An engineer by training and a Taylorist, Person framed his approach to the university business curriculum around "three zones" of business activity, ranging from administration through management to operation. The workers and clerks of the bottom operations zone required little more than on-the-job training, and were unlikely to rise above that level. The job of collegiate and university business schools was to train a class of managers, who might begin their careers in Zone I, but would quickly rise to the managerial functions of Zone II thanks to an ability to "interpret his experience in Zone I with a grasp of the functions and problems of the next higher zone" (1920, 112). Person allowed that leading administrative positions were occupied by men with "ripe judgment" developed from extensive business experience. However, the business school–trained managers were expected to rise ultimately to Zone III, since their preparation in managerial functions laid a foundation for the development of ripe judgment through experience.

We have here a glimpse of the heroic manager, who comes into sharper focus over the twentieth century. Although specific attributes shift over time, the business manager is marked by a potent competence comprising training and innate instinctive talent that allows for the effective administration of risky complexity and the rapid progress through a professional career. An agile jack-of-all-trades, interdisciplinary and flexible, many qualities of the MBA manager appear already in Eliot's 1908 introduction of the HBS project to the Harvard Club of Connecticut. Presenting the Harvard Graduate School of Business as part of a broader turn toward professional education at

Harvard, Eliot remarked, "The future in our country is for those professions, gentlemen. They are to be the leaders of the people, the controllers of our industries, the directors of our finances and our commerce, the managers of the great public services" (Cruikshank 1987, 35).

Civic Capitalists

At the turn of the twentieth century, technical knowledge of business and finance was seen as increasingly necessary to good governance and informed civic engagement. A *New York Times* article from 1908 reporting on the increasing number of college business programs makes a case for the greater civic need for training in business. Noting that college business training may serve to establish basic ethical standards in business practice, the article goes on: "Nor is it only in a private, moral, and individual sense that these schools have a high function at a time when our public affairs are so largely economic." The article laments poorly informed Congressional action around matters of currency, railroads, and tariffs, and suggests that the business schools will help produce graduates and faculty who can provide authoritative counsel on "business ideals" and "commercial methods."

Alongside this sense that business held answers to domestic policies was a preoccupation with the standing of the United States as a newly self-conscious power on the global stage. In 1891, Edmund James, director of the recently established Wharton School, was commissioned by the American Bankers' Association for a research trip to study methods of business education in Europe (James 1893; Daniel 1998, 32). Congressional testimony concerning commerce and education and conference proceedings of professional societies such as the National Education Society similarly reflect concerns about international competitiveness and comparisons between the preparation of businessmen in the United States and that of those in Europe.

Efforts over the 1910s and 1920s to frame business curricula position the manager as sitting astride and integrating a welter of diverse interests and forces, many deriving from the sharpening class politics of expanding industrial capitalism. This was only intensified by the Great Depression and its aftermath, as the rivalry between the Soviet Union and the economically shaken United States amounted in the eyes of some to a profound challenge to Western capitalist civilization. Business schools cast themselves as rising to meet the challenge. Wallace Donham, the second dean of HBS, wrote in a 1931 book critical of the malaise of American business, *Business Adrift*,

It is my belief that the only hope for Western civilization centers in the ability and the leadership of American business, and on their recognition of the fields in which government action is necessary to secure sound results, in their capacity to make and carry out a major plan conceived in the largest terms by men of the highest ability and social objectives. (Donham and Whitehead 1931, 154–55)

Public regard of business schools was changing as well. In 1932, Thomas Watson (of IBM) told the *New York Times*, "If business, finance, and science had known the right thing to do three years ago, we would never have reached our present low economic estate. . . . I believe young men should go about the study of business as never before" (Daniel 1998, 117).

The (Social) Science of Business

In 1926, Wallace Donham recruited Elton Mayo, a leader in the emerging field of industrial psychology, to HBS. Mayo had come to the United States from Australia in 1922 for a Rockefeller-funded appointment at Wharton and quickly made a name for himself through studies approaching factory workers as damaged by industrial work conditions and by the stresses of working-class life. Mayo's work as a psychologist and a social theorist helped shape a new facet of the figure of the MBA manager, whose enlightened administration might ameliorate the afflictions of the working class, which were impacting industrial productivity.

Psychology lent a cloak of science to the fields of business education. It also introduced "the social," or at least a voicing of it, into the science of business, and it did so at a time when social strife in industrial society, in the form of management–labor conflicts, was a primary preoccupation for government and industry. Taking on these issues helped HBS establish its merits in the eyes of industry leaders, with the result that economics, long dominant in the development of business education, was gradually rivaled in some programs by social sciences (Daniel 1998; Gabor 2000; McDonald 2017; O'Connor 1999).

Business school curricula over the 1920s and 1930s saw the appearance of courses like "Personnel Management." The *Annals* of the American Academy of Political and Social Science devoted its entire November 1923 issue to "Psychology in Business." The introduction, written by former Wharton faculty C. H. Crennan, noted "At the heart of every business situation is a human nature problem. . . . the psychologist is in business to stay because business involves human nature" (Crennan 1923, 1; Daniel 1998, 98). Alongside a range of technical competencies in accounting, finance, and so forth, the MBA thus became an engineer of the social.

Note the sleight of hand by which the virtues of the MBA are always established in a reciprocal reading of the social challenges of the day. This turn to the social in a field that came to stand almost seamlessly with American modernity was deepened through connections with a confluence of cultural developments crystallizing over the decades after the Depression. Along with the emergence of the business manager as an American cultural type, this period also saw the ascendance of the idea of the "American Dream" as an explicit ideology of upward mobility and potential. The consolidation, often within the multidisciplinary framework of business schools, of academic disciplines such as human relations and industrial psychology, intensified the engagement between business education and the mid-century cultural milieu (Frederick 1964; Hegeman 1999; O'Connor 1999; Susman 1984).

Corporations are People

By mid-century, the corporation stood at once as an exemplar of modern capitalism and the embodiment of modern US society. This was, of course, a racially-privileged and class-privileged and gendered part of US society standing for the whole. The hegemony of that framing—the widely accepted view of "business" as quintessentially "American," or of corporations as organic extension of US society—included business schools and MBA programs, which had become fairly routinized parts of the production and reproduction of managerial capitalism in the United States. To some degree, then, the struggles to establish the legitimacy of collegiate-level business schools were over: business schools and MBA programs were unquestioned parts of the educational and social landscape for aspiring businessmen. But the cultural work of bounding the MBA was ongoing—particularly given the essentially inchoate characteristics of the MBA—making it highly responsive to, and in many ways dependent upon, frequent accountings of the world. The post–World War II world was especially consequential for the MBA.

A figure at the intersection of all of these strands—the management of the modern corporation, the continuously developing ideal of the MBA manager, the political and economic challenges of the post–World War II world—is Peter Drucker, whose book *Concept of the Corporation* (1946) is a seminal work in the modern management canon. Born in Austria, Drucker was among a group of European émigré intellectuals arriving in the United States around the time of the Second World War. Drucker studied international law in Germany, where he also worked as a journalist. When an essay regarding legitimate forms of state authority was banned by the Nazi regime, Drucker left for England. He took up work as a banker, while continuing his more sociological and philosophical reflections on contemporary capitalist society.[8] In a biographical timeline on the website of the Drucker Institute, Drucker describes "an epiphany" in Cambridge during a lecture by economist John Maynard Keynes: "I suddenly realized that Keynes and all the brilliant economic students in the room were interested in the behavior of commodities while I was interested in the behavior of people."[9] Drucker came to the United States in 1937. He took up a sequence of teaching positions in economics (at Sarah Lawrence) and in political philosophy at (Bennington College), before joining the school of business at NYU in 1950.

Concept of the Corporation was based on a quasi-ethnographic study of corporate management at General Motors (GM), only after a long list of corporations rejected his unusual request to have a stranger come to talk about management.[10] Indeed, it was GM that contacted Drucker on the initiative of one senior executive who had been intrigued by Drucker's earlier publication, *The Future of Industrial Man* (Drucker 1942). There Drucker had posited the mass-production plant and the corporation as the emblematic institutions of contemporary Western society and argued that crises of Western society (such as had been experienced through the rise of Fascism in Europe and the Depression) could be averted only if such representative social institutions were legitimately in harmony internally and with the values of contemporary society. Drucker proposed exploring this through a study of a corporation, and GM's interest enabled a two-year study of management practices across the company.

In *Concept*, Drucker casts "Big Business" as the representative American social institution, poised structurally between the scattered individualism of free enterprise and statist economic planning of the New Deal. The collective power of the corporation marked a new capacity for coordinating human productive power and economic activity, but risked violating the strong social ideals of individualism, which Drucker understood to be the core value of American society and therefore the source of any legitimacy for the corporation as a social institution. Drucker returns throughout the book to the cooperation and coordination of industrial production during World War II as an exemplary case of the aligning of individual motivations and collective effort, often discussing the experiences of GM, which reorganized their manufacturing activities in support of the war effort.

Drucker's interest in the balance of individual freedom alongside the planning and control of corporate institutions and states reflects a similar preoccupation by a contemporary and fellow Austrian, F. E. Hayek. Twenty years Drucker's senior, Hayek, along with other Austrian economists (Mises, Schumpeter), was a regular guest at the Drucker household when young Peter was growing up. Hayek's 1944 collection of essays *The Road to Serfdom*, initially published in Britain but republished with a new foreword for US readers in 1956, helped to popularize his stridently anticollectivist views, articulating a reassertion of elements of classical liberalism in twentieth-century social, political, and economic contexts. Consolidated under the banner of neoliberalism and elaborated through a network of scholars and business leaders, these views became ascendant over the second half of the twentieth century. Drucker's interest in the role of institutions in harmonizing individual and collective interests is sometimes contrasted with the more singular profit motive often ascribed to neoliberalism. Nonetheless, the mid-century managerial ideal Drucker helped establish would facilitate the implementation of neoliberal capitalism in the United States through the generalized recognition of managerial action and expertise (as opposed to, say, labor) as a primary site for value creation (Gilman 2006; Hanlon 2016).

In *Concept*, Drucker compares the official management model of General Motors, as it was presented by senior company officials and in organizational charts, with actual company practices. Drucker notes that the model is neither a plan implemented from the top down by senior management, nor a completely accurate representation of the corporation. Instead, Drucker argues that the particular structures of GM, founded in a set of principles (favoring decentralization), "were developed gradually and in dealing with concrete situations and concrete personalities" (Drucker 1946, 70). What is more, he underscores that the current abstract model of the corporation is not how it really runs. "General Motors is a functioning and moving organization of human beings and not a static blueprint" (71). Drucker turns to the tensions and contradictions of GM's blueprint in practice, looking at the model from differently positioned actors in the system: from top and middle management, to factory foremen and workers, to car dealers. As Nils Gilman notes, "Ducker's key methodological innovation was to conceive of the corporation as a social entity and to analyze its social function in political terms" (2006, 119).

Drucker's work calls us back to the influence of Elton Mayo nearly half a century earlier, and suggests a reassertion in mid-century contexts of the conviction that MBAs must be technicians of the social. Drucker called for a fuller realization of principles of decentralization as corollary to ideals of greater worker participation in setting goals and policies. His more democratized vision of the workplace was not well received at mid-century. Nor was his sense that workers ought to be able to rise through managerial ranks. However, in the absence of an authentic or harmonized corporation, Drucker's analysis throws into relief the vexed position of managers, who must undertake the structural alchemy of integrating the business and social functions of a corporation.

By 1950, a few years after *Concept* was published, business education was a well-established part of higher education in the United States. The number of business bachelor's degrees awarded increased from 1,576 in 1919 to 72,137 in 1949—a rate of increase higher than the general rate of increase of all bachelor's degrees over that time. The stability of business education was further indexed by the adoption in 1949 by the AACSB of a resolution on the core fields of business education.[11] The MBA, however, remained a relatively lagging part of this boom. MBA degrees had increased from 110 in 1919 to 4,335 in 1949; the degree was gaining popularity, but much more slowly than undergraduate business education. That was about to change.

In an essay published in *Fortune* in 1950, Drucker (who was starting his position at NYU) wrote about the postwar "arrival" of graduate business education, and the challenges and limitations of the relationship between American business and its newly accepted "professional school." Large corporations, he reports, increasingly look to graduate business programs for new managerial talent. The influence of business schools is registered with a "Wall Street joke ... that the center of financial decisions has not, as it is commonly believed, shifted to the Federal Reserve Bank, but rather to Professor [Marcus] Nadler's money-market seminar" (1950, 93). The joke reflects the changing environment of postwar American capitalism and the place of graduate business education within it.[12] In Drucker's view, professional business education in 1950 reflected a general consensus around training focused on three goals: the economic performance of the enterprise, "the problem of the human organization, which is the productive unit in our industrial society," and the relationship of business and management to society and economics. Further, most programs agree that "education for leadership" requires an integrated approach, combining a range of functional areas and broad "liberal education" rather than a focus on specific technical knowledge or skills.

With the changes in American business practices, the accelerating tilt toward MBA training, as well as a generational shift in the leadership of collegiate business programs, business schools were at a turning point. Drucker reviews three key difficulties facing business education of the time. The first is the challenge of teaching business to MBAs fresh out of college and with limited life experience. This is particularly the case for the rapidly expanding focus on "human relations" in the business curriculum. Drucker cautions that it is difficult for "young men without adult experience" to avoid the misunderstanding "that manners, honeyed words, and the right gestures constitute 'human relations.'"[13] The second difficulty is the challenge to produce forward-thinking entrepreneurs rather than administrators of a routine status quo. Without the entrepreneur, Drucker warns, "the large corporation turns arteriosclerotic." The final difficulty has to do with the nature of MBA "himself," as many are taught to consider themselves "crown princes." Some of this stems from the tendency of business classes to teach business problems always from the point of view of top management. But Drucker also faults businesses for essentially outsourcing the work of managerial training to business schools. Graduate business education had indeed arrived, with "the MBA" an ambivalent cultural type already familiar (at least to the readers of *Fortune*) by 1950.

The postwar period, then, was a time of considerable ferment in business training, particularly at the MBA and doctoral levels. Convergence of a number of factors amounted to a rebranding of the MBA along contours recognizable to this day. Academic policy initiatives, postwar economic expansion, the consolidation of the firm as the metonymic institution of US economic might, the heady sense of the United States as a major world power, and the counterbalancing uneasy sense of the postwar world as a rapidly changing environment requiring ever-advanced modes of understanding, all informed a critical reassessment and reorganization of business education that gave rise to the cultural figure of "the MBA" as a social type as much as a professional degree. Also at issue during this period were the initial institutional efforts to internationalize business education in the United States. The following sections turn to these mid-century processes of critical reinvention, which brought additional familiar contours of "the MBA" into view.

MANAGING THE POSTWAR WORLD

The 1950s and 1960s saw a set of landmark publications critically reviewing the state of business education and calling for its transformation in accord with what were seen as the rapidly transforming demands of the postwar world. The more coordinated efforts to reimagine a professional business curriculum in the United States were a pair of reports commissioned by the Carnegie and Ford Foundations (Gordon and Howell 1959; Pierson 1959). In 1953, Ford had established a Program in Economic Development and Administration, with objectives that included strengthening business training at the graduate level. Under this initiative, Ford made grants to various business programs seeking to support the application of behavioral sciences and mathematics to problems of business administration, the development of new programs in international business affairs, and the redesign of the business curriculum to respond to "new and changing demands for administrators in education, business, and government" (Carroll 1959, 156–57). The Foundation also sponsored a national conference in 1955 in coordination with AACSB,[14] established doctoral and faculty fellowships in business administration, and commissioned Berkeley economists Robert Aaron Gordon and James E. Howell to prepare a report on ways to "relate the objectives and educational methods of schools of business education to the requirements of business and society." Alongside this 470-page report, economist Frank Pierson (Swarthmore) led a separate study commissioned by the Carnegie Foundation.

A central question for both the Ford and Carnegie studies is how to rework the business curriculum in order to produce better-prepared and more capable managers. Both studies key on the rapidly expanding field of business administration, stressing the integrated knowledge of the recently consolidated MBA model over specialized functional training of accountants, operations specialists, finance experts, etc. In what may be the founding accounts of the "can't-get-no-respect" origin story of business education, the two studies review the history of business education as a struggle for credibility and both position their aims along the lines of similar efforts earlier in the century, consolidating the standards of other professions such as medicine or

ACCOUNTING FOR BUSINESS · 81

law. Yet, the sense of the emerging and rapidly changing need for new sorts of managerial talent makes the challenges of business education qualitatively different than the professional consolidation of law and medicine. And this is reflected in the figure of the manager being produced, who must be ready for anything. Pierson writes, "Broadly speaking, careers in business management require technical skills, general background, and 'strategic capacities,'" defining "strategic capacities" as

> the ability to grasp relationships among jobs, activities, physical magnitudes, and human beings in a business environment, to reason about business-operating problems with precision and imagination, to see immediate and future possibilities in situations, to use general principles to illuminate concrete problems, and to achieve workable solutions in complex cases. (1959, 10)

Using surveys of managers, Pierson notes changing trends among the managerial class. A generation of executives without college education, or with an education focused on engineering and science was being replaced by a generation with training in business and economics. College education was not a general criterion for hiring in many firms, although there was a growing preference for a liberal arts education among employers hiring college graduates and a preference for undergraduate rather than graduate degrees. "Those companies that do prefer graduate majors," wrote Pierson, "are frequently the larger ones, which view the principal asset of applicants with a Master's in Business Administration to be their broader educational background and greater potential for long-term career development" (1959, 12). Pierson reports that arts and science majors advance more quickly and are quicker to say that their college education contributed to their careers. He argues that undergraduate business training is too narrow and calls for the development of undergraduate programs focused on broad background preparation and graduate programs focused on solving management problems.

> Only in this way can business schools provide graduates who can meet the present trends and projected needs in our society: the expanding role of science, technology, and mathematics in business; the growing complexity of internal operations within business organizations; the increasing attention to human aspects of internal company operations, to relations between a firm and its external environment, and to a firm's social responsibilities; the increasing variety and complexity of this country's economic ties with other countries; and the need for maintaining the growth rate of the American economy through the development of new products, cheaper methods of pro-

duction, new materials, improved quality, and wider distribution—in essence the continual search for the new and the untried." (Pierson 1959, 14)

Gordon and Howell also recommend an increasing emphasis upon the MBA degree, arguing that this should be constituted as a *professional* rather than a graduate degree.[15] Similarly, they frame the MBA as something other than an extension of undergraduate business training. In the process they advocate for what became a standard two-year MBA curriculum, with the first year devoted to condensed coverage of core functional areas of business, with electives and some specialization in year two. The list of core functional areas follows the AACSB 1949 curricular recommendations. As we have seen, the condensed presentation of core business subjects, along with the totalizing view encouraged by the comprehensive survey amount to something of a paracurricular element of MBA training, instilling other sorts of sensibilities and subjectivities held to be integral to managerial practice.

In consolidating the contours of the MBA as a professional degree for business, the mid-century reports respond to shortcomings of business education as it had developed to date. But they also respond to an assessment of the needs for particular managerial qualities in the postwar setting and so signal the advent of the manager as a figure condensing a particular understanding of mid-twentieth-century business and its future. Gordon and Howell offer a listing of the "important trends that have been 'professionalizing' the practice of business," each compelling new managerial skills. Their list rehashes some familiar characterizations of twentieth-century business, including the growth in size of business firms, resulting in increased need for the coordination and planning of decision-making; the separation of ownership and management as described by Berle and Means, resulting in the increased role of the salaried executive; the accelerating pace of technological change, requiring "enterprising and competent leaders of industry and society, capable of facing up to the demands of the increasingly complex and science-based economy"; the increasing role of social science and statistics as part of Tylorian management science; and the need for "human relations engineers" to help to balance the needs of individuals alongside their integration within organizational environments. The final point on their list merits quoting separately.

The increasing complexity of the firm's external environment has steadily added to the difficulties of the businessman's task. This is by now a familiar story: the increase in the power of organized labor and the steady upward pressure on wages; the expanding role of government; the Cold War and the precarious state of international relations; changes in the distribution of political and economic power and in the climate of public opinion; and so on. (Gordon and Howell 1959, 13–15)

This is the job description for a Master of the Universe! Tasked with synthesizing the gamut of "hard" and "soft" knowledge, charting a successful course into the new and uncertain postwar economic frontier; resolving or ameliorating both long-standing and emerging tensions between labor and management, individualism and human fulfillment and conformity, free enterprise and government; and developing brand "USA" within a self-consciously unstable and shrinking world, the MBA became a repository of promise, and the answer to every question. And insofar as "business" or economy functioned as imperfect but undeniable surrogates for the social, managerial insight knew no bounds. It is little wonder, then, that honorifics such as "management guru" or "business guru" were introduced in the 1960s and 1970s to reference the profound wisdom of the leading theorists of management of the time.

The "guru" label, part of an orientalist appropriation of the idea of a spiritual master, energized in the 1960s and 1970s through the US counterculture, already reflects a wry cosmopolitanism in its adoption to refer to a management sage. That it has become such a routine way of thinking about management expertise (there is a subsidiary branch of business journalism focused on producing profiles and definitive lists of the top management gurus) also indexes the very tight connection in the United States between business management and personal fulfillment. This has roots in the industrial psychology work of Mayo along with mid-century concerns about the alienation and anomie of the "Organization Man" (cf. Whyte [1956] 2013). But the staying power of the term seems to me to disclose something more about the ways business management has become more than a corrective for the damage done by industrial capitalism, and become a site for the generation of a new and prized kind of sociality, and even an approximation of human perfectibility through managed quality control regimes.[16]

It is a short step, of course, from guru to rogue, and the MBA emerged as a profoundly ambivalent figure over the later twentieth century. On the one hand, the MBA remains at risk of the drawbacks of the system he is expected to surpass: the dullard corporate functionary. On the other, as the very model of a modern capitalist subject, the MBA is celebrated or scorned as a transgressive agent of system-bucking positive or negative transformation. Like other tricksters/heroes, the MBA condenses tensions, maps and, indeed, manages the boundaries and frontiers of social processes.

The Ford and Carnegie reports had a mixed reception by business schools, some of which were already embarked on some reforms called for in the reports, while others complained that the recommendations were so broad as to be meaningless.[17] The next few decades saw an accelerating rise in the number of MBA programs and MBA enrollment. The number of MBA-granting programs increased by an average of twenty per year between 1950 and 1975, with a rate of increase of thirty-five per year by the end of the period; more MBAs were awarded during the 1970s (over 387,000) than in the previous seven decades combined (Daniel 1998, 196ff.).

Also in line with the call for a focus on graduate training, there was a sharp increase in the number of PhDs awarded in business. This had a set of implications for MBA education. While the wall between professional MBA training and scholarly research remained in place, it was also the case that these PhD programs were training the next generation of business school faculty. And they couldn't train them fast enough. By the later decades of the twentieth century, MBA faculty were often scholars with limited business experience. Another result was that the focus on PhD training created a cohort of specialist scholars, feeding a tendency toward new specializations or departmental silos within business schools, where it sometimes seemed that the only real "generalists" were the MBAs themselves. The introduction of rankings in the 1970s and an aggressive hierarchy of corporate recruiting led to folklore about spectacularly lucrative positions for hotshot MBAs from the top programs and a corollary competition among firms to prove their standing by hiring MBAs from those programs (cf. Ho 2009). Against the economic malaise of the recession and inflation of the late 1970s, the MBA degree increasingly seemed like a golden passport (cf. McDonald 2017; Van Maanen 1983).

MANAGERS ABROAD

In June 1980, NBC broadcast a documentary titled *If Japan Can, Why Can't We?* Hosted by Lloyd Dobyns, the documentary contrasted the late 1970s economic malaise in the United States with the booming economic situation in Japan, which had gone in just a few decades from a country in postwar ruin, and an economy known for making low-quality products, to a nation renowned for its modern manufacturing processes producing high-quality goods at low cost. After reviewing complaints about the ways government regulation and union–management antagonisms limit economic productivity in the United States, the documentary turns to the case of Japan to present the postwar rise of an economic power. It is offered as a story of government and management committed to policies and practices supporting growth and innovation with workers fully involved in the process and loyal to the long-term goals of their companies.

The documentary highlights the work of an American consultant named William Edwards Deming as key to Japan's postwar success. Deming was a statistician and engineer, who developed over the 1920s and 1930s a statistical approach to quality control premised on the difference between normal and abnormal variation in a system. Any system will have some amount of variation or imperfection, and statistical analysis can help identify the normal range or occurrence of imperfections. While these might be accepted as a normal feature of the system, occurrences outside of the normal range should be investigated and corrected. Corrections result in a new system, which is subject to another round of statistical analysis. For Deming, blame for quality problems lay with management, not with workers, since quality problems were about a statistical variation built into the system. Management is responsible for the system and Deming advocated a continuous feedback process as workers are empowered to inform management about ways of improving productivity.

Deming was one of two statistical quality "gurus" who spent time in Japan in connection with postwar administration and rebuilding efforts with significant impact on the postwar development of Japanese industry. The other, Joseph M. Juran, was an engineer, similarly committed to practices of quality control and improvement. Juran's approach helped to popularize in business education the "Pareto Principle": a statistical rule of thumb indicating that 80% of the variation in a system is normally connected to 20% of the sample. Thus, effective quality control involves identifying and fixing the relatively small parts (20%) of a production process that are responsible for the vast majority (80%) of the defects. Juran cited anthropologist Margaret Mead as an influence, crediting her 1953 edited volume *Cultural Patterns and Technical Change* with helping him appreciate the ways ingrained cultural habits shape the reception of new technologies and ideas (Juran 1956, 1957, 1964; Mead 1953). For Juran, enlightened managers played a crucial role in the successful implementation of quality control measures.

Note that both Deming and Juran key on the figure of the manager and both connect the managerial point of view with the big-picture, commensurating vantage of their statistical approach. (Recall the aphorism "If you can measure it, you can manage it," presented in chapter 2.) In this regard, their respective critiques blaming management for poor product quality were nonetheless an affirmation of the necessary and productive role of the manager, connecting it directly to the physical manufacturing process and the properties of the final product.

Like Deming, Juran spent time working with Japanese industries, beginning in the 1950s. Biographies cast them as heroic figures in Japan, recognized with state honors and, in Deming's case, memorialized by a prize awarded by a Japanese industry group (Gabor 1990, 2000; Hoopes 2003). A common line in biographies of these two "quality gurus," ironic in the light of the focus of the Mead volume on the resistance to change in "traditional" societies, is that they each received warmer receptions in Japan than they did in the United States, where manufacturers were slow to see the value of their teachings.

The 1980 Dobyns documentary makes much of the fact that the secrets of Japanese success came from American innovators, although the documentary points as well to other elements of Japanese business practices and workplace culture—from worker loyalty and teamwork ethos to an openness to assimilating ideas from outside of Japan—that contributed to the impact of Deming's quality revolution. Juran similarly credited his observation of "quality circles" in Japanese industry—small work teams that discuss quality control issues and make recommendations—with shaping his approach to total quality management. And the documentary concludes with a few case studies of US businesses that have rediscovered Deming through the Japanese miracle and incorporated practices developed in Japanese industries such as quality control circles. In this regard, the hybrid practices of Japanese industrial success stood as something culturally other to US manufacturers, for whom the 1980s were marked by an imperative to emulate the foreign.

Accordingly, the 1980s marked a rapid intensification of the internationalization of business school curricula, driven in large measure by the postwar ascendance of Japan as a threat and a model. The field of operations management was particularly impacted here, as the application of statistical methods of quality control through changing workplace practices and the adoption of other Japanese innovations such as "the Toyota Way" of *kaizan* or "just in time" production, was heralded as the key to turning around the floundering auto industry and other manufacturing fields. James Womack, Daniel Jones, and Daniel Roos (1991) report on a study, begun in 1984, of Japanese "lean production" techniques, casting these as a world-changing revolution in industry for which the United States could have no response but to learn the Japanese way or be left behind as a global competitor. International Business textbooks similarly cast the period as one of an epochal shift, in which the intensifying global economy exhausted settled patterns of international business behavior (Bartlett, Ghoshal, and Birkinshaw 2003). Business faculty of a certain age—particularly those in operations management fields—would often talk to me about the 1980s as a time when everyone was talking about Japan, or when Japanese cases were de rigueur for MBA education.

From such tellings, it might appear that international business education began with the postwar rivalry with Japan and diversified over the late twentieth century to reflect the increasingly complex conditions of globalization. That periodization certainly captures part of the story. But the international focus of business education and the international concerns of US business in the 1980s and 1990s were not strictly new. This changing orientation to national and cultural differences, and a changing sense of the global field of business practices, emerges from a longer concern with international business and regional specialization. As part of the continuous cultural process of accounting for business, business programs repeatedly reencountered the global contexts of capitalism, periodically reinventing the meaning of the margins, with profound implications for the experts trained to manage them.

Special Agents and Country Hands

The early decades of the twentieth century saw the systematic employment of regional specialists in the Departments of State and Commerce, as in the Commerce Department's "Special Agents Series," providing country- and region-level information about trade and investment opportunities and strategic advice about getting things done on the ground in specific countries (e.g., Halsey 1918; Schurz 1921). These Special Agents crossed between government and academic work; some wrote textbooks on their regions of expertise (e.g., Schurz 1941). These initiatives reflect the concerns we have seen about international competitiveness and the growing international economic role of the United States at the time. Similarly, some of the early business schools had faculty with scholarly connections abroad, and some financed expeditions to survey world regions. For the most part, as with the Special Agent Series, these involved country-level knowledge or regional specialization. As the AACSB curricular consolidation of the 1950s advanced, these more specialized and area-focused international courses were left behind for the canonical functional areas of business (Daniel 1998, 138–48).

International Business (IB) thus had to be rediscovered at key moments over the century of business education. The earliest IB concentrations in US business schools developed over the late 1950s and 1960s, with programs established at Columbia (1956), Indiana (1959), Harvard (1961), and NYU (1963) (Robock 2003). As a component of the professionalization of US business training, these programmatic developments reflect the geopolitics and political economy of the postwar period and the strategic interest of the United States in shaping the economic recovery of regions impacted by the war. Initiatives such as the Economic Cooperation Administration (ECA), established under the Marshall Plan, facilitated interactions between European economists and business faculty in the United States and helped routinize and broaden international perspectives and expertise in US business programs (Fayerweather 1994). Under the auspices of the ECA, for instance, European business leaders and scholars attended programs with business faculty at Indiana, Columbia, and NYU.

These postwar entanglements created international professional networks of business scholars and a cosmopolitan consensus among academic business elite that constrained apprehension of national and cultural variations. By the 1970s, NYU had established a tripartite consortium for faculty and student exchanges (Program in International Management) connecting them with the École des Hautes Études Commerciales in Paris and the London Business School. Such international institutional networks built upon exchanges started immediately after the war. Faculty I interviewed pointed to periods of international residence or teaching exchanges that brought them to European campuses as triggering something of a conversion experience, leading to more profound internationalization of their teaching or scholarship. Some point to these experiences as leading them to prepare case studies on international themes, or to undertake research collaborations with European scholars. Some point to their experience as a foreigner on a European campus as heightening their sensitivity to international and cross-cultural themes in business. Comparable decentering experience is today increasingly packaged as essential to the value of the MBA curriculum, and particularly through the experience of short-term international study abroad (see chapter 5).

Another notable initiative during the postwar period was the American Universities Field Service (AUFS) program. Established in 1951 as an extension of the work of Institute of Current World Affairs, the AUFS was intended "to give young men of promise an opportunity to study, firsthand, foreign areas about which there is a general lack of knowledge in this country." With the participation of institutions including Brown University, the California Institute of Technology, Carleton College, Harvard Business School, University of Kansas, Stanford University, Tulane University, and the University of Washington, an early report announced:

> The field staff is expected to be built up to a strength of some 20 men. These men will prepare regular reports for the staffs of cooperating institutions, and will be available for consultation by visiting professors and graduate students. Each man will return home every 2 years, and will visit the campus of each participating institution to take part in seminars, faculty discussions and conferences, give lectures and meet with local bankers, businessmen, and journalists. As the plan expands this will mean that four or five field men will be visiting each university each year, to expand and enrich the university's existing courses of instruction with their direct reports on conditions in various sections of the world.[18]

AUFS reports were taken up in business school classrooms, where they served as the basis for case studies (Fayerweather 1994, 3).

The founding in 1958 of the Academy of International Business and the debut of the *Journal of International Business Studies* (1969) gave further scholarly coherence to the field, indexing an increasingly felt need for professionalized experts with international knowledge. As embodied by "special agents" or the intrepid "field men" of the AUFS, this expertise stemmed from traditional area studies scholarship: "country hands" leveraging a detailed knowledge of place to produce reports of strategic relevance for business practices. This was echoed in corporate organizational structures, where international posts were typically staffed by managers with long-term connections to a foreign country. Although these posts are remembered today as dead-end middle management positions, there was a sense that "our man in Buenos Aires" was an adept of the place, with deep knowledge deriving from long-term personal immersion.

CIBER Business and the Global Order

The push toward IB gained additional momentum in the 1980s, spurred—as we have seen—by the challenges to US international competitiveness in the face of the rise of Japanese manufacturing. The rise and consolidation over the 1980s of neoliberal "free market fundamentalism," supported by shifting policy priorities at the IMF and World Bank, as well as a series of "Structural Adjustment Policies" implemented in developing nations, facilitated and in many ways compelled the increasingly routinized engagement of US capital across the world (e.g., Harvey 2005; Mirowski and Plehwe 2009; Stiglitz 2003). This emergent reframing of the international space of capitalism had the dual effect of establishing international engagement as an inevitable component of business practice, and thereby created a new conceptualization of risk and a requirement for its management across physical and cultural space.

One indication of the perceived critical need for the retooling of US business training in view of a new landscape of global capitalism is the participation of US federal government funding in the efforts. By the late 1980s, US business schools were competing for federal support to establish CIBERS: Centers for International Business Education and Research, dedicated to fostering international business competitiveness. The CIBER program was constituted in 1988 through an amendment to Title VI, Part B of the Higher Education Act of 1965; that is, as a component of the Congressional Act that also provides National Resource Center and Foreign Language and Area Studies (FLAS) Fellowship funding. With average annual awards of $304,700 supporting faculty and curriculum development, international business research, and outreach to US businesses at fifteen centers around the country,[19] the CIBER program constitutes an effort to routinize the production and application of international knowledge in business training and practice.

That the institutional "slot" for this initiative is the administrative home for the federal area studies project—itself an effort to harness the production and circulation of knowledge about international spaces to the perceived national interests of the United States—is telling. The alignment of IB training with area studies certainly reflects the earlier characteristics of international business knowledge concentrated in country hands. However, over the course of the 1980s, the texture of international expertise—in business as well as in area studies—was changing under the ascendant frame of "globalization" (cf. Dirlik 1999; Escobar 1995; Guyer 2004; Pletsch 1981; Rafael 1994; Szanton 2004).

Theodore Levitt's 1983 article, "The Globalization of Markets," discussed in chapter 1, is representative of the time: taking the intensifying interactions across cultures as a symptom of a dawning ecumenical modernity, in which successful global firms would develop and market products standardized to emerging global norms. Two decades later, this vision of global standardization is widely considered by influential business scholars to be inadequate.

Pankaj Ghemawat, for instance, writes of "semi-globalization," detailing the various ways in which the majority of people are *not* globally connected, and challenging managers to do business in a world "where differences still matter" (2007). Alan Rugman and Alain Verbeke (2004) have argued that regional units of analysis (defined by geographical and cultural proximity), rather than "globalization," better fit the actual business activities of multinational enterprises. And in an international business textbook used in some MBA programs, Bartlett, Ghoshal, and Birkinshaw (2003) present a (native) periodization of four "evolving" stages of internationalization: "international mentality," "multinational mentality," "global mentality" (here they reference Levitt), and the "transnational mentality." The current "transnational" business mentality is a strategic response to "countervailing forces of localization" and reassertions of "national preferences" that emerged in response to the powerful threat of global homogenization made patent over the 1980s (Bartlett, Ghoshal, and Birkinshaw 2003, 10ff.) This trend was echoed in the theme of the 2007 Annual Meetings of the Academy of International Business: "Bringing the Country Back In."

Of course, in the context of MBA education especially, this is not a return to the in-depth local knowledge of the classic area hands. The challenge as Bartlett, Ghoshal, and Birkinshaw frame it is

> for companies to become more responsive to local needs while retaining their global efficiency. . . . In such companies, key activities and resources are neither centralized in the parent company, nor decentralized so that each subsidiary can carry out its own tasks on a local-for-local basis. (2003, 12)

This magical middle ground, balancing standardization with the nuances and niches of localization, is familiar from other discussions of the neoliberal moment. And this literature has shown that the world of such a "transnational mentality" is made rather than found (Ho 2005; Tsing 2000, 2005; Wilk 1995). Indeed, much as the very idea of "the global" requires the cultural constitution of specific places and their scalar connections to national, regional, and global circuits of capital (Ho 2005; Tsing 2000), the renaissance of place and region in global business thinking is a blueprint as much as a map.

．　．　．

MBA curricula, at any given point in time, crystallize a particular reading of the exigencies of contemporary capitalism: the managerial subjects required and the curricular subjects and methods adequate to produce them. In the current moment they are calibrated to the production of standardized international competencies adaptable to multiple local contexts. This is coordinate with what the programs understand to be trends in corporate hiring. Where international and cross-cultural expertise may once have been the purview of expatriate managers, viewed as having limited career prospects beyond their place-specific experiences, the expectation increasingly is that a wide range of mid- and lower-level managers will be involved in international activities in a range of places. In this view, all business is global, and the core competencies of any MBA ought to include the ability to work as part of business teams that span borders and cultures. In turn, MBA curricula have moved away from a pedagogy that might present international and global business issues as supplements (electives or additional themes for the final week of a module) and toward one in which international themes are taught as part of the basic condition of business practice.

A core goal of this curriculum is the production of MBA managers attuned to the dimensions of cultural difference newly understood as integral to the global order—a value-adding feature rather than a backward bug. As we shall see in subsequent chapters, the effective management of otherwise irreducible cultural difference is a source of value to be harnessed by globally adept MBAs. As a step toward that discussion, and to get a better sense of what MBAs mean when they talk about culture, the next chapter reviews the assimilation of the culture concept in business training over the twentieth century.

FOUR

The Currency of Culture

It is preterm orientation for an entering MBA cohort. Over the course of a few days, MBA administrators with the help of second-year students have put the new group of some sixty excited MBAs through their professionalizing paces of team-building, trust-building, norm-setting activities. There have been formal receptions with benedictions from the dean and leading faculty, and slick videos with thrumming up-beat soundtracks to show the students the condensed seven-minute version of the challenging and rewarding journey on which they are embarked. There have been speed-networking exercises—interpersonal scavenger hunts as we try to collect different kinds of biographical facts from different kinds of people in the cohort—and Myers-Briggs personality assessments to sort the group in other ways. ("Raise your hands if you are orange," instructs an associate dean.) There have been outdoors team exercises with blindfolds and other props to inspire trust, and classic scavenger hunts to bond the first-year study teams.

Presentations from MBA clubs give us a glimpse of a broad silent curriculum of professionalizing and networking activities for students interested in learning more about Latin America, golf, or wine. The abundance confronts us with personal and professional choices to be made in the extracurricular marketplace, and announces the hyperscheduled MBA life we are about to begin. The orientation events call for different gradations of professional dress—business formal/business professional/business casual/casual—keeping us on our sartorial toes.

As part of the orientation, the group gathered to learn about culture and diversity. We started with a version of a card-game-based exercise often used for diversity training in academic and corporate settings. Here, students are arranged in small groups around a set of tables. Each table has a deck of cards and each player gets a set of rules for the game. Students read the rules silently and begin play, with the additional rule that they are unable to speak to one another while playing. After a couple of rounds, one student from each table moves to another table in the room. Each table begins play again. However, unknown to the participants, the rules at each table are different, meaning that the newcomer at each table is continuously doing things wrong: playing out of turn, valuing the cards incorrectly, etc.

This is our introduction to culture. More precisely, this is our introduction to culture as a limitation, a liability, a source of failure. Culture drives mistakes: playing the game the wrong way. Culture is a font of inside information, hidden from view, and unequally available to all participants, particularly outsiders. And culture confers a different set of blinders on insiders, who find themselves frustrated by the counterproductive play of the idiot who just joined their table, ignorant of the fact that at her home table her card playing makes perfect sense.

DISCOVERING CULTURE WITH FIRST-YEAR MBAS

The MBAs then convene for a formal presentation on "managing cultural diversity," led by a professor, Tim, with expertise in organizational design. Our conventional understanding of diversity is too narrow, he explains. "Diversity is a resource." Differences "mark unique skills." But we encounter barriers of ignorance and convenience in managing diversity: "ignorance" in the form of negative stereotypes; "convenience" because it is easier to work with people similar to us. Now more than ever, Tim tells us, managers need to be aware of these barriers. Cross-cultural experience is essential to contemporary business. The MBA program, he promises, will give us cross-cultural experience without having to travel.

Tim launches into a set of varying dimensions of culture—manifestations of difference managers may encounter: time, dress, eye contact, eating habits, ways of greeting. There is a strongly territorialized sense of culture as illustrations evoke broad regional types (Mediterranean culture, Latin American culture) with nested country-level examples (Italy, Mexico). Against a set of examples of other people who may be late for appointments, kiss at the start of a business meeting, eat noisily, defer to authority, and not signal disagreement, he elicits the cultural norms of the MBA program, which we have been striving to embody all preterm. "We" are individual-focused, we expect punctuality, we are encouraged to ask questions, we respect one another's personal space. This complex and reflexive field of difference is boiled down to a four-quadrant graph, mapping two dimensions of variance: individualist versus collective orientation and a high degree of vertical hierarchy versus a more horizontal or egalitarian social hierarchy (figure 4). This is our first glimpse of the graphs and tables we will be seeing in our course classes starting in a few days.

The United States, we decide, is to be placed in the upper left quadrant, reflecting a high degree of individuality, and a relative low focus on status differentiation. Tim polls international students among the MBA cohort to ask where their home countries/cultures fall. China and India, for instance, are placed in the lower right quadrant (low individualism, high status differentiation). A student from Jamaica suggests that Jamaica be placed in the upper right quadrant (high individualism, high status differentiation). Our professor declares that Jamaica can serve "as a bridge" between the cultures in the neighboring quadrants. The summary of takeaways from this part of the session includes this turn toward engineering the multicultural spaces of the MBA program: (1) Cultural difference is a manageable resource; (2) Managers should avoid ignorance about differences; (3) Managers should embrace difference and find synergies; (4) The MBA program is an opportunity to learn about cultural differences.

As if to hammer home this fourth point, the session concludes with a "cross-cultural quiz" presented by the MBA program dean. On one side of the sheet are questions challenging us to identify the local cultural meaning of a variety of behaviors.

- *An Indian student is shaking his head from side to side as you are talking to him. This gesture means. . .?*
- *If a Korean friend gives you a gift, you should not open it in front of her. True or false?*
- *In the United States, it is acceptable to ask someone their salary. True or false?*

On the back is a set of paragraph-length scenarios. Each describes a cross-cultural interaction that ends in some sort of failure, followed by three or four possible explanations of what went wrong. Every case involves a national culture represented among the MBA cohort, and the dean tries eagerly to bring international students into the conversation. (She asks an Indian student to demonstrate the "head bobble." Where are my Japanese?! she calls out at another point to help explain the meaning of slurping soup.) These are all

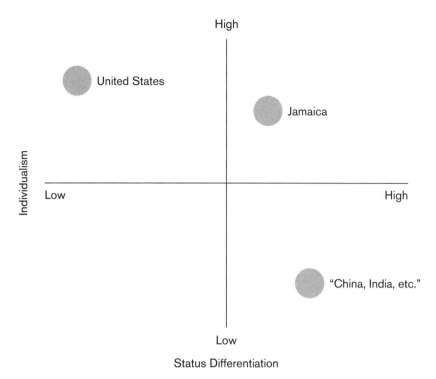

High

United States

Jamaica

Individualism

Low —————————————————|————————————————— High

"China, India, etc."

Low

Status Differentiation

FIGURE 4. This complex field of difference is boiled down to a four-quadrant graph.

of a piece with other socializing efforts during preterm as the cohort is figured as a space of cultural difference from which MBAs can extract important managerial lessons.

. . .

This chapter focuses on the shifting preoccupation with culture in the world of business training. The ideas about culture evident in the MBA orientation reflect the current state of culture-talk in the business world. One goal of this chapter is to present a genealogy of such culture-talk in business since the 1950s. That periodization is connected with the emerging post–World War II global political and economic order. In this regard, I am also interested in this chapter, as I am across this book, in thinking about globalization as a context for business practice. Obviously, globalization generates intensified forms of crosscultural contact in the world. In addition, globalization is generative of new kinds of difference and new kinds of consciousness of difference. Among these new kinds of consciousness of difference is the very contemporary idea that everyone has a culture (cf. Hegeman 2012; Sahlins 1999). It seemed quite obvious to the MBAs in the room, for instance, that each had a culture to be located on the four-quadrant graph. One upshot of this in MBA training is that "culture" has become integral to the valuable expertise MBA programs confer and authorize. And, insofar as this culture-talk is connected with (culturally apprehended) understandings of risk and the specific challenges of global business, this chapter sets the stage for the remaining chapters of the book, which examine the globalization of MBA education in ethnographic detail.

What MBAs mean when they talk about "culture" at once reflects and shapes the world of business MBAs seek to engage. Over the decades reviewed in this chapter, "culture" has become increasingly crucial to the managerial legitimacy so carefully and continuously cultivated by MBA programs. "Culture" plays an important role in the shifting conceptualization of, and orientation to, international difference in business practice beginning in the mid-twentieth century. The dawn of culture-talk in the 1950s and 1960s lines up with a broader turn in applied social science to the end of a more engineered modernity. And, from that watershed, "culture" serves as a very telling barometer of the shifting native worldview of late-capitalist, neoliberal global business.

CULTURE IN CONTEXT

There is another story to tell about culture, this one rooted in my home discipline of anthropology, which has long claimed scholarly ownership of the small-"c" culture concept. Over the last few decades, as culture's stock has risen in the field of business and in popular conventional wisdom, it has declined precipitously among anthropologists, many of whom are ambivalent about the idea. Without getting too far into the weeds of (largely) intradisciplinary debates about culture, it is helpful to review the vicissitudes of the concept because anthropologists have played important roles in the translation of the culture concept for business, and because anthropologists' questioning of the concept and business schools' embrace of it are shaped by the shared context of globalization and neoliberal capitalism.[1] Additionally, it may be helpful for anthropologists to keep in mind the purchase of culture-talk in the field of business as we sharpen our own analytic tools, and critical reflections on the culture concept from within anthropology may be useful in making sense of and productively critiquing culture in the business world.

The modern anthropological concept of culture is principally linked to the "American" school of anthropology. The American focus on culture is often cast in counterpoint to a British anthropological tradition that has focused rather on "society," and it is usually characterized as having roots in German romantic scholarship conveyed through the immigrant father of the American school of cultural anthropology, Franz Boas. Over the first half of the twentieth century, Boas and a number of his students elaborated a relativist, geographical culture-area-focused understanding of culture as a shared ethos shaping peoples' experiences and organization of life in ways that varied from society to society.

Systematic critiques of the concept of culture emerged forcefully within anthropology beginning in the 1970s and 1980s, and turn around three principal sites of dissatisfaction. One of these has to do with the boundedness of the culture concept, which seems at times to refer to a stable and objectively discrete group of people, represented in the stereotypical anthropological text titled "The X." This view of culture (if it ever uncritically existed) was increasingly unsettled by the empirical reality of social change in the context of colonialism, and, especially in the wake of World War II, by the integrating postwar, postcolonial global order. A corollary critique of culture concerns the exoticizing West/rest contrast implicit in some framings of the concept. Such a view was unsettled by the dawning small world of the 1960s and developments such as the inclusion of newly independent nation-states within global organizations like the United Nations, underscoring the contemporaneity of all extant societies in contrast with an ethnographic tendency to describe some as frozen in time. Additionally, this systematic questioning of anthropological concepts and practices was energized by the increasing participation of multiple voices in the anthropological project. Scholars of color, female scholars, native scholars, queer scholars, and scholars from the Global South at once brought new perspectives to anthropological scholarship and helped illuminate the degree to which anthropology had been shaped by the largely white and male points of view of its practitioners and its colonial contexts.

Running through all of these points of critique are the complexities of post–World War II modernity, taking shape over the final decades of the century as globalization. For many current anthropologists, who came of age in a discipline reshaped by these critiques, culture is understood to be inadequate to the social dynamism and complexity of globalization. The movement of populations, the new possibilities of economic and affective connections across diasporic settings, the appropriation and circulation of distant cultural forms (music, television, clothing styles, etc.) through new technologies, make it impossible to ever talk about "The X" as a bounded stable culture. This was matched by calls for increased attention by anthropologists to the hybridizing, syncretizing processes ("cultural flows") by which culture was uprooted from any stable connection to place or people, to be blended or taken as a resource for creative improvisation by individuals the world over. Anthropology shaped by this critique of the culture concept has tended to focus on highly particularized sites of individual subject-making, with larger scales of analysis informed by concepts such as globalized flows, modernity, or neoliberalism. Culture has been a relatively silent partner for many anthropologists of late.

It is important to the story I am telling to note that by the 1990s, anthropological critiques of culture in the face of globalization reflected an understanding of the world apparently identical to that held by other social scientists, business theorists, and commentators. At the core of this consensus was a sense of a dawning ecumene, discussed in chapter 1, in which national and cultural boundaries were decreasingly relevant in the face of an ascendant global culture—a flat world.[2] And yet, while culture remains a point of contention among anthropologists to the present day, the idea has had a renaissance in the field of business. I return to that story now.

CULTURING THE UGLY AMERICAN

By the middle decades of the twentieth century, a set of Franz Boas's students[3] were engaged in public discussions drawing upon the culture concept in ways that made it a cross-disciplinary referent for a modern educated engagement with the world (cf. Hegeman 1999). In a host of government institutions connected to the Second World War and its aftermath, as well as in a broader set of public discussions, culture-talk was very much in the air, evident, for instance, in the coining and adoption in public discourse of terms like "culture shock" (attributed to Cora Du Bois and Kalervo Oberg) and "enculturation" (Melville Herskovits).

A set of postwar institutions helped to frame spaces of implicitly or explicitly marked cross-cultural exchange taken as integral to US engagement with the postwar world. These included programs like the Economic Cooperation Administration and the American Universities Field Staff, discussed in chapter 3, which posted area and country specialists from various disciplines around the world to send back correspondence and periodically visit a consortium of sponsoring universities. Additionally, the State Department's Foreign Service Institute included cultural competency training among its programs for foreign service officers.

Other symptoms of the moment include the success of the 1958 novel *The Ugly American*, which detailed the provincial incompetence and ineffectiveness of Americans working abroad (Lederer and Burdick 1958). The circulation of the phrase over the postwar decades amounted to a wry recognition in some social circles of the shortcomings of Americans abroad—at least in the eyes of a host of critical others who were inevitably part of American senses of self. And the emergence over this time of the institutionalized project of area studies provided at once a broader ethos of interdisciplinary cross-fertilization in the service of producing strategic international knowledge and the conceptual grooves and rails of translatability across disciplines and comparability within and across formally enshrined regions.

One influential point of connection between mid-century anthropology, these institutional developments, and the emerging preoccupation with culture in the nascent field of business training is the work of Edward T. Hall, a linguistic anthropologist often cited as a founder of the field of intercultural communication (Pusch 2004). Hall was trained at Columbia (PhD 1942), then the institutional center of the Boasian world.[4]

After a brief stint at the University of Denver, Hall took a faculty appointment at Bennington College. While much is often made of Hall's exposure to psychology during his early career (particularly his association with the psychological anthropologist Abram Kardiner at Columbia, and with Erick Fromm, who was on the faculty at Bennington), it may be more relevant to this story that among the faculty colleagues he recalled as close friends during the Bennington years was a young philosopher and political scientist named Peter Drucker. Hall's two years at Bennington were just after Drucker published *Concept of the Corporation* (1946).

Hall left Bennington in 1950 to take up service as the Director of the Point IV Training Program of the State Department's Foreign Service Institute (FSI). "Point IV" referred to a bullet point in a 1949 speech by President Truman calling for a US effort to provide global foreign aid and technical assistance to postwar recovering and other developing nations. Hall's work at FSI involved preparing Foreign Service officers for postings abroad. The training focused on the links between culture and communication, and stressed an approach to communication that went well beyond words, to underscore proxemics, kinesics, and other cultural orientations and bodily habits implicated in meaningful interactions.

Hall's 1959 book, *The Silent Language*, reflects this focus on the tacit dimensions of culture and their impact on communication. Hall's work attracted notice in the business world, which was itself increasingly preoccupied by the challenges of international difference, as "trade," along with "peace" and "freedom" were the rallying points of US engagement with the postwar world. In 1960, Hall published a condensed adaptation of his book in the *Harvard Business Review* (HBR), "The Silent Language in Overseas Business" (E. Hall 1960). In 1962 he was appointed as a Leatherbee Lecturer at the Harvard Business School.[5]

In the HBR article, Hall sought to assist Americans, as "relative newcomers on the international business scene," in decoding "the many variables of foreign behavior and custom" that "complicate" their efforts. Although "the American" is familiar with a variety of behaviors through the "peculiar" habits of "the man next door," those venturing overseas must be prepared for a difference of another order. Hall uses a series of vignettes. An American executive is left waiting in the outer office of a Latin American official. "What the American does not know is the point at which the waiting becomes significant." An American in Cairo to meet with a "highly recommended" potential Arab business associate is unsettled by the contrast between his modern hotel and Western amenities found in "the new part of town," and the "crowded," "dilapidated," "smelly" environment of his potential business partner, whose meeting with him is marked by constant interruptions. (E. Hall 1960, 87–88)

> One minute everything looks familiar and he is on firm ground; the next, familiar landmarks are gone. His greatest problem is that so much assails his senses all at once that he does not know where to start looking for something that will tell him where he stands. He needs a frame of reference—a way of sorting out what is significant and relevant. (E. Hall 1960, 87–88)

Hall goes on to illustrate five dimensions of silent language through which tacit cultural communication is achieved or frustrated: "the language of time, of space, of material possessions, of friendship patterns, and of agreement" (E. Hall 1960). For each dimension, Hall provides an example from another society in which standard American expectations of the meaning of time, personal space, the entailments of friendship do not hold. His discussion is relativizing in that he calls attention to US assumptions as an example of the silent language he is discussing.

The discussion proceeds through a series of thumbnail examples. The section on time, for instance, invokes the United States, Ethiopia, the Middle East, "the Japanese," and "the Indians of South Asia," imparting practical knowledge of these specific cultural contexts. Thus, "When the Indian makes a place in his time, it is yours to fill in every sense of the word if you realize that by so doing you have crossed a boundary and are now friends with him." Or, "[The Japanese] have learned that Americans are vulnerable to long waits. One of them expressed it, 'You Americans have one terrible weakness. If we make you wait long enough, you will agree to anything.'" "The point of all this," Hall concludes, "is that time communicates just as surely as do words and that the vocabulary of time is different around the world. The principle to be remembered is that time has different meanings in each country" (1960, 89).

Hall's checklist of five dimensions of tacit culture, and his brief vignettes of failure have retained currency in contemporary discussions of culture in management education. Tweak some of the masculinist language of the American "businessman," and a few other more dated references, and Hall's HBR piece could easily accompany the handout on cultural diversity described in the introduction to this chapter. Time, personal space, impersonal individualism versus the relative importance of family and social ties remain at the core (and, for some, comprise the entirety) of culture-talk in the world of business.

But some elements of Hall's discussion betray his (relative) outsider status to the world of management training and also reflect the historical moment of his writing. For instance, at the end of his HBR essay, Hall cautions against the assumption of easy takeaways. The lesson to be learned about doing business in any one culture is not likely to be one-dimensional. "The point is simply this. It takes years and years to develop a sound foundation for doing business in a given country." Here, he betrays a more classic anthropological sense of long-term field research as the basis for a more holistic sense of culture. He also advances this point to suggest that when a firm finds someone developing competence in doing work in another country (our man in Cairo), the "home office" should heed their insights about how to do business in X and not hobble them with demands about narrow time frames for getting agreements signed, or business decisions that do not take into account local relationships.

Despite Hall's warnings, this holistic sense of culture was quickly jettisoned in favor of more instrumentalist views of the managerial engagement with cultural difference—a "good enough" understanding of culture. Hall's message of cultural complexity has certainly been received. But, as I argue below and in subsequent chapters, the complexity of culture has been embraced—indeed quite literally priced-in—as an incommensurable excess inevitably at stake in cross-cultural contexts. This irreducible difference is valued as a component of risk—deriving from the sort of communications failures and misunderstandings illustrated in Hall's examples and in the orientation exercises during MBA preterm—and MBAs who learn this lesson enhance their own value insofar as they can manage the cultural margins.

A Good-Enough Sense of Culture

What I have in mind with "good-enough" involves the instrumental use by other professions of shorthand poachings of the culture concept.[6] Focusing on medical anthropology, and building on the work of Didier Fassin (2001, 2010), Elizabeth Durham (2016) describes the adoption by nonanthropologist international health workers of "concise ethnographic soundbites" ("cultural keys," in Fassin's terms) to make sense of cross-cultural medical interventions. The tendency here is to find in other cultural practices the root cause of the problem being addressed. Durham refers to "a second version of anthropology at play here," by which she means the ways nonanthropologists in the medical field make use of selected insights attributed to anthropologists, while rolling their eyes at the slow pace and self-referential detours of scholarly anthropological production. Encoded in the eye-roll is an appreciation of the insights of ethnography, which includes some additional detail that the nonanthropologist practitioners recognize as important, but cannot make use of.

I don't intend "good-enough" to suggest some arch commentary on anthropology under way in business programs. Few MBA faculty, and fewer MBAs, have a developed sense of the work of ethnography or anthropological discussions of culture. This is not about "us" anthropologists, except as an instructive illustration of the afterlives of the culture concept, as some anthropologists give it up for dead. For it is a short step from the borrowing of culture among international medical workers to the cultural insights taken as integral to the making of global MBAs. Thus, I mean to call attention to culture-talk in the field of international business as it at once adopts shorthand cultural keys to define manageable dimensions of difference and evokes a broader excess of difference always at the margins of manageability.

This cusp of manageable difference staked out by a good-enough sense of culture is the space MBAs are being prepared to transit. And they are being prepared to do this in a good-enough way, not through the hard-won expertise of long-term immersion, but through a nimble global flexibility enabled by a general cultural competence. MBAs are challenged to become adepts of cultural difference if not masters of any particular case. Here, to my ear, the qualifier good-enough also resonates with shades of the verb "to manage," implying doing just enough to clear a basic acceptable threshold (there being little marginal value in doing any more).

From Specificity to Cosmopolitanism

Hall's work came during a period of remarkable ferment in international business activities.[7] The year 1959 marked a turning point for business education in the United States, with the publication of the Ford and Carnegie studies discussed in chapter 3. The late 1950s were also something of a watershed for international business training. The Academy of International Business was founded in 1958.[8] The inaugural issue of the journal *The International Executive* was published in 1959. The managing editor of the journal, and one of the earliest members of AIB, was a business scholar widely considered a founder of the field of international business, John Fayerweather. In 1960, Fayerweather published the first textbook focused on international business, *Management of International Business Operations: Texts and Cases*, which drew on his 1959 monograph, *The Executive Overseas*. Fayerweather's work reflects some of the earliest and more business-oriented assimilation of the culture concept.

Initially trained as a geological engineer, John Fayerweather attended Harvard Business School after service in World War II. Fayerweather's studies were interrupted when he was recalled as a reservist for stateside service during the Korean War, but by summer 1953 he started his doctoral research on foreign mine management in Mexico and Canada. He cites this as a productive first experience of fieldwork, noting that he and his wife were exposed to "the range of Mexican society from cosmopolitan Mexico City to the remote back mountain country where mines tend to be found" (Fayerweather 1994, 3).

Back at Harvard, Fayerweather was assigned to the teaching rotation in the "Business Responsibilities and American Society" course. That course was under revision to include sessions on international business topics, and

Fayerweather, based on his emerging international experience (a summer of field research), was tapped to coordinate that part of the class. In that capacity, Fayerweather hosted AUFS scholars and also had contact with European faculty visiting HBS as part of a program to increase European competitiveness. A few Mexican colleagues from his research connections there were also in residence at HBS at the time.

Fayerweather was subsequently assigned to the "Foreign Trade Management" course, and was given some freedom to update the curriculum. As he describes his thinking, "It seemed clear that the major feature of international business our students would encounter was not export management but running operations spread around the world—factories, banks, mines, and the like." He renamed the course "Management of Foreign Operations," reflecting the objective of developing in students "a sense of the adjustments in business methods needed to function effectively in foreign economic, political and cultural environments" (1994, 5).

Fayerweather describes a course focused around a set of five detailed country studies,[9] reflecting his belief that students needed a "deeper" understanding achieved through a "cumulative sense of the context." He saw this as an extension of the case study approach, and some of the cases used in the course were developed in collaboration with his AUFS and Mexican colleagues. He also used films (some produced by companies with operations overseas) to achieve the "intimate, personal experience" he sought to evoke in his students. After developing the course in 1953 and 1954, Fayerweather intensified his research focus on the Mexican case, undertaking more systematic open-ended interview-based research with a set of Mexican and US managers in US firms doing business in Mexico. Fayerweather refers to this phase of his research as "cross-cultural" and he also reports a different kind of cross-cultural scholarly experience: growing collaborations with non–business school affiliated scholars, including Edward Hall.

Hall and Fayerweather each had brief essays in the third issue of *The International Executive*. Hall's piece, titled "The Anthropology of Manners," summarized an essay published in *Scientific American* and is close to the "Silent Language" material. Hall concludes *The International Executive* essay saying, "The role of the anthropologist in preparing people for service overseas is to open their eyes and sensitize them to the subtle qualities of behavior—tone of voice, gestures, space and time relationships—that so often build up feelings of frustration and hostility in other people with a different culture" (1959, 10).

Fayerweather's piece, "The Executive Overseas," is drawn from his book of the same title, and summarizes the opening vignette of the book. Harry Grey has been sent to Mexico to help solve a problem with a parts supplier for his firm's local manufacturing operation. Grey wants their local Mexican manager (Pedro Gomez) to break relations with a supplier who has been occasionally late in delivering parts and work with a different local supplier. Gomez seems to agree with Grey, but never follows through to either insist on better service from the current supplier or contract with a new one. Grey's posting to Mexico drags on for months as he makes little headway in working with Gomez to solve the problem.

Fayerweather unpacks the problem. Business relations in Mexico are anchored in friendships; Gomez has close relations with his supplier. Although some deliveries may be late, there is an underlying dependability that he is not willing to give up for a new relationship. Compounding that is resentment toward his US boss. Fayerweather explains, "In most of the underdeveloped countries, especially those which have gone through extended periods of colonial domination, feelings of inferiority and insecurity are common in relations with US executives." "To work effectively overseas," Fayerweather concludes, "the US executive should develop an understanding of the differing administrative attitudes found in other cultures, an appreciation of the feelings toward him as a foreigner abroad and a capacity to adjust his actions to function effectively in this environment" (1959, 6).

Like Hall, Fayerweather sees cultural differences as a way to account for "difficulties in relations between United States and foreign executives" (1959, 6). Like Hall, Fayerweather uses a set of vignettes to illuminate management failures that can be traced to ineffective communication and incomplete understanding on the part of US executives abroad. In this regard, Fayerweather, like Hall, is conceptualizing an interactional intercultural space. Within this space, Fayerweather, like Hall, is intent on pointing out that US executives are themselves shaped by a specific set of cultural conventions and values, of which they must be aware. And, like Hall, Fayerweather asserts a holistic, multidimensional sense of culture, advocating that doing business across cultures requires some degree of specialization in a particular national culture, and that this is acquired over time and through immersive experience.[10]

At the same time, Fayerweather takes up the difficulties of intercultural communication more specifically as a business management challenge. Alongside Hall's list of silent languages, Fayerweather discusses four dimensions of cultural attitudes: attitudes toward other people, values, social status attitudes, and attitudes toward individual work. Fayerweather introduces an understanding of culture based not only on tradition and relativism, but also on the efficacy of certain cultural attitudes as a way to get things done. He encourages the overseas executive to take a step back and consider local customs in the larger scheme of things. Such habits emerge because they served to meet certain challenges. This is an instrumentalist view of culture, and it echoes a definition popularized in the 1950s by anthropologist Clyde Kluckhohn, emphasizing the "distinctive achievements of human groups" (1951).[11] Seen in this light, the executive should be flexible to consider local ways as potentially useful. But Fayerweather also notes that the challenges local cultures confront change over time, and that local cultures therefore are also undergoing processes of change. "Inevitably," he points out, "there is some lag" between the requirements of a new historical moment "and the formulation of new attitudes at the cultural level" (Fayerweather 1960, 21).

With this dimension of change and the accountability of culture to some sort of historically appropriate effectiveness, Fayerweather introduces a new kind of managerial subjectivity to the discussion of culture in international business. Fayerweather's executive is tasked with fully analyzing a given management problem. Removing cultural blinders improves the analysis, but it does not mean that adapting to local culture is the correct answer. Of the Mexican case with Harry Grey and Pedro Gomez, it may be that the traditional approach favored by Pedro is the best one to follow. At the same time, Grey has data indicating that at least *some* Mexican suppliers operate more in accordance with conventional US expectations. "There is an evolution in business relationships underway in Mexico," Fayerweather explains, "and [Grey] may also be right" (Fayerweather 1959, 7). Here, the payoff of understanding other cultures may be better managing their modernization. Seeing cultural difference has become an especially acute way of seeing change.

Fayerweather comments on the success of some US executives in working with foreign associates. Some, he notes, are instinctively flexible in modifying their expectations and actions to achieve results. Others, "have gone so far" that they've lost their initial cultural attitudes and "gone native." Fayerweather continues,

it does not appear, however, that the men who have gone that far are in an over-all sense the most effective executives overseas. They are inclined to lose sight of company objectives and to have difficulty in relations with other United States executives and with the home office. The effective men seem to be those who have retained their own attitudes and values intact, but are able to depart from their dictates sufficiently to take positions in relations with foreign executives which are realistic in that they are capable of producing useful results. (1959, 9)

Culture here is an input to the managerial decision process. Managers are students of cultures (including their own), but slaves to none (including their own). "Avoiding these pitfalls requires three things of a man," writes Fayerweather: "1) understanding his own positions—his objectives, his expectations and the effect of his actions on others; 2) understanding the point of view of the foreign executive; and 3) enough flexibility and self-discipline to modify the first to fit the second." The upshot is that changing practices in other countries "may be encouraged or discouraged by the actions of United States executives" (1959, 11).

With Fayerweather, then, we have a particular mid-century uptake of the concept of culture in the field of business—a field that was itself at the time in the process of a dramatic professionalization and legitimation with respect to a domestic society and a dawning international order seen as an increasingly salient and unavoidable challenge and opportunity for US business. Culture emerges as a tool of business decisions, with two connected implications. One involves engineering the postwar economic order, with culture as a medium—and eventual remainder—of the dawning small world.[12] At the same time, cultural awareness is connected to the newly engineered manager, who, thanks to exposure to the culture concept, acquires new analytic capabilities and managerial options that make "him" superior to previous iterations of the US executive and superior to his counterparts abroad.

BUILDING A BETTER INTERNATIONAL MANAGER

The decades of the 1960s and 1970s were a time of contentious institutionalization of international business. Debates about IB turned on whether it should be a specialized curricular track or an element of business training infused across the curriculum. Those debates notwithstanding, the concept of culture as an explicit component of managerial practice became more firmly entrenched. This next section looks at this through two illuminating studies: Maison Haire, Edwin Ghiselli, and Lyman Porter's 1966 study, *Managerial Thinking: An International Study*, and Geert Hofstede's 1980 publication, *Culture's Consequences*. Together, these publications illustrate a second phase in the assimilation of culture within business theory and practice, with vital implications for the contemporary currency of culture.

From the more interpersonal and ethnographically holistic tone of Hall's discussion of culture, and the more instrumentalized framing in Fayerweather, this next phase rests on a statistically derived rendering of the managerial salience of cultural variation. This approach, focused on managing cultural variation by measuring it, reflects the continuing influence of psychology as the house social science of management theory. It emphasizes selected dimensions of variance and the clustering of national cultural types in quasi-geographic regions. This period marks the emergence of what I will dub the "cultural derivative." This is a register of culture-talk that presupposes culture, but is once removed from it; that gestures to on-the-ground complexity and context sensitivity, yet distills these into a canon of core dimensions of managerial practice; that resolves the dilemma of immersive specialization in an individual culture by rendering cultural knowledge in graphical units that no longer refer directly to a given society, but rather are derived from statistical relationships across societies. Such an approach remains influential through the present day, albeit in increasingly nuanced frameworks for measuring culture as an engine of distance.

The Cultural Derivative

Haire, Ghiselli, and Porter's *Managerial Thinking* (1966) is hailed today as a pioneering work in international and cross-cultural management studies (Jack and Westwood 2009). It is based upon an international survey conducted with 3,641 managers across fourteen countries by three psychologists at the University of California, Berkeley: Mason Haire, Edwin Ghiselli, and Lyman Porter. They introduce their study as evidence of the increasing contribution of the behavioral sciences to the study of management. Their Ford Foundation–funded study takes as its point of departure the question, "When managers think about managing, are their ideas all pretty much the same, or does managerial thinking differ from country to country?" (Haire, Ghiselli, and Porter 1966, 1). They begin their study acutely attuned to the challenges of country-level differences, including as part of their discussion of their survey methodology the various challenges they experienced translating their survey instruments, and including as appendices surveys in eleven different languages.

One rendering of their results is a remarkable map that precedes their first chapter (see figure 5). The map is a distorted projection that reflects their determination that certain countries "are close to one another in terms of the similarities of managerial attitudes." Offered somewhat tongue in cheek—the map is titled "Map of the World after the Explorations of Haire, Ghiselli, and Porter"—it nonetheless announces one takeaway from their research: that the systematic study of cultural attitudes is generative of a new view of the world, one potentially more relevant than a conventional map based on physical distance. "As spatial geography shrinks with transportation and communication, it becomes doubly important for us all to concern ourselves with the psychological geography of neighborhoods and clusters" (Haire, Ghiselli, and Porter 1966, viiif.).

In addition to reflecting the small world zeitgeist of the time, Haire, Ghiselli, and Porter seem equally concerned to address or take stock of the managerial malaise identified in the 1958 study "Organization Man" (Whyte [1956] 2013). Invoking the "specter of the 'organization man,'" they report that "across all countries, the needs least felt to be satisfied are Autonomy and Self-Actualization" (Haire, Ghiselli, and Porter 1966, 175). There is a sense of crisis in management as they fret that "talented men" may turn to other professions to better express themselves.

The surveys use Likert-scale questions to probe for respondents' views about specific managerial techniques (e.g., providing detailed instructions or setting goals and letting subordinates figure out how to achieve them), about the qualities of their current position (e.g., prestige, opportunities for personal growth), and about their attitudes toward a set of prompts ranging from professional positions (e.g., Physician, Factory Foreman) to actions (e.g., to decide, to cooperate, to reprimand). Haire, Ghiselli, and Porter summarize their surveys as evoking managerial assumptions and attitudes around a set of four dimensions:

1. Capacity for leadership and initiative (including whether people desire to be directed by others; and whether everyone has, or can develop, the capacities to be a leader);

2. Sharing information and objectives (whether leaders should tell people what to do or set goals for them, and how closely information should be controlled);

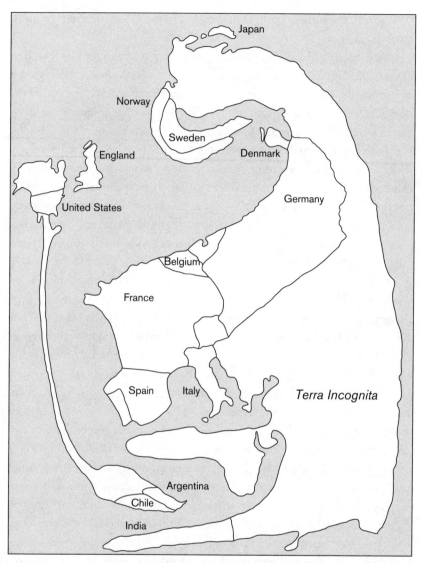

FIGURE 5. "Map of the World after the Explorations of Haire, Ghiselli, and Porter" (Haire, Ghiselli, and Porter 1966, viiif.) (reproduced with permission of John Wiley and Sons, Inc., from *Managerial Thinking: An International Study*, Haire, M., E. E. Ghiselli, and L. W. Porter, John Wiley & Sons, 1966; permission conveyed through Copyright Clearance Center, Inc.).

3. Participation (whether leaders should be influenced by their subordinates, and planning done in groups); and

4. Internal control (involving how to motivate employees—through economic incentives or other rewards/punishments).

At stake, they believed, were managerial assumptions about human nature. That they undertook the study presupposing that these were culturally derived and would vary across countries indicates the groundwork done by the likes of Hall and Fayerweather.[13] With the surveys, they aimed to look systematically at whether and how these cultural differences impacted managerial practice (Haire, Ghiselli, and Porter 1966, 19ff.).[14]

Haire, Ghiselli, and Porter computed this by calculating the variance of all of the 3,641 responses to each of the survey questions. At the same time, they calculated the mean score for each country for each item and compared the standard deviation of the country means against that of all respondents. From this they determined that some 25–30% of the variation in managers' reported assumptions and attitudes was related to country differences—a finding that told them that cultural differences are not "overwhelming," but are "real and substantial" (1966, 9f.). They next correlated the country means for each survey item across the fourteen countries represented in the study to look for groups of countries that scored similarly across multiple survey items. The upshot of this analysis—which is already two or three calculative steps away from the respondents pondering the survey prompts—was their designation of five country clusters:

• Nordic European (Norway, Denmark, Germany, Sweden);
• Latin European (France, Spain, Italy, Belgium);
• Anglo-American (United States, Great Britain);
• Developing countries (Argentina, Chile, India);
• Japan.

The Haire, Ghiselli, and Porter study thus recast a welter of diversity as a more manageable set of country clusters, each with their modal orientation toward the management challenges defined in the survey. As the "terra incognita" and the language of exploration on their map indicate, they cast their study as a preliminary effort to get some data-driven understanding of country/cultural differences, and call for the expansion of such studies to more countries. "Present statistical techniques—with a boost from computer technology—make the data manageable" (1966, 180).

Of course, they mean "manageable" in every sense of the word. For Haire, Ghiselli, and Porter, a world "growing rapidly smaller and more interdependent" requires refined understandings about how this process of change interacts with cultural differences. In their final sentences, they turn to a language of "development" and "industrialization," to tell us that we need to understand that other developed

> neighbors see the process through their culturally-tinted spectacles. [...] And if we are to help and nurture the growth of less-developed countries, we need infinitely more information about the way their traditional values and practices will interact with the culture of industrialization. (Haire, Ghiselli, and Porter 1966, 181)

The systematic turn to international and cultural themes contributed to the production of MBAs as engineers of a dawning postwar world. The Haire, Ghiselli, and Porter study illustrates this turn, consolidated over the 1960s and facilitated by the analytic manipulation of the cultural derivative. In his 1969 book *International Business Management*, Fayerweather similarly characterized the manager in a multinational firm as "a cross-cultural change agent," introducing innovations through international business activities (Fayerweather 1969, 73).

Alongside this call for the manager to be a modernizing industrializing agent of cultural change, Haire, Ghiselli, and Porter present cultural variance among developed "neighbors" through the more benign, relativizing metaphor of "culturally-tinted spectacles." There is a sense here of a workable détente, that these variations in attitudes and assumptions can all be encompassed within a neighborly ecumene. This is a relativized sense of cultural differences as entailing higher or lower barriers to interaction depending on the relationship of the two interactants. The country clusters render this spatially, as some differences are generative of greater distance, whereas cultural variations within some clusters do not amount to significant distance-making difference. This framing of relative distance is a function of a statistical rendering of cultural variation, which effects a convenient sleight-of-hand by which culture is replaced by its derivative. This cultural derivative reaches its fullest expression in the work of another pioneering theorist of culture for business: Geert Hofstede. Hofstede reframed the idea of a cluster through the canonization of key dimensions of difference along which relative variations across national cultures can be plotted.

Dimensions of Culture

Since the 1980s, Geert Hofstede's framing of culture for the purposes of management has been a go-to reference for culture-talk in the world of business. Although his work has attracted numerous critics, and was sometimes invoked by MBA faculty I interviewed with the sort of eye-rolling resignation ("of course we talk about Hofstede") often used for tired but still unavoidable disciplinary chestnuts, his work is assigned and referenced in MBA classes, it is included in the chapters of international business textbooks, and it is a touchstone for current publications taking on the concept of culture in the field of business management. For the purposes of this chapter, I cast Hofstede as the culmination of a trend evident from the 1950s, characterized by the ascent of the cultural derivative reflecting the assimilation of the culture concept in managerial discourse and practice.

Hofstede is a Dutch social scientist. Initially trained as a mechanical engineer, he undertook doctoral study in social psychology at Groningen University (1964–67) after having worked a series of managerial positions for Dutch firms. He has described his interests as based in a concern with the "internal productivity" of workers, with his thesis work focused on the impact of standards and budgeting processes as tools of employee motivation (1997, 47). Hofstede's doctoral work was undertaken at around the same time as Haire, Ghiselli, and Porter's study, and reflects a psychology-driven concern in management theory of the time with tools for motivating subordinates and supporting the "self-actualization" of employees.

Hofstede's doctoral research—semistructured interviews in five Dutch companies—included work at an IBM typewriter plant in Amsterdam. IBM recruited him in 1965 to lead a new Personnel Research Department for IBM Europe. Working with his Europe-based team of researchers and eventually collaborating with the New York headquarters of IBM's Personnel Research Department, Hofstede undertook a systematic survey program intended as a tool for organizational development. By 1973, Hofstede's group had administered some 117,000 questionnaires in twenty languages to IBM employees in seventy-two countries.

Over the 1970s, Hofstede moved between a number of teaching and research positions at European business schools,[15] while retaining connections to IBM and working on the statistical analysis of the survey data. The results, published in his landmark 1980 book, *Culture's Consequences*, reflect three significant analytic developments. Two of these deal with the survey material and reflect an extension of the practices connected to the framing of the cultural derivative. First, Hofstede found that his individual survey data in fact revealed country-level characteristics. Country thus became the salient unit of culture and the salient boundary across which statistical variation was analyzed. This connects to the second analytic development. Hofstede analyzed the variations across national cultures along selected dimensions of contrast. The result was a value assigned to each national culture for each dimension of contrast. Thus, a more recent publication includes a table for "Long-Term Orientation Index Scores" ranking twenty-three countries, ranging from China (Rank: 1; Score: 118), to Brazil (Rank: 6; Score: 65), to the Netherlands (Rank: 10; Score: 44), the United States (Rank: 17; Score: 29), to Pakistan (Rank 23; Score 00) (Hofstede, Hofstede, and Minkov 2010, 240). Those values were cultural derivatives, reflecting not the country-specific data (already aggregated from the individual interviews) but the relative position of countries/cultures with respect to others along each dimension (see Table 1).

Hofstede initially presented his findings using four dimensions of contrast:

1. *Power-Distance* (higher scores indicate more acceptance of hierarchical, unequal power relations, such as those between parent and child, boss and subordinate, government and citizen; lower scores indicate discomfort with it).

2. *Individualism* (higher scores indicate loose ties between individuals, less group integration, orientation, and the idea that everyone has to take care of themselves; lower scores indicate stronger group orientation, less emphasis on individual successes, more emphasis on loyalty).

3. *Masculinity versus femininity* (associating assertive, competitive, and money-driven behavior with masculinity, and caring, modesty, and selflessness with femininity).

4. *Uncertainty Avoidance* (pertains to people's tolerance of uncertainty and ambiguity. Societies with a high uncertainty avoidance score have low tolerance for ambiguity and diversity and a lot of rules and a lot of stress as a response. Societies with low uncertainty avoidance are more open and accepting of diversity of ideas, religions, opinions, etc.).

TABLE I. A value assigned to each national culture for each dimension of contrast (reproduced with permission from the author from Hofstede, Hofstede, and Minkov 2010, 240, Table 7.1).

Long-Term Orientation Index Score for 23 Countries Based on the Chinese Value Survey (LTO-CVS)

Rank	Country/Region	Score
1	China	118
2	Hong Kong	96
3	Taiwan	87
4	Japan	80
5	Korea (South)	75
6	Brazil	65
7	India	61
8	Thailand	56
9	Singapore	48
10	Netherlands	44
11	Bangladesh	40
12	Sweden	33
13	Poland	32
14	Australia	31
15	Germany	31
16	New Zealand	30
17	United States	29
18	Great Britain	25
19	Zimbabwe	25
20	Canada	23
21	Philippines	19
22	Nigeria	16
23	Pakistan	00

He subsequently added a fifth dimension: *Long Term versus Short Term Orientation* (a future-oriented focus characterized by thrift, humility, perseverance vs. a focus oriented on the present and past characterized by tradition, pride, and an emphasis on social obligations). This was developed with a collaborator (Michael Bond) based upon additional research undertaken in the 1980s, specifically focused on reproducing the original survey while controlling for the "Western values" of the researchers. Accordingly, they arranged to have a survey designed by Chinese scholars administered in Asian and non-Asian countries. Hofstede and Bond found the results confirmed Hofstede's four dimensions, but also revealed the new dimension (originally dubbed *Confucian Work Dynamism*). Hofstede added a sixth dimension in 2010: *Indulgence versus Restraint*. Developed in collaboration with the Bulgarian sociologist Michael Minkov, *Indulgence versus Restraint* contrasts the degree to which there is a "tendency to allow free gratification of basic and natural human desires related to enjoying life and having fun" versus the degree to which there is "a conviction that such gratification needs to be curbed and regulated by strict social norms" (Hofstede, Hofstede, and Minkov 2010, 281).[16]

Hofstede borrows explicitly from mid-century approaches to culture as broadly shared patterns, an approach popularized beyond anthropology in the work of Clyde Kluckhohn and Ruth Benedict. He cites Kluckhohn as offering a "consensus of anthropological definitions":

> Culture consists in patterned ways of thinking, feeling and reacting, acquired and transmitted mainly by symbols, constituting the distinctive achievements of human groups, including their embodiments in artifacts; the essential core of culture consists of traditional (i.e., historically derived and selected ideas and especially their attached values. (1984, 21, citing Kluckhohn 1951)

Hofstede updated this in ways fitting for a former employee of IBM: describing culture as "the collective programming of the mind which distinguishes the members of one human group from another" (1984, 21) and more recently as "software of the mind" (Hofstede, Hofstede, and Minkov 2010). With this metaphor he presents culture as relatively determining of individual behavior. He takes national frameworks as more enduring and self-sufficient units of culture.

This is the basis for Hofstede's third analytic development. He deploys this definition of culture to distinguish his level of focus from ethnic and subnational regional groups, and from the application of the culture concept to refer to organizational culture, which he views as superficial, voluntary, and impermanent. These have turned out to be strategically useful analytic moves, enabling Hofstede to make his study "about" clearly defined national units, and enabling him to generalize from an original study that, after all, was focused on executives of a single multinational corporation.[17] For Hofstede, national cultural differences are relatively stable; they undergo change but only very slowly. He has used this point to argue for the long shelf life of his cultural dimensions against criticism that they are outdated or rendered obsolete by globalization.

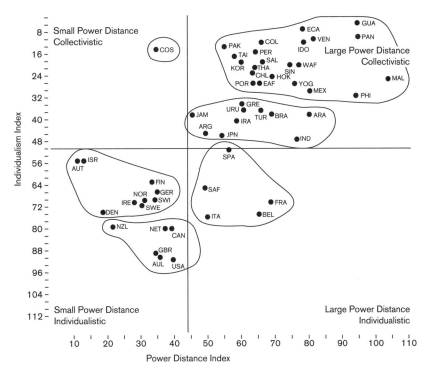

FIGURE 6. Country scores are characterizations of their relative position with respect to the positions of other countries along the same dimensions (reproduced with permission from the author from Hofstede 2001, 217, Exhibit 5.2; cf. Hofstede 1984, 159, Figure 5.3).

The nature of Hofstede's country scores as culture derivatives is also relevant here. In an argument for the insignificance of change in national cultures, he points out that the country scores are not absolute characterizations of national cultures but rather characterizations of their relative position with respect to the positions of other countries along the same dimensions. For instance, in the second edition of *Culture's Consequences*, Hofstede presents a graph plotting the relative position of some fifty countries along the scales of "power distance" (horizontal axis) and "individualism" (vertical axis). The similarities and differences across national cultures are underscored by circles enclosing the graphed positions of countries in each quadrant. (Hofstede 2001, 217, Exhibit 5.2; cf. 198, 159; see figure 6). Ultimately, for Hofstede, it is about the distance, not the details. In this regard, just as some financial derivatives can serve as a hedge against change and volatility, the country scores in Hofstede's system (like other expressions of the cultural derivative) preserve a certain degree of fabricated stable legibility in the face of the otherwise murky, changing, and unknowable quality of culture on the ground and in time.

Hofstede has had a contentious relationship with critics from a number of related fields.[18] He often writes about critics who sought to replicate his research with an eye toward unsettling his dimensions or showing them to be inapplicable to a given country. As the Hofstede accounts have it, these studies often find minor variations while largely affirming the salience of the Hofstede dimensions and country rankings. His encounters with his critics from within anthropology, apparently, have had fewer happy endings. Hofstede makes a point of criticizing contemporary anthropology as an increasingly irrelevant field focused on small and obscure populations and questions. Much as national cultural characteristics remain relevant over the *longue durée*, Hofstede continues to embrace the mid-twentieth-century anthropological framings of culture that helped inspire his understanding of culture in terms of patterns, national character, and computer programming.

Hofstede's Consequences

Hofstede posits culture as an inevitable feature of an otherwise integrating world. In ways similar to Hall, he stresses the implicit, hidden nature of culture and casts his work as revelatory: providing "a better understanding of invisible cultural differences (Hofstede 1980, 8)." Driven in part, perhaps, by his position as a Dutch scholar, there is a decentering move in *Culture's Consequences* as Hofstede decries the global spread of "American" management theory, which he suggests takes US business culture as the global norm. In his analysis, the United States is assigned country scores and correlation points along each of his cultural dimensions just like any of the other nations represented in the study.[19] In this regard, Hofstede's dimensions are all-encompassing and universally relativizing. This holds, with some caveats, for the nations consigned to the "developing world." The sixty-six countries surveyed in the initial IBM research include nations from Africa, Latin America and the Caribbean, the Middle East, and the Pacific. Data for twenty-seven countries were excluded from the findings in *Culture's Consequences* because of small or incomplete sample sizes. Excluded countries were disproportionately from the developing world and regions not likely to have robust business connections with IBM. That said, Haire, Ghiseli, and Porter's "developing countries" (Argentina, Chile, India) along with Colombia, Pakistan, Philippines, and Thailand are all among the forty countries included in the 1980 study, where they appear as a coequal set of points on his graphs. In Haire, Ghiseli, and Porter's terms, we are all bespectacled neighbors now, opening a global space of interaction premised on the informed crossing of cultural boundaries rather than modernization.

Hofstede's core message—that cultural difference and distance are part of the environment of business and that management training must be about building capacity to work across cultures—is integral to contemporary approaches to MBA training. If I am posted to a country with a different position on the Power-Distance axis, how should I modify my leadership style? What sort of incentive structure is likely to be effective in motivating subordinates from a country with high "femininity" ranking and weak "uncertainty avoidance"? (See Hofstede, Hofstede, and Minkov 2010, 213f.) Although there are benefits to be gained from a full immersion in the complexities of a national culture, Hofstede's dimensionalizing approach operationalizes the recognition that it is not necessary and certainly not practicable to do so. Instead, Hofstede's dimensions provide managers with a graphical rendering of the relative cultural locations and distance of managerial self and others to provide cues to how managerial policies and practices should be adapted across country/culture boundaries to increase their efficacy. Good enough.

It bears underscoring that Hofstede's dimensions are a tool for *intrafirm* management. This is fitting given their development over the 1960s and 1970s, decades that marked the apogee of the large multinational corporation, as well as their emergence out of a study commissioned by an exemplar of such firms: IBM. Although Hofstede's sense of culture appears stable, the model of the firm has been anything but. As we have seen, the 1980s and 1990s saw the undoing of classic multinational corporations and the managerial class that ran them, victims of the celebrated ideology of shareholder value and a sort of ruthless technocratic financial managerialism that saw downsizing and intensified mergers and acquisitions and an itinerant career model for top-line MBA CEOs. The model of a corporate MBA that had emerged in the context of mid-twentieth-century managerial capitalism was upended. But reports of the death of the manager turn out to be exaggerated. For, to the extent that MBA managers were adepts of the social, and brokers of the tensions and stresses of capitalism, and to the extent that MBA programs have continuously invented and reinvented themselves through aligning the ideal of the manager with the dominant challenges of the day, this moment marks another refiguring in the idea of the manager. As a technician of the social, the turn-of-the-century MBA was recast as an adept of international difference. With the retreat of the organizing frame of the large multinational corporation, the need for managing the resulting space only increased.

Dashboards and CAGEs: The Firm in the World

Hofstede's dimensionalizing rhetoric of cultural distance continues to influence culture-talk in MBA programs. Indeed, note that the graphical representation of cultural difference from the MBA orientation meeting discussed at the start of this chapter (see figure 4) echoes Hofstede's presentation of his country scores as described in figure 6. His prolific publication program, his promotion of his work through his website and through aggressive responses to his critics, and his ability to find verification of the fundamental contours of his approach to cultural difference across the decades surely contribute to the staying power of his ideas. There have been other frameworks for representing relative cultural difference in terms of management challenges. For the most part these, like Hofstede, build up from fundamental Hall-ian discussions of culture as a shared and largely implicit system of meanings and pattern of behaviors. There are three core characteristics of such culture-talk as I encountered it in contemporary MBA programs.

The first of these is a synoptic rendering of culture as a set of measurable dimensions. The ability to quantify features of the murky silent realm of culture through the relativizing calculus of the cultural derivative provides a sense of calibrated certitude to managerial decisions. This is often done through four-quadrant charts, weighted scatterplots, and other graphical representations, and suits a managerial aesthetic favoring "dashboards" providing concise and visually elegant snapshots of key performance indicators.

A second entailment of such culture-talk is that contemporary MBA discussions of culture present it as an instrument or exercise in the calibration of the managerial self. Part of the graphical renderings, and baked into the relativizing derivative function, is a decentering self-awareness through a "you are here" position on the dimensional grids. The culturally aware manager transforms culture from a boundary or a barrier to a resource manifest as a quality or attribute of the self. Facility with that alchemy is the fullest expression of the contemporary global manager.

A teaching note on "national culture" published by Harvard Business School Press in the mid-1990s illustrates these first two points.

Rather than merely acknowledging that people from another national culture are "different" in some undefined way, managers should be able to identify specific ways in which various cultural groups may exhibit distinctive behavior. Just as importantly, they should develop an awareness of their own cultural behavior. They should ask, "What are *my* implicit assumptions about time, about expressions of agreement and disagreement, about individualism and about power distance? How do my cultural norms manifest themselves in the ways *I* behave in a business setting? How am *I* likely to be perceived by someone from another country? Culture, after all, is not something that only affects the behavior of others, but is a basic component that shapes each of us. (Rosenzweig 1994, 13, emphasis in original)

A third enduring takeaway of culture-talk in business is the framing of culture as an obstacle: a source of misunderstanding and friction (as in "culture eats strategy"). Approaches like Hofstede's offer an ameliorative sense of culture linked to recognizing and overcoming difference. It is tactical in the sense of avoiding errors and facilitating the execution of a larger strategic goal. This sense of culture constructs it as a remainder, as the trailing edge of progress and innovation, compartmentalized from real engines of history, or maladapted to the challenges of the present and future. Indeed, the 1994 HBR teaching note on national culture endorses the view inherited explicitly from Hall and Hofstede that cultural differences can pose challenges to the relationships between firms and in intrafirm relations. However Rosenzweig makes a distinction between "social" and "technical" business operations, suggesting that "culture" applies only to the former, and warning as well that "cultural differences" can sometimes be a language for expressing disagreements that have a noncultural basis. In this regard, Hofstedian and similar dimensionalizing discussions of culture are entirely congenial to a Levittian sense of globalization as a dawning flat ecumene brought about by the shrinking of difference and distance over the late twentieth century. Documenting cultural distance is a step in its overcoming.

By the turn of the twenty-first century, we have seen the view of the flattening ecumene was increasingly considered inadequate (e.g., Bartlett, Ghoshal, and Birkinshaw 2003). In the IB literature, this is reflected in work giving the lie to generalizing claims about globalization and focusing rather on intensifying regional and cultural differences and on the need to balance standardization with localization in international business endeavors. In chapter 3, I reviewed work by Alan Rugman and Alain Verbeke, arguing that regional units of analysis (defined by geographical and cultural proximity), rather than "globalization," better fit the actual business activities of multinational enterprises. Pankaj Ghemawat has drawn insightfully on data detailing the limits of globalization—90% of the world's people will never leave the country where they were born, 2% of all calling minutes are international, trade between countries that share the same language will be three times greater than between countries without a common language—to argue for the "rootedness" of business practices and examine the ways that "distance still matters" (Ghemawat 2007, 2011).

These discussions are not describing delays or speed bumps on the road to globalization. While some of these discussions may invoke straw-men criteria of totalizing globalization to make their point, neither are they denying the impact of globalization nor implying that the localizing forces, regional frameworks, or rootedness they are tracking in any way escape or negate global contexts. This is nicely captured by Ghemawat with the term "semi-globalization," and more recently with his use of the designation "globalization 3.0" to evoke a post–flat world (globalization 2.0), but still global, moment. Instead, much of this work revoices long-standing IB concerns with difference, now incorporating distance and difference as a feature and not a bug. In this conceptual environment, awareness of culture and dimensions of difference shifts from the realm of tactic to that of strategy, scaling up the calibrated self-awareness of the problem-solving manager, to inform a strategic understanding of the relative opportunities available to a given firm within the variegated field of international business.

Perhaps the most influential voicing of this in the context of MBA training is the CAGE framework developed by Ghemawat (2007, 2011). CAGE is an acronym for four dimensions of distance: Cultural, Administrative, Geographic, and Economic. In brief, *Cultural Distance* refers to differences or similarities in language, religion, and "social norms" familiar from the other discussions reviewed above; *Administrative Distance* considers historical relations of colonizer and colonized, as well as contemporary trade pacts, common currencies, and regulatory systems; *Geographical Distance* refers to physical distance between potential trading partners, but also considers internal distances within a country, access to ports, as well as the sensitivity of a given product to physical distance; while *Economic Distance* refers to the impact on trade relations of relative differences in wealth and income between consumers in different countries.

The CAGE framework thus bundles "culture" as a component dimension of difference alongside other contextual factors shaping country-level differences. A CAGE analysis enables an assessment of relative closeness or distance along each dimension, tailored to specific products and specific characteristics of a firm, and so allows a manager to identify lower risk (low-distance) opportunities and recognize specific high-distance (higher risk) challenges. As a resource for CAGE analysis, Ghemawat has developed a website generating distance figures for selected countries along selected CAGE dimensions.

As an anthropologist I am inclined to see all four CAGE dimensions subsumed by a more expansive sense of culture. But I accept this as reflecting the place of "culture" in a native conceptual system. MBA students are socialized in a Hofstedian vocabulary of dimensions of cultural difference, and International Strategy courses will often include a discussion of the CAGE framework. Alongside these various iterations of difference as distance is a quality of culture as a business resource.

This culture-talk involves three broad claims about difference and its implications for contemporary capitalism. The first concerns culture as a claim about the texture of the world: characterized by local rootedness, semi-globalization, and so forth. Such differences entail new challenges and opportunities for marketness, and imbue the world with risk and excess to be managed by appropriately attuned managers. This is the second implication: when MBAs talk about culture, they are invariably talking about themselves—calibrating their skills to manage across cultural difference and leveraging their unique experiences and points of view as part of their own talents and tinted glasses for engaging the world of business that always exceeds the technical models for its measurement and management. This leads to the third claim bound up in such culture-talk: insofar as the reenchantment of the local interrupts the global ecumene once envisioned by Levitt and other earlier theorists and practitioners of globalization, the recalibration of the manager implies another sort of ecumenical magic available in the social world of MBAs.

I am referring with this last point to the idea of "cosmopolitanism" as a self-consciously cultivated quality of managers and the companies they lead. "Cosmopolitan" still conveys a traditional sense of the term denoting a citizen of the world. But recent uses of the term in the business literature underscore cosmopolitanism as an ability to deploy culture as a relational resource. This, after all, was the takeaway message from the preterm introduction to culture described at the start of this chapter. The diversity of our MBA cohort was a resource, a strength in and of itself.

A "cosmopolitan mindset," then, involves an "active interest" in local differences (Javidan, Teagarten, and Bowen 2010). A recent essay reflecting on the "rise of nationalism in Europe and the United States" defends cosmopolitanism by distinguishing it from globalization: "One is a fragile personal attitude, the other is a relentless socio-economic force. One strives to humanize the different, the other to homogenize it" (Petriglieri 2016). As a business strategy, "global managers and firms must adopt a cosmopolitan approach of understanding and working with differences rather than against them" (Ghemawat 2011). This last quote is from an essay by Ghemawat connecting his sense of the "rootedness" of business and the salience of difference to a call for a "cosmopolitan corporation." Among his recommendations is the development of diverse management teams filled with "rooted cosmopolitans" (cf. Appiah 2007). Managers in this view are always partial heroes—mastering the world one cross-cultural relationship at a time.

The following chapters turn to the enactment of these late capitalist managerial imperatives entailed in the rediscovery of culture, through a close ethnographic examination of a new and an old feature of MBA training. Chapter 5 looks at short-term study abroad classes, which have emerged in the past two decades as a ubiquitous component of global MBA education. Chapter 6 examines a more classic component of MBA education, the case study method, for what that may show us about the cultivation of managerial subjects through the engagement with the "real" world through stylized presentations of excess and difference.

FIVE

Managing the Margins

IN 2007 I ACCOMPANIED A GROUP of US MBA students on a study abroad trip to Mexico. We were hosted by an elite business school in Mexico City. Our hosts had developed a two-week program around the theme of "Doing Business in Mexico," combining a series of lectures presenting a narrative of recent Mexican political and economic history with more standard MBA curricular fare: case studies focused on Mexican businesses, corporate visits, and team exercises. These last intermixed the US MBAs with their Mexican counterparts and assigned us to undertake business analyses of a set of enterprises in Mexico City. These assignments all involved restaurants, bars, and nightclubs, so the feel of the "work" was a bit along the lines of spring break party tourism, with young Mexican elites as our guides and pals. The restaurant my team was assigned marketed itself both for fresh and well-prepared seafood, as well as a genre of bartending known as free-pour: tableside bartending with rum or whisky poured until you say "when." I still have the hat and polo shirt we each received after our visit and tour of the Corona brewery, where, in addition to a sampling of their product line, we saw a preview of an upcoming marketing campaign.

The classroom component of our trip was also memorable. In the course of an introductory lecture sketching the recent history of the Mexican economy and Mexican economic policy, one of our hosting professors reviewed the Mexican financial crisis of 1994 and the subsequent liberalization of the Mexican banking system. One outcome was the increasing participation of European and US banks in the Mexican retail banking market. Our professor observed that this was especially beneficial for the development of Mexican banking because US banks like Citibank brought needed experience and expertise in assessing credit risks, enabling Mexican banks to expand their loan activities.

The timing of the presentation could hardly have been worse. In 2007 the global credit bubble was stretching to the breaking point, but not yet burst. With hindsight, it is clear that US banks may not be the source of "best practices" in credit risk assessment. But it is equally clear that the Mexican business adepts were not really interested in Citibank's abilities to detect credit risk. They were interested rather in Citibank's efficiency in creating manageable risk by pushing out credit to as many people as possible (cf. Williams 2005). One of the case studies featured for the US MBAs involved a small messenger service who had leveraged their reputation for intrepid deliverymen on bicycle, motorcycle, and horse, negotiating an illegible warren of back roads to make deliveries no one else could, into a multimillion-dollar enterprise. A key part of their spectacular growth was that they had the contracts with new retail banks to hand-deliver shiny new credit cards to legions of new users of consumer credit across the country.

Short-term study abroad (STSA) trips like the one I joined have become an integral part of MBA training over the past two decades. Business study abroad experiences are especially potent because of the ways they at once provide an experiential "executive summary" of frontier spaces of capitalist potential, while also shaping and ritualizing the alignment of the emergent selves of US business professionals within a geography of business practices now seen inevitably to require such spaces. US MBAs thus learn to manage the margins: developing a transnational habitus of engaging with other professionals and negotiating foreign places, and cultivating capacities of self that enhance the transiting of risk-bearing difference in ways that realize or create value. This alignment of mobile expert subjects within a landscape of value-adding places is at the core of contemporary global capitalism, the production of which is the business that business schools are in (cf. Ho 2005; Tsing 2000).

. . .

This chapter is about the staging of the international as a space of difference in US MBA programs. Focusing on STSA courses, this chapter twines together three primary discussions. The first concerns the ways the space of international business is presented as requiring the apotheosis of the managerial subjects produced by MBA programs. That is to say that international business compels a performance of the qualities celebrated in the MBA ideal of the managing leader, combining skills of art and science. In a similar vein, international space emerges as a very particular setting for the application of business fundamentals. This is especially the case for the ways the framework of the market compels business managers to work always on the cusp of the future. This is my second point. As framed in MBA programs, to do business internationally is to travel in time. This is nowhere more evident than in so-called emerging economies, where MBAs learn that they can know the future in some world areas insofar as they are embarking on processes that have been completed elsewhere. Additionally, thinking with international space provides an opportunity to push the future at home insofar as the culturally nimble manager can see in international contexts qualities, opportunities, and products that can be brought home.

Finally, the staging of the international in US MBA programs frames global space as an especially dense site for prospecting for risk. Insofar as risk is a necessity for productive business practice, international spaces beckon as the frontier of the known, presenting capitalist potential entangled with—and indeed constituted by—uncertain complexity. MBA students prospect for risk in other ways in connection with the STSA courses, which are often packaged for them and by them as physically risky ventures. By attaching these experiences to their professional selves, they demonstrate managerial capacities to render the risky margins manageable.

STAGING THE GLOBAL INCOMPLETELY

The internationalization of business curricula takes a number of forms, from courses devoted specifically to IB themes, to the inclusion of international cases in standard functional courses in the MBA curriculum. As we have seen in chapter 4, programs also leverage the high percentage of international students in MBA cohorts to claim that they offer a virtual international experience for US MBAs. International students are urged to be ambassadors of their cultures and to help contextualize IB discussions by sharing their experiences in their home countries.

Discussions about international content in MBA curricula have typically unfolded in a space marked by the tension between two poles of thought: specialization (treating IB as a distinct function of business, like accounting, finance, marketing, etc.) and infusion (integrating international content across the curriculum to reflect the common refrain that "all business is global"). Most programs do some of both. MBAs take elective courses explicitly labeled as "international" or "global" in their second year or in one of the spring modules of year one. At the same time, you would be hard-pressed to find an MBA program that does *not* claim to offer international or global content across the core curriculum. In practice, this usually means a session or two, or a case or two, taking up "international" matters. In a functionally focused course like Accounting, it may mean periodic marking of US accounting practices and regulations as but one of a set of varying international standards for accounting.

No one I spoke with among faculty or MBA students felt the core presentation of international content was adequate. Faculty cited the time pressures of compressed MBA modules to explain their limited treatment. Robert, who was preparing to teach a core strategy class in a program he recently joined, told me he planned to devote two class sessions out of a twelve-session module to international issues, and that those two days would be a "CliffsNotes"[1] version of an International Strategy course he offered as an elective at his previous school. MBA students tended to recall one or two cases or an invited guest speaker as constituting the international content of their core classes. Kaitlin cited her first year Management Communication course, in which international MBAs gave presentations on business practices in their home countries, as the primary examples of international content in her core courses. Other international material was in elective courses—an STSA to India, in her case—and via the paracurriculum in the international milieu of her MBA program. "I hear different languages every day and it doesn't faze me," she told me, adding that she was currently on a team "with a woman from Thailand and a man from Taiwan."

The apparent "limitation" of the presentation of international content is integral to the staging of the international in MBA programs. As with other elements of compression in MBA training detailed in chapter 2, the distilled exposure to international content—especially in the formative core courses—sets up a particular framing of "international" as an arena, and indeed as a *quality* of business practice. The lament by MBAs and faculty alike that their compressed treatment is inadequate further reifies international business space as always entailing an excess beyond the fundamentals conveyed in the MBA programs.

More senior faculty often contextualized contemporary IB content as an expansion of the field from the 1990s, when the international focus was

principally on Japan. George is a professor of management and former director of his business school's CIBER. He cast a pendulum swing in IB education from the postwar focus on country studies to a focus on the preparation
of managers who can "integrate their business across all national borders."
Where there was "lots of Japan in the 1990s," coursework today "should have
a good representation of different types of economies in case studies." In this
view, the cumulative exposure to difference through "studies from around the
world, allow[s] students to see some common threads." For instance, George
told me, "if you do enough diverse cases, you see that countries that were
former colonies have quite different mindsets about how business is done."

Here, the framing of global business announces a world of compounding
complexity, in which country-level knowledge is necessary but insufficient
for managers preparing to integrate business practices across national borders. The presentation of IB content, especially in the compressed context of
the core sequence, discloses shorthands for bundling different countries. At
the same time, they gesture toward a space of country-level complexity never
fully engaged.

Peter is a younger professor of strategy, who was still in school in the
1990s. He framed the shift in IB education along two dimensions. The first
encapsulates the extension of IB over the past decade or two from one premised on US rivalry with an economic superpower—as in Japan, or earlier
concerns about the Soviet Union—or the hegemonic US-centered expansion
of global business across many borders, to what is seen as a situation of more
reciprocal influence. "I think the big shift . . . is the two-way flow of what's
going on, especially the two-way flow with emerging or developing economies." He was referring particularly to the size and influence of emerging
economies, especially as measured by growth projection in gross domestic
product (GDP) and foreign direct investment (FDI). In these representations, and indeed by their very designation, "emerging economies" stand as
the embodiment of a changing status quo, and signal to the savvy analyst the
contours of the future. But he was also gesturing to the point that business
practices in and from other places hold lessons for Western managers. Peter's
work focuses on Europe and he used that to point out that "central European
countries are teaching countries in western Europe to be more competitive."
He had made a similar point earlier that day to the MBA students in his
International Strategy course. There he pointed out that the strategies being
developed by globally successful firms from emerging economies offer lessons
to their US-based competitors.

Recall Robert, preparing to teach the core MBA Strategy course in which two of the twelve sessions will cover international material. "I have two objectives," he told me. The lesson for the first session "is to try to understand how . . . different ways of organizing your firm . . . balance various objectives. So, one objective would be adaptation to local circumstances and something that would kind of rub up against that would be economies of scale." His approach is "to outline four different structures a multinational can adopt and talk about the extent to which each of these achieves some objective, but usually at the expense of others." By now, we can imagine this dichotomized rendering of the challenges of international business (which stand at once for the vicissitudes of globalization) rendered along two graph axes, with each ideal type of organizational structure (or perhaps a series of corporate examples) plotted out to illustrate where they fall in a space defined by local adaptation versus global standardization.

"The second day," Robert continued, "will be on institutions." This is close to his own line of research, which focuses on the ways different country-level institutional environments—political, legal, regulatory systems—shape business practices. For scholars like Robert, part of the study of these institutions involves how globally modular institutional practice, such as those associated with neoliberal reform agendas, play out differently in different national contexts. In this regard, "institution" stands as a derivative indexical proxy for historically contingent country-level culture, values, or norms. Although Robert's work involves country-level variation, he told me that he typically does research that spans upward of seventy countries.

> So I can't go into depth for each country. No question that there are idiosyncrasies at the country-level having to do with history (let's lump all into "history"), economists would call "path dependence," which we probably miss. But I think the payoff is that we can generalize. When we find empirical support for a particular story we're telling or a particular conceptual mechanism, you can take it to the bank.

The sort of "story" he tells might involve the kinds of countries in which a certain sort of regulatory practice—say, the deregulation or privatization of an industry sector like education, healthcare, or electricity—is likely to be accepted or to encounter resistance. For a manager deciding on an international project, this sort of analysis is something you can "take to the bank" because the relative conformance of a given regulatory environment in a particular kind of country might give you some sense of the likelihood that current policies will stay in place. Put differently, this can help assess (i.e., measure and price) policy risk: changes in a business environment connected to dramatic political change or instability.

For Robert's class, the "idea will be to talk about how political institutions, regulatory institutions, legal institutions differ from country to country and what that implies for management practice." "The message you want to get across that day is, 'be careful about the assumptions you make, be very self-conscious when you go to a different environment, and recognize that lots of the things you take for granted and just assume are not going to be valid there.'"

There is a strong conformance, then, between the sort of reengineering of the self that is a core function of MBA training—in terms of the management of complexity and the decentering of self and nurturing of managerial talent through engagement with diversity—and the qualities of international business space as presented through the staging of international material in the MBA curriculum. The complexity of international space is quite literally where business is going and this is a future cast explicitly as never fully in hand—and productively so.

The managerial challenge posed by international content is fundamentally twofold. On the one hand, Robert's core strategy course, with two international-focused sessions tacked on at the end, frames the challenge as the extension of more settled business fundamentals to manage less settled international business contexts. Reflecting on the balance of two international sessions at the end of a twelve-session course, Robert told me, "There's a lot of really core stuff you have to cover. Maybe two days of international stuff is all you can hope for.... I do think that most of the tools that you learn in the first part of the strategy course are things you can take with you." Coordinate with this is the challenge of managing an excess of information. This is the second way that IB is cast as pushing at the limits or edges of business basics. The real world of business may never be completely captured (that is one reason compelling the managerial blending of artful talent and technical expertise); the international context, even in its staging in the curriculum, stands as the epitome of this always imperfectly apprehended condition.

International contexts are always presented as settings of compounding complexity. And that complexity is scaled and spatialized through the invocation of country-level details. Here, the effective international manager is always moving between the nuances of country-level detail and a higher order analysis seen to be required for managerial action. Much as the presentation of international business in the MBA core curriculum acknowledges greater complexity while offering a good-enough summary, international business teaching acknowledges a wealth of country-level detail, only a selection of which can inform managerial analyses and decisions. International management entails rendering from the incommensurable excess of country-level contexts the generalizable patterns that can, in Robert's phrase, be taken "to the bank."

When I spoke with Robert about teaching international cases, I asked if he brought additional contextual information in through supplementary readings. He suggested that the cases they read were already too long and that students complain about the length and level of detail. He told me,

> I think that one of the skills we want students to develop is to cull the information from the case. Students aren't very good at that. . . . I always tell them, "When you're a manager you're going to be confronted with all this information, and you're going to need a way to make sense of it." So the way I pitch the whole course is, "here's what we're going to do: we're gonna talk about these conceptual frameworks and then we're going to actually apply them using the cases." And the whole point is to use the frameworks to identify what the right questions to ask are and what elements of a situation you have to emphasize. That's what we're trying to do. There will always be contextual information and the country-level. And then there are people like me trying to do broad patterns. We are encouraging students to meld those two things.

Prospecting for Risk

Cutting across all of this is the potentially productive specter of risk. The value added of the provisional commensuration of international business contexts stems precisely from the otherwise incommensurability of country-level settings, which endows them with risk. Two examples illustrate this.

In his Global Management course discussed in chapter 2, Kevin explicitly introduces "transitioning" and "emerging" economies as "markets of tomorrow." And while his approach follows MBA conventions of taking what his syllabus promises to be "a top management perspective," he also stresses that international business decisions are no longer exclusively the purview of senior management. Rather, mid-level managers and functional specialists (the likely starting positions, he points out, of many of his students) are increasingly responsible for global strategic thinking. Kevin's syllabi present this as an index of "twenty-first-century" business, as well as a change that is responsive to the heightened risk and fast pace of international business.

He told me,

> Given the need to react more quickly, I think everyone needs to be aware of the international implications of something. They may not be the decision-makers, but it's their responsibility to see that x, y, or z is happening and to react upon that. If you look at some of the biggest mistakes—international ones—a lot of them occurred at the lower level, or could have been prevented at the lower level. . . . In that sense, being aware of what a company's doing, it may not be as much on implementation as much as avoiding a mistake, and I've told that to them [MBAs] as well, "you're going to have a lot of competitors from business schools that know how to implement, but if you can avoid a problem, that may be much more valuable than being able to implement something well."

Echoing Robert's comment about not assuming that things you take for granted apply in other countries, Kevin stressed the importance of training students to be skeptical of "standardized approaches" to help them identify potential risks. Of course, identifying risk does not necessarily mean avoiding it; it can also mean managing it. Indeed, one rationale for doing business internationally is to tap into greater rewards available through well-managed risk.

> Some of the difficulty with international that doesn't come up as much I think in a domestic situation is, as you expand into a foreign market, the less assets you invest, the less risk you have and pretty much always the lower reward you're gonna have. So, this risk-reward trade off becomes much more apparent when you're trying to do something in a foreign country, 'cause there's more risk factors and more reward factors probably coming up.

Perhaps the clearest illustration of the ways the excess and idiosyncrasies of international contexts are converted into value comes from the field of finance. Anthropologists Edward LiPuma and Benjamin Lee have written about the ways representations of emerging economies along criteria of inequality, or political instability, become a risk premium to be priced into globally circulating financial derivatives (2004, 56ff.). In Finance courses, MBAs are habituated to a set of calculative practices for assessing and comparing present and future value and factoring in levels of risk. Staple finance formulas such as the Capital Asset Pricing Model (CAPM) and its variants provide frameworks for analysts to assess the value of a given project through a combination of accounting measures to evaluate equity and debt and estimations of future equity values by forecasting likely market returns. The forecasting involves a comparison of effectively risk-free investments (typically using the returns on US government bonds) with a statistical analysis of the variation in equity prices for a stock or bundle of stocks that simulate the investment under consideration compared against general market averages. As an algorithm for commensuration, CAPM requires a variety of choices on the part of the analyst, and therefore an element of creativity. Financial forecasts involve "a mix of guesswork and spadework" in the words of one of my finance professors. Experience and managerial talent also play a role here, as Sarah Hall shows in her analysis of a similar financial algorithm used in business analysis (2008).

International projects are presented as inherently more difficult to value. In my interview with Barbara about her approach to teaching international finance to MBA students, she echoed a common view of "international" as an extension from the basics.

> Now business schools are wrestling with, How do you teach finance these days when the market is international? Financial markets are global. We still have the old mindset that you teach a basic finance course and then a follow-up course as an international finance course that delves more into detail. I happen to think that's a little bit old and dated way to approach financial markets. But that's still the way it's done, I think partially in the interest of time: there are so many concepts that need to be introduced that it makes it difficult to bring in some of the international issues.

Among the different international issues, she cited "exchange rates" and the "cost of capital."[2] Exchange rates "add an extra element of risk" and an "extra element of complexity."

> Exchange rates permeate so much of finance, and you can look at it from the influence on asset prices, from how it affects your ability to manage risk, your ability to value a company. So you take your basic capital budgeting, that risk can be built in to the discount rate, it gets built in to the cash flow analysis that you're looking at.

Regarding the cost of capital, she focuses in her course on

> how that's evaluated in an international context versus a domestic context. And I try to make students aware of the literature on international asset pricing. But again, a lot of that is drawing on how well risk is diversified

internationally. Exchange rate risk comes into that. But that does add another dimension. So, instead of just looking at the basic CAPM, how is CAPM modified in a global environment, or is it? And what are the additional risks that need to be taken into account when you're trying to evaluate an international project?

The international finance literature is filled with efforts to address this question. The key point for our purposes is that the CAPM method of pricing assets—itself already mysterious if we look closely at the quantitative rendering of forecasted risk based upon "spadework and guesswork"—appears as a relative point of solidity requiring some supplement to evaluate international business projects. Far from adding certainty or precision, that supplement stands for the opacity of international contexts so that it can be priced. It is a strategy of producing legibility that requires itself to remain incomplete, with some remainder. International business requires a constant production of the boundaries of legibility, for it is at that edge that the significant margins can be found.

Virtual Regions

In her ethnography of Wall Street investment bankers, Karen Ho makes a remarkable observation about global business (2005, 2009). Banks that call themselves "global" often base that claim on a single or small set of offices (sometimes lightly staffed or even vacant) in one or a handful of other countries. Globalization, in this sense, is not really globalized. It is "lumpy" in texture, with key places standing as metonyms of an ideal but nonexistent condition.

In the context of certain authoritative rhetorics of globalization, a strategically selected set of parts stands for the global whole. "Global business"–talk rests on a sleight of hand by which a limited set of places often stands as an index of a broader international or global quality.[3] International content in MBA programs effects a similar sleight of hand, as a little goes a long way toward evoking a larger class of economies with comparable qualities. Over the last fifteen years, the rhetoric of international business practices has been shaped by a series of shorthands, bundling emerging economies through catchy acronyms. BRICS is the best known of these, although a series of others—MINTs, CIVETS, EAGLEs—have emerged since the coining of BRICs in 2001.

BRICs—Brazil, Russia, India, China[4]—was coined in 2001 by Jim O'Neill, then an economist at Goldman Sachs. In a paper titled "Building

Better Global Economic BRICs" prepared as part of Goldman Sachs's economic forecasting, O'Neill identified Brazil, Russia, India, and China as emerging markets with a "healthier outlook" as measured in GDP growth than the G7 economies. O'Neill's discussion was focused in part on the ways these growing economies might merit greater consideration and even direct participation in forums for economic policy planning such as the G7. The paper worked through a set of recommensurating calculations—such as converting raw GDP numbers into a comparison of purchasing power parity (PPP)[5]—which showed the BRIC nations to be stronger economically than reflected in standard GDP rankings (O'Neill 2001). However, the discussion had consequences beyond conference tables and global economic policy meetings. O'Neill's presentation framed a select group of emerging economies as embodying at once the dynamic growth of a developmentalist frontier with a promise of all-but-G7 success and stability in the near- to mid-term future. The upward trajectory seemed to offer the arbitrage-like dream of risk on the cusp of vanishing, and therefore an all-but-certain higher than average return. The acronym "BRICs" in O'Neill's playful title evoked the elemental solidity and security (cf. the three little pigs) of business fundamentals of capitalism. (The brickmaker appears only a few paragraphs after the parable of pinmaking in Adam Smith's presentation of the division of labor.) As O'Neill has commented, people are "scared of all these places" (Korn 2011).

These shorthands create a manageable legibility of international space, effectively flagging a group of emerging economies as embodying most fully the business promise of international contexts.[6] And while the BRICS group has fallen somewhat out of favor since their early-aughts coining,[7] the habit of bundling sets of emerging economies—often casting them as "the next BRICS"—remains popular. In 2005, the Goldman Sachs group identified a set of countries as the "Next Eleven (N11)";[8] in 2009 the Economist Intelligence Unit coined the acronym CIVETS,[9] identifying these countries as especially promising based upon their rising FDI levels and young populations; and in 2011 O'Neill was advocating a subset of the N11 as MINT or MIST economies.[10] Alongside these newer partitionings of the world, South Africa joined the BRICS in 2010.

There is a strategic modularity to these acronyms, which amount to virtual regions, cohering mainly by comparative criteria considered key to the future at a given time. They are diversified across actual regions, and you can trace the regional representation as Brazil is replaced by Mexico; South Africa by Nigeria. In each case, these are cast as gateways to wider regional investment.

Of course, these shorthands participate in the making of the world they claim to describe: driving investment in these serially favored groups often through the development of targeted investment funds.[11] The logic here is that some international exposure is crucial to help boost returns, and these favored economies are likely to provide the benefits of international investment with little of the negative risk. A 2011 article published by Wharton School of Finance reported that a survey of corporate executives, investors, and business leaders revealed that a majority

> would be interested in doing business with multinationals in the CIVETS countries. Respondents said they were most attracted to CIVETS because of low labor and production costs and the countries' growing domestic markets. When asked to identify weaknesses, the survey participants cited political instability, corruption, a lack of transparency and infrastructure, and homegrown companies without much of a reputation or brand identification.... A significant set of respondents (42%) predicted that by 2020, the CIVETS countries would be on a level playing field with the BRICs in the global economy. (Knowledge@Wharton 2011)

According to one management professor, "An acronym is a simplification, but it calls attention to growth opportunities in rapidly growing markets abroad that managers need to come to understand." Others remarked on the opportunities of these "frontier markets": "With emerging markets there is always risk. But whenever you have risk, if you are savvy you are going to make a nice return. This is a difficult game, but it is an interesting one" (Knowledge@Wharton 2011).

The intensification of international training in MBA programs correlates quite closely with the rise of the BRICS and their successors. The curriculum shares in the virtual metonymic quality of these strategic simplifications. The buzz of the BRICS helps shape student demand and contributes to the rise of case studies focused in these nations. The itineraries of short-term study abroad programs conform closely to these gateway economies.

SHORT-TERM STUDY ABROAD

On a damp late February afternoon, I joined a course of some two dozen MBA students preparing for a trip to India. With just two more weekly class sessions left before their departure, scheduled to coincide with spring break, there is a note of urgency in the announcements made by the supervising faculty and student leaders. The student leaders are trying to finalize a schedule of corporate visits during the time in India, and they are reminding their classmates to review the list on the class website, to provide any feedback or suggestions, and to signal their interest in being part of a team with some responsibility for one of the corporate visits. Each team is expected to prepare some overview material about the industry and the specific corporate host, and also to take a lead role in making a formal statement of thanks and presentation of a small gift to the corporate host on behalf of the class and the business school. They are aiming for eight visits over the two-week study tour, with teams of two or three students for each corporate visit.

The other MBAs have their own demands for the student leaders. They want a finalized itinerary with contact information for hotels. Some report that their families are pressuring them for this information. The student leaders have a final meeting with the travel agents scheduled for later this week. They promise to have a packet with the day-by-day itinerary and other travel advice ready by the weekend.

The course is directed by Pradeep, a native of India, who has led two previous study abroad trips there. Pradeep chimes in to also remind students about written work due for the class: he wants a project statement from each student prior to departure. This prompts some more discussion as one student asks what to do if she really has no project idea for the trip. Pradeep responds with mild exasperation: "This is a business school elective," he begins. "We tend to forget that." The class chuckles as he goes on "You have to come up with a proposal that relates to business in some way." As if to index how wide open that condition is, he says, "It can be religion in the workplace. . . . Anything to do with business is fair game." He wants the students to prepare a three-page proposal for their project. (Here, he throws out a more typical example: "Say you want to set up a wind farm off of Mumbai.") He explains that the point of the exercise is to develop a proposal based upon what they can learn about the project "from here," and then, "when we go on the trip, look for what you learn that would change your proposal. What can you learn from here? What can you learn from there?" In this regard, the assignment formalizes the takeaway of all such MBA study abroad experiences: codifying the value added of international managerial experience. He also encourages the students to use their observations to inform an evaluation of the STSA course: what details should be kept or changed, would they recommend the course to future cohorts? Conveniently, next week's class will be a panel presentation by students from last year's trip to India. These second-year MBAs are effectively the CliffsNotes personified for the class, embodying as they do the transformation, or the value added, through the STSA experience.

STSA courses like this one are ubiquitous across MBA programs in the United States. By developing a condensed overview of the country or region to be visited, these courses frame and make the world of business. The courses also make the students, engaging them in a ritual coproduction of the international context as a risky but promising and potentially manageable space for business. At the core of that promise is the cultivation of the MBA student as a manager with personal qualities and capacities apt for the challenges of global business leadership.

The repertoire of STSA destinations for MBA programs replicates closely the roster of global exemplars enshrined as BRICS, CIVETS, etc.: India, China, Mexico, Brazil, South Africa, and Vietnam are all represented in the sample I covered. My interviews also put me in touch with faculty and students participating in programs to Cuba, Argentina, Peru, Poland, and the Czech Republic.

As with other international content in MBA programs, STSA are at once central to the MBA experience and marginal. This is evident in Pradeep's wry reminder that "This is a business school elective." And MBA students themselves often see in the STSA the peril of (appearing to be) wasting time with a frivolous trip.[12]

I also detected a whiff of this in a pattern of junior international faculty being tasked with these courses. This surely reflects a process of generational change among business school faculty and increasing diversity among the younger ranks of faculty. Yet, the tendency to outsource STSA courses to younger and international faculty replicates in the register of faculty hierarchy the tension between the pressures of compressed professional time and the cost of engaging with international contexts, which always challenge the MBA outlook with marginal excess. When I raised it in an interview, I was told that more senior faculty are busy with other programmatic responsibilities, journal editorships, and so forth, and therefore the extended trip abroad in the middle of an academic year would be especially onerous for them.

STSA courses are rituals of commensuration. Most programs run multiple trips in a given year, and the menu of options already suggests an interchangeable seriality—a marketplace, even—in which any of the country experiences on offer are potentially exchangeable, give or take any idiosyncratic discounting on the part of a given student. Some programs run information sessions in which students interested in upcoming STSAs can learn about each of their options. Some programs offer full-blown STSA fairs with informational booths set up to inform/recruit students to different STSA courses. Booths might offer country-specific decorations, music, and food as part of the marketing of the course. I have also seen sleekly produced videos with images from previous trips, and testimonials from students recounting their more memorable takeaways. There is competition for enrollment among courses. Student leadership experiences with STSA courses are counted among the simulations of professional life in the MBA paracurriculum.

Commensuration by Decomposition

As with other analytic habits in business education, the STSA courses effect a form of commensuration through decomposition. If the totality of the experience promises a sort of salubrious excess, energizing managerial capacities, the supplementing coursework enacts a coming to grips with the foreign context through a review of salient component parts. The most common format has five to eight weeks of preparatory courses prior to a trip of one to two weeks. An alternative format is focused principally on the study trip with a preparatory meeting or two and some classroom presentations during the time abroad. Preparatory study usually focuses on generalized categories of local knowledge (history, religion, culture [in the sense of local arts: say, tango in Argentina]) as well as standardized categories of business or economic analysis (financial and banking systems, key industry sectors, marketing and consumer behavior, etc.). This thematic segmentation certainly follows the specificities of each target country; I have heard MBA team presentations on microfinance and outsourcing in India, on adventure tourism in Peru, on biofuels in Brazil, and the wine industry in Argentina. But these more locally salient topics nonetheless function as part of a ritual disassembly and reassembly of the target nation. It is in this decomposing and reconstituting of the foreign that the commensurable and the (value-adding) excess are defined. And this ritual reassembly of the foreign as a space subject to conventional managerial practice and as an experience of excess shaping and requiring less conventional managerial talent is constitutive of the agile global managers whose production is the goal of the STSA.

Faculty for STSA courses often work alongside a team of two student leaders, who have a hand in shaping the study abroad experience. In one program, students compete for the position of team leaders by submitting proposals containing ideas and itineraries for scheduled study abroad courses to be offered in the coming term. In another program, the student role is even more entrepreneurial: a team of two students develop a proposal for a study tour and then recruit a faculty member to lead the class. Team leaders help recruit other students to the class, they work to set up many of the corporate visits and other activities to be undertaken in-country, and they coordinate communications with the travel agent and relay the emerging details of the itinerary to the class.

The planning of the course is itself a performance of business subjectivity. Student leaders I spoke with seemed to take some pleasure from the competitive, entrepreneurial experience of forming a successful partnership and winning the leadership positions. One man, who had been part of a successful team organizing a trip to South Africa, noted that he and his partner had been selected over another team that included a woman who had an area studies background focused on the region as well as knowledge of a local language. Although many details of the course are standardized from year to year—particularly when the same faculty member is involved—students experience the course as an emergent team project reflecting their interests and expertise.

Most of the STSA teaching faculty I interviewed told me they have a few set presentations of their own and a list of invited speakers they draw upon. However, the bulk of the preparatory meetings are devoted to student presentations on specific componential themes. Like so many other MBA presentations, these are extremely condensed communications, supplemented with PowerPoint slides. Students reported that most of their research was conducted online, and the presentations I observed were typically compilations of data already reduced to tabular form online to represent the size or rate of growth of a certain industry sector, or, say, the increase over the past five years in the amount of money outstanding through microfinance arrangements. In class they cited analytic materials published by consultants such as McKinsey & Company or Boston Consulting. Of course, there is a high degree of conformance between the analytic categories of industry sectors and characterizations of the BRICS, CIVETS, etc., economies found in these publications and the organizational categories of the STSA lesson plans. In some cases, the presentations are further compiled into a "briefing binder" as a resource for the aspiring executives to take on their trip. STSA students also have a chance to flex their networking prowess. Corporate visits are often planned by mobilizing networks of MBA alumni as well as family and professional connections of current MBA students.

In addition to the preparatory classwork and team reports, most STSAs involve MBA student teams in projects to be developed in-country. Pradeep was reminding his class about this in the session I observed. These projects are often framed as consulting exercises with deliverables, including a set of recommendations about developing the targeted industry sector—as when an MBA team studying the banking sector in Peru was asked by a Peruvian banking chain for their recommendation whether they should compete for customers by offering zero-interest transfers of credit card debt. My visit to the seafood restaurant with the open-pour practices in Mexico was connected to our team project. I have also heard MBA reports on projects that involved white water rafting in Peru and visits to beach resorts and ultra-high-end luxury hotels in Brazil.

While this prompts some eye rolling and sarcastic commentary on the "tough life" of the global MBA, these STSA activities merit some thicker description. For starters, they exist alongside other projects focused on banking and biofuels, wind farms and supermarkets, and other more "serious" themes. More fundamentally, the suite of MBA projects in any given STSA course enacts a highly reflexive process of discovery, connecting young adult MBAs with foreign business settings. As with the preparatory research, the set of projects performs commensuration through decomposition. Moreover, the carrying out of the project, including the reporting back to the MBA group, further entails the performance of an elite global subjectivity. Meeting with managerial counterparts in local industries (many with MBAs from the United States or Europe), engaging in participant observation focused on sites of cosmopolitan recreation (upscale bars, high-end adventure tourism), US MBAs are encountering recognizable versions of themselves.

So, too, for MBA team projects involving social entrepreneurship: AIDS education in South Africa, microfinance in India, etc. Entrée to these worlds is often through professional brokers in NGOs who have MBAs or are MBA-fluent. The number of MBA programs featuring social entrepreneurship has increased since the tarnishing of the finance-associated MBA brand in 2008. Presentations about social entrepreneurship and philanthropic activity typically cast it in neoliberal trickle-down terms. This is so locally, as an MBA team cast the emergence of microfinance in India as a natural extension of recent decades of economic growth. "And clearly economic growth leads to philanthropy." It is equally so globally, as these initiatives are seen to be energized by executives who have become spectacularly wealthy and now seek to "give back," applying their talents to social entrepreneurship. Here again, MBAs literally exploring this career space are attaching themselves to their aspirational futures (see chapter 7).

Research reports are presented to the study group at the conclusion of the trip—often as part of a final follow-up session back on campus, although some programs schedule presentations as one of the final events in-country, particularly when there are mixed teams of US and local business students. These performances concatenate with other framings of the target destination and, since many of these framings involve stylized experiences of personal discovery—through individual research, through being there (and back)—these performances enact the ritual production of internationally competent MBA subjects.

Mapping the Margins: Business Fundamentals

STSA courses operate on the margin of commensurability, framing the country-level specificities as renderable in terms of capitalist fundamentals with an excess that informs and requires managerial talent. As Pradeep pointed out, STSA courses *are* "business school" courses, and a primary order of business is presenting country-level specificities as opportunities to affirm and illustrate what are taken as basic capitalist truths. Thus, in a presentation on microfinance in India, which involves small loans to support small-scale entrepreneurial activities, Jennifer contrasted microfinance with a local practice of moneylending. She decried the practice of moneylending, which was often to help meet subsistence needs, not only because of exorbitant interest rates but also because the borrowers were "not using that money to create money; they're not making any profit . . . so, offering them ways to use that money appropriately is really a huge social impact." An orthodox capitalist worldview is also evident in an MBA report on the banking industry in Peru. Their recommendations included textbook prescriptions for restructuring burdensome tax regulations and accelerating trends toward privatization to put key industries like mining, agriculture, and fishing "into the private sector where there's an economic incentive to create efficiency."

On the Mexico trip, morning lectures by local business faculty began with a historical overview of the Mexican business climate. A history of a succession of Mexican political administrations was rendered a narrative of progress in the consolidation of free market capitalism in Mexico. This was done graphically on a chart with two axes: "democratization" and "economic liberalization." Taking the balance of the two as the best possible condition, the political and economic history of Mexico was presented as a series of lurching steps, not always in a straight line, but tending toward a neoliberal sweet spot on the graph. This was, of course, a strategic rendering of the singularity of Mexican history, intended for the consumption of US MBAs there to assess the prospects of doing business in Mexico.

The response of the US MBAs to this presentation was striking. The initial reaction was that this historical narrative greatly clarified the current situation in Mexico and more than a few students remarked that they wished their home MBA program included a similar discussion of political history and economy in the United States.[13] By the end of the program, however, this reflexive insight was lost. In follow-up interviews, students I spoke with were left with the takeaway lesson that a distinctive feature of countries "like Mexico" was the tight link between politics/government and the business climate. In an inversion of the Lévi-Straussian categorization of "hot" and "cold" societies, they were hot societies, where dynamic historical events were part of the lived fabric of contemporary Mexican lives. The United States, on the other hand, is a cold society: absent dynamic history or politics.

A similar framing is evident across the range of STSA courses I surveyed, as the link between government policy and the economic environment is foregrounded. Much of this follows neoliberal conventional wisdom, with governments blamed for regulatory policies that inhibit economic growth or cause the "shocks" that make up much of the risk of doing business internationally, and doing best when they get out of the way of capitalism. However, I also heard calls across many STSA sessions for certain forms of increased governmental action, particularly in terms of infrastructure investment to provide roads, ports, airline hubs, and so forth that would facilitate the scaling up of business activities.

Carol, an MBA student on the Mexico trip, suggested that we would have to look to the post-Depression policies of the New Deal to have a comparable example of the link between government and business climate in the United States. She stressed the vast distance between this historical moment and her own lived experiences. Her analogy is thus particularly resonant as it creates commensurability and incommensurability at the same time. Mexico can be related to as going through their own version of a process that the United States went through previously. However, for contemporary US citizens, that lived experience is radically other. For their part, the Mexican business faculty had other genealogies in mind: using Mexico's record of sustained economic growth over the 1950s and 1960s (the Mexican Miracle), they explicitly positioned Mexico as the "China" of the time—an odd enfolding of time and space to endow contemporary Mexico with the fully developed potential expected for the future of contemporary China.

Growth and Opportunity: Managing the Future

A key part of the STSA process involves the framing of rapid economic change. This dynamism is the primary criterion for entrance in the BRICS and CIVETS club. The sense of rapid change is evoked with statistics and graphs. Biotech in India is expanding by 40% annually; 75% of multinationals in the United States or Europe consider outsourcing some functions to India; Peru is described as one of the fastest growing economies in South America; the number of women participating in microfinance activity in India has increased tenfold in the last decade; the amount of money being loaned has increased nearly 700% in the five years prior to the trip.[14]

The result is a condition of opportunity to be developed out of a situation of rapid change and related precarity. This typically entails managing with an eye toward the near future. MBA presentations underscore the crucial next steps to secure or realize the potential being identified. Thus the repeated stress on infrastructure investments as a necessary correction to a national economy stretched thin by a business boom. And the engineering challenges are not only in the realm of roads and ports. Discussions of emerging economies inevitably raise what is often a condition of growing economic inequality—usually presented with reference to the Gini index. This is cast as unsustainable in MBA classes and linked to an increasing risk of political instability. I return to this focus on poverty and the so-called "bottom of the pyramid" in chapter 7. For now, I want to note that MBAs saw in such socioeconomic inequalities the potential for a trickle-down transformation, in which the poorest might become a consumer class. This is described as "turning the pyramid into a diamond," in the words of an MBA student talking about India, with the goal of cultivating a consumer middle class with bank accounts, credit cards, mortgages, and enough steady income to attract the expansion of commercial activity and to establish a viable tax base to support modest government incentives to promote further economic growth.

Similarly, an MBA team focused on consumer behavior in Brazil reports that the Brazilian consumer market is conventionally segmented into five socioeconomic groups: A through E. Segments A, B, and C are glossed as comparable to wealthy, middle-class, and working-class slots in the United States. Segments D and E are categories of more extreme poverty, largely off the radar of most conventional marketing. The team observes that while multinational firms for the most part are mainly focused on marketing premium products to the A and B classes, which comprise only 6% of the population, their recommendation is to offer products to all socioeconomic classes, underscoring that the C class, in particular, is where the action is. "The C class is like 57% and [thanks to economic growth] they're getting 20 million new consumers in that class," reported the MBA spokeswoman for the team. "So, clearly, that's where the opportunity lies!"

Deploying similar reasoning, the banking sector team for the STSA to Peru recommended that the bank *not* offer zero balance transfers to acquire new credit card companies. Carl argued, "Because Peru is a growing economy—it's not mature like the US—you don't have to go after this type of a strategy, mainly because with new entrants and people who are developing their personal income, there's going to be a growing market out there. You don't have to steal that from others." The point is made more concisely by an MBA team focused on the tourism industry in Brazil, for whom the BRICS designation says it all: "Brazil is a BRICS nation, so the economy is becoming more modern and cosmopolitan."

As such comments reveal, the dynamism of emerging economies is harnessed to narratives of capitalism to create story lines that might be anchored by the template of the United States, or reckoned through comparative reference to other archetypal places. MBA programs trade in, and help produce, those narratives. The future of the CIVETS can be gleaned from the BRICS.

Ordeal or No Deal

While these presentations line up the BRICS and other emerging economies as knowable through the prism of business logic and imbued with potential, the presentations also weave a sense of the exotic in their framings, endowing the STSA countries with an element of opacity and risk. Sometimes this is linked to the macropolitical contours of a given country; the other shoe to fall, next to all of that focus on the importance of good government policies, is the specter of a return to less stable or promising times. But it is also marked through the immediate experiences of MBAs, who relate a personal odyssey of engagement with the (almost) indecipherable otherness and apparent confusion of emerging economies and endurance of a host of dangers and discomforts.

A presentation on marketing and distribution channels for consumer packaged goods in Peru describes narrow wholesaler storerooms dramatically stacked from floor to ceiling with goods. "It's like a very narrow garage that's rather tall, and so they stack up as high as they can get it, probably two stories with just products stacked on top of each other, and you have to be pretty claustrophobic as you walk through there." The MBA jokes that a slide showing her in one of these storerooms depicts her "look of horror," thinking "I'm going to get killed in the space." The image is a dramatic one and elicits chuckles and gasps from the class. She continues,

> and you have a lot of kittens running around these shops, and we're thinking, "what in the heck is going on there?" And the kittens are there to catch mice [*a soft, "ah!" from the class*]. Of course, mice and rodents are an issue in any market place, but you probably won't see cats that are typically brought into a wholesale market for that purpose and left where customers can see that.

Such war stories of otherness—even built around banal details of cats and mice—mark the STSA spaces as different but decipherable. The same student remarked later in her presentation on the heavy presence of women in commercial activities, reporting that this reflects the role of women "in Andean culture" as responsible for the financial management of households, and, by extension, likely to be in the front of the shop attending to business matters.

A team studying banks in Peru describes being surrounded by heavily armed guards when they tried to take a picture of the bank. The professor reported that on a previous trip he was once asked by guards to delete pictures he had taken of an upscale hypermarket in Lima. He added that this was a vestige of a time of terrorism and instability in Peru and suggested that it underscored the importance (and precarity) of the present trend of stability and economic growth.

As this last example illustrates, while students actively weave their engagement with and decoding of otherness and risk into their accounts of STSA experiences, STSA faculty and program administrators also actively highlight this dimension of the trip. For example, in preparatory classes in advance of the India trip, Pradeep illustrated the financial precarity of the rural poor by discussing the burden of providing dowry for daughters, telling the class that the shame of not marrying your daughter drives some poor farmers to suicide.

He also follows up on a presentation about the environmental impact of rapid economic growth, promising the students "we'll see pollution when we're there." He described particulate matter in the air around Delhi as ten times the healthy limit, adding "that sounds great, man! It used to be one thousand times [when I lived there]." And, with their departure looming in a week and a half, he included some advice about hygiene, cautioning students that the way they have been sharing a tray of sandwiches and fruit during class would be unthinkable. "I would never eat these things there," he said, adding "don't touch anything that is liquid." He reports delicately that based on previous trips "despite all precautions, each of you will experience one round of 'adjustment.' . . . It is not a question about if, but about when." Finally, following a discussion about fragmented land holdings in India and government regulations as an obstacle to doing business there, during which a Korean MBA student compared the situation to "red tape" and corruption familiar to her from Korea, he offered a brief lecture on "corruption":

> This sounds bad when I say it, but take it with a pinch of salt. . . . When you go to India and you're doing business in India, you follow different rules than what is written down. [*Long silence*] There are different rules, which, by the way, are not rules that you or me as entrepreneurs can use. If we try to set up a business, we'll die before we get even one permission. But people who are the big business houses, they know their way around. It's a very, sort of, very high entry barriers kind of a business. But, they manage to get the things done, whether it is by connections or bribery, or whatever it is. So there is a lot of corruption and things hardly work, but still, somehow, who knows why, this idea outsourcing thing has come up over there.

In a separate conversation, Pradeep told me that witnessing students' shock at points of otherness—particularly related to poverty—during previous class trips helped him identify teaching objectives. "I try to keep track of things that are surprising them," he said.

An information session for the Mexico trip I joined focused almost exclusively on the grave dangers students would face from the moment they exited customs until we were ensconced in our swanky hotel. Warnings about avoiding unofficial taxis, not traveling at night, or not wearing jewelry on the street are good advice, and helpful advice is certainly necessary for many US MBAs, who have surprisingly little international travel experience, according to my sample. Still, I was struck by the ways danger seemed to be the defining frame of the trip. This is poor marketing, I initially thought. Or, maybe it wasn't. While most of these STSA trips are comfortable and privileged glimpses of other countries—excellent hotels, corporate visits, private buses, and hired taxis—the discourse of fear and risk burnishes the authenticity of the experience. It also mutes any discomfiting sense of privilege that might taint the experience. And the haze of danger and fear that envelops this international activity intensifies a sense of triumphant capability and productive risk-taking recounted at the other end of the experience. One MBA invoked Hofstedian cultural dimensions of self-understanding to talk about striking out on his own to explore Buenos Aires. "It is risky. For me being in that situation was exciting. It fit with what we learned about cultural attitudes." Speaking to a hypothetical employer, he said, "You can throw me on an airplane and I'm not going to die if I get off the airplane at Buenos Aires!"

Such survival is not an individual accomplishment. During the Mexican trip, our more intimate immersions in the place occurred within the collegial cocoon of transnational case study teams. The Mexican MBAs, more thoroughly internationalized, and dealing with their own elite anxieties about safety, confirmed our concerns, while also heroically shepherding us around town in convoys of their own cars, in hypervigilant subway rides, and for the most adventurous of the group, in a memorable trip to a *lucha libre* event. Students from other trips reported minders or guides from sister business programs in-country or from travel agencies that now specialize in such global business tours, as well as relationships established through alumni networks and corporate contacts over the course of their trip. The buffer of local professional guides thus constitutes and brokers the margins of the commensurable and incommensurable experiences of Mexico, India, Argentina, and so forth. On the Mexico trip, the totality of the experience was assimilable to the professional selves of the US students through the staged collegiality of the team projects: the frame or excuse for many of the adventures, sealed with an all-nighter before our team presentation was due, an earnest exchange of business cards and personal cell numbers, and heartfelt embraces at the end of the trip with pledges of open-ended hospitality (If you're ever in Chicago . . .).

Products and Placement

MBA STSA trips, then, stand as a ritual of ordeal. In this challenging rite of passage, in which the chaotic and risky liminality of the foreign is broken down and reassembled as a legible manageable business space through the transformation of the MBA participants, local touchstones provide calibration and commensuration. I have in mind the ways MBA student reports weave mention of familiar global corporate landmarks and actual or aspirational professional and socioeconomic peers as components of the emerging economies they are exploring. The effect is to temper the otherness of the place, hedge the risk with evidence of participation by other economic actors, and coimplicate the MBAs within the social and economic worlds of these target countries. The target countries thus become plausible contexts for the MBAs, and the MBAs are affirmed as plausible actors within those contexts.

One way this is achieved is through dropping references to familiar brands and labels. Coca-Cola is globally ubiquitous and a master brand at negotiating local consumer contexts (e.g., Foster 2008). So it is not surprising that it is identified often in MBA reports. The team discussing consumer behavior in Brazil used Coke as an example of efforts to market across socioeconomic classes, by describing the ways different sized bottles of Coke enable purchases by poor consumers who may not have enough expendable income to make larger weekly or monthly purchases. They also invoked Coke as an example of aspirational status brands, describing a family who might drink a local brand of soft drink, but keep a bottle of Coke on display to be served to an important guest.

Teams visiting supermarkets in various countries remarked on the presence of high-tech scanners at the cash registers, and the presence of familiar brands. The tone here was one of surprised admiration, with one student commenting that she had never seen as many varieties of Head & Shoulders hair care products in one place as she saw in an upscale hypermarket in Peru. These corporate touchstones balance some of the more intimidating exotic details and unsettle stereotyped views of an emerging economy.

If these known brands are not out of place, neither, perhaps, are the MBAs. Alongside the reassurance of familiar products are the ways the STSA courses embed the MBAs within transnational professional networks. As I have already noted, corporate contacts on STSA trips are often alumni of their business programs; many trips involve network-building interactions with faculty and MBAs at local business schools. Through elite hotels, fancy dinners, hired buses and cars, and entrée through the gates of well-guarded corporate campuses, MBAs transit the stark juxtaposition of street life in a city in the Global South and enclaves that are almost indistinguishable from familiar environments back home. Such agility is part of the power believed to be imparted by these rituals.

A key payoff of the cross-cultural competencies being established and enacted by MBAs was the cultivation of new relationships. At a meeting of Pradeep's class in which a student team was discussing outsourcing as an industry sector in India, one of the MBAs, Kenneth, related his previous experience with outsourcing projects prior to pursuing the MBA. The first had been a disaster marred by poor quality work and communication failures. He continued,

> I decided to never do it again. But as I thought more about it, reflected more about it, I decided that it was really all my fault, that the expectations I had about the communication barriers and the working styles and what I needed to provide to make the project successful were unrealistic. And I think that's the problem that a lot of companies see in these kinds of projects. And I think the second project that I had where I was much more successful, was much more hands-on with the team, treated them more like I would treat a team that was there on the ground with me; that was an extremely successful project. A lot of good ideas came out of the offshore team, very high-quality work, and I would absolutely do it again.

Another student, Ed, recounted to me in glowing terms his successful meeting with a business contact in Thailand. He had learned the formal word for "hello"—adding as an informative aside that the word varied according to the gender of the interactants—and also rehearsed the appropriate posture for a formal greeting. He continued triumphantly,

> She was ready to shake my hand to accommodate for *me*. But I did that and she just smiled and said, "how did you know?" And I had just been watching people at the hotel. So, it was appropriate to do. . . . It made a good impression and we talked . . . and it went really well.

Other MBAs recounted their impressions that doing business internationally was a much more social endeavor, describing business contexts where family life is valued and time is devoted to really interacting and getting to know your business associates.

This strong functional focus on building relationships reflects the decentering impact of business travel abroad. The social dimensions of business, tacit and invisible in a more familiar setting, appear in relief in other contexts. The emphasis on relationships also squares with the ascendant model of a cosmopolitan organization and a vision of global business as constituted out of a network of self-aware and culturally savvy managers, adepts of working at the limits of their rooted selves.

STSAs are rituals of transformation, producing global MBAs through the decomposition and reassembly of emerging economies as manageable business spaces. Crucial to my argument is the point that international business compels the fulfillment of the managerial ideal melding talent and skill, art and science, and that MBAs mobilize their STSA experience as evidence of these key managerial qualities. This became clear in my interviews with MBAs after their trips.

Unsurprisingly, students cast their decisions regarding the course selected and their level of participation in terms of market metaphors and professional development. Often surprised by how "academic" the coursework was, most make sense of this hard work less as a way of learning about another place than as an index of their personal investment in the experience—they speak of "buying in" and gaining a sense of "ownership" in the trip.

A number of students discussed their experiences by first describing the lighter-weight trips they *didn't* go on, or more cuttingly, telling me about a friend in a different (clearly softer) MBA program who went on a less challenging trip—a vacation for credit. Their skepticism of trips involving beaches or Anglophone countries set in relief the sober professional value of their own experience. The calculus that many MBAs reported involved assessing a destination as both a plausible IB location and one that was remote or otherwise challenging enough that they could not imagine going there themselves outside of the structured STSA context. Indeed, the value added of the STSA experience, in the accounts I have collected, was a shift in the boundary of competence.

Diane, who traveled on an STSA to India, told me, "I might go to Brazil for a vacation, but not to India." She had gone to business school after working for a large consulting firm, where she saw an increasing number of professional activities moved to offices in India. "You expect to see this in the service sector or manufacturing," she told me, "but these were accountants and actuaries." Diane mentioned repeatedly that this had created bad feelings among professionals in her US office and that part of her motivation to go to India was to "see the other side of it. I was getting a very American picture and didn't have the opportunity to talk to my Indian counterparts about it."

David, whom we met in chapter 2 (and who went to Brazil), told me of his experiences at the STSA fair:

My initial take: this is a glorified field trip. You see the Cuba booth and you think, "I'm going to be smoking cigars and drinking mojitos on the beach." It was exciting, but I felt I really want to do something. I'm making a huge upfront cost to go back to school. I want to have something that I can at least use in a story. I thought South America was a fairly strong story because I believe that's where tech is going.

David had worked in the computer industry before going to business school. He had been through some turbulent ups and downs at the end of the dot-com bubble. Although his situation prior to entering the MBA program sounded pretty good to me ("I had achieved my goal of hitting six figures by the time I was thirty"), he experienced his position as precarious. "I was non-billable," he told me. "Not being billable is a second-class citizen. They are the first to get cut." Business school training was a way "to attach myself back to revenue."

In such comments, we find a reckoning of a different sort, rooted in the relentless unease of managerial subjects in the new economy (Thrift 2000). Diane, threatened by outsourcing and troubled by the anger she experienced in her office, feels compelled to expand her "American" view of the economy. David, with the experience of "cratered" dot-coms in his past, seeks both the credentials that will give him a structurally more secure position, as well as an informed sense of the future of the tech marketplace, which, he has come to believe, lies to the south. In this regard, the STSA experience serves to mitigate risk, affording students a glimpse of the business future and supplying them with "outside" information, rather than "inside" information. Presupposed in all of this is the expansive nature of capital, converting unaccounted risky singularity at the margins into manageable future value.

The international milieu of MBA student life is another factor shaping MBAs' motivations to study abroad. Some students I interviewed spoke positively about the presence of international students as an inspiration to undertake an STSA. Some students get travel advice and assistance in preparing their team reports from classmates from the intended country, and I have heard of one case where a student extended his trip to India by an additional week to travel and stay with the family of a classmate. Others, however, react to the large numbers of international MBA students from India, China, or Korea as competition—effectively closing off those areas of the world as regions where a US student might gain a competitive advantage. As one MBA student put it: "There are so many people here already who are Chinese or Indian. They are fluent in English and have work experience. They bring more value to the table." Because there were fewer Latin American students at his program, he concluded there would be "more opportunity for me" pursuing a study abroad trip to Argentina.

At the same time as he was recognizing these international students as adepts of international business, whose competence he could only hope to approximate in a different regional niche, this same student raised reservations about the ability of international students to convey to US students the local cultural flavor of business in their home countries.

> I don't think you get as good a feel unless you're immersed in it. Walking down the street, seeing how people talk and interact, going to restaurants. So much of it is—I don't want to say soft skill—it is something you just have to experience. In terms of students who come here, day-to-day interactions at school don't give you that great of a feel for how things work in a country. And what you hear are very stereotypical.

A Value Chain of Culture

An important anchor of transnational commensuration on many STSA trips—another familiar corporate touchstone—is a visit to the local stock exchange. Reflecting on his trip to South Africa, Kyle described a tour of the Johannesburg Stock Exchange where they met the founder of a South African entrepreneurial success story: a company producing backfill bags used to help prevent mine cave-ins. What is more, the company employed disabled miners to produce the bags. He summed up the experience as providing a glimpse of a "value chain of the culture."

> We saw how the stock exchange was slightly different and what they were doing to bring in these entrepreneurs, we saw a consulting organization that was working with this lady at [the company] and how she was developing her concept and how she was employing people from difficult situations in Africa. . . . It's on its own local timeline, it has its own local characteristics, and so that was really important for us [to see].

Here the distinctive attributes of the South African business climate concatenate into a "value chain"—distinctly South African, but structurally commensurable, with respect to any other business practice. By "culture," Kyle was gesturing to "the distinct characteristics of the people and maybe how they're different than some of our habits, concepts, ideals that exist in the States, where those concepts, ideals, experiences are different. I guess when I say 'cultural' it is what makes their people and their heritage unique." Viewed as a resource in a value chain, this irreducibly singular quality is aligned and rendered commensurable with activities anywhere.

Something comparable was at stake in the packaging of Mexican cultural distinction in the 2007 trip. The formal case studies we discussed in class were almost all selected to showcase specific "Mexican" entrepreneurial qualities along with the business potential charted in the thumbnail economic history of the country. Recall the success story of the messenger service that renders the illegible warren of Mexican neighborhoods (places our MBAs' hosts would not take us to) receptive to consumer credit and other commercial communications. Their success rested on the can-do ingenuity of their intrepid messengers. A second case involved a company that produces rail frames for trucks, buses, and RVs. Founded in the 1970s by a man who had worked for a US-owned steel mill in Mexico, the company has grown to be one of the three largest producers of rail frames in North America. With the now elderly owner present for our discussion, faculty extolled the company as anchored in family values, with loyalty to customers and concern for workers. They celebrated a spirit of artisanal ingenuity, developing innovative production processes to meet customers' needs, implying that such problem-solving ingenuity and creativity was not possible in the US firm that originally employed the founder. These are the qualities you get when you access Mexican (or global) markets with Mexican partners; this is the marginal value of doing business in Mexico.

For traveling MBAs, familiar institutions like stock exchanges, or romantic frames like the family-owned business help them manage the differences at the margins, some of which they find quite troubling. A student from a trip to Brazil, Edward, described the stark differences he experienced between the pace of business life in Brazil and in the United States. With some disapproval, he described the "lax," disorganized, "thrown together" quality of the corporate visits. This was unsettling for the student, and it was the primary example he offered when I asked him to expand on his comment that the trip had given him a sense of cultural differences and the different ways society works "down there." This laid-back approach was different from in the United States, where "we're very driven here to work a lot and produce a lot." The only exception to this impression was a trip to BOVESPA, the Brazilian stock exchange, which "was really driven."

I found Brazil incredibly depressing. Such a black and white division—a horrible pun!—of economic division. Areas of beautiful houses next to favelas. . . . It was just crappy. You see that kind of thing and it does make you appreciate where you live because there is no general poverty here. I mean you see Appalachia and you see homeless people in metro areas. We saw families of eight—not one crazy homeless person—living in stick huts. . . . You see someone here and you can say that guy did something to screw up his life, he's clearly a crack addict or an alcoholic, and then you're in a position where you're seeing—we went on a jungle tour doing canopy rides, and the farther we went out of town the more things went downhill. And you get to a point where you say I just don't want to go any farther because I don't want to see this out here.

"It sounds elitist," he went on, "but I guess to some point you can hope to insulate yourself from that. In certain areas you don't even see it. If I were [posted there] I wouldn't take my family to see that. Or if I did it would be just before we hopped on the plane to leave." Such things may be important to see (his analogy was a troubling trip he took to the Holocaust Museum in Washington, DC), but these were "things you only need to do once."

This longed-for once-ness is instructive. The trip to the margins confronted Edward with a set of more and less manageable experiences. Alongside the serial familiarity of BOVESPA and the more rehearsed indulgence of stereotyped Latin American colleagues running late and disorganized, he struggles to make sense of the scenes of poverty he glimpsed. Analogies from home—"Appalachia," the homeless "crack addict"—are inadequate, and he is left saying "I just don't want to go any farther because I don't want to see this." As the saying goes, you cannot "un-see" something. The task, rather, for MBAs like Edward, is managing the singularity: maintaining its marginality as a potential terminal link in a "value chain of culture" or as an experiential emblem of global managerial competency.

The STSA experience as an emblem of global managerial competence is a theme that has surfaced in virtually every interview I have conducted with MBA students with study abroad experience. In almost every case, students told me that the greatest value of their study abroad experience had little to do with direct knowledge of a particular place. Sometimes this comment stemmed from an awareness that the short study abroad experience was inadequate, that more time in-country, knowledge of the local language, and travel off the well-appointed beaten paths of MBA study tours would be necessary for any claim to detailed knowledge of the region. Sometimes this comment reflected the fact that the student had no particular interest in the country to which she had traveled; rather, she had a generic interest in international experience.

For most students, the greatest value of the study abroad experience stems from what the experience reveals and cultivates about attributes of their selves. A number of students told me that their study abroad experience was a great "ice breaker" in recruitment interviews: that anecdotal information about a given city or the casual display of linguistic sophistication by correctly pronouncing a recruiter's "foreign" name, served to establish rapport in these interactions. And as a marginal addition to the standard business school résumé, these study abroad experiences were understood to signal their adventurousness, their inquisitive spirit, their flexibility and willingness to take risks, their capacities to work in cross-cultural environments.

Recall David's interest in going to South America because he could "use it in a story." "What do you mean, 'use it in a story?'" I asked him.

> When you interview with people. Things like that. There's got to be some kind of a reason you do things. . . . I think the international aspect is very valuable and I think bringing South America to the table for me is much more compelling if you know I have some kind of an international exposure, some kind of a vision, [that] I get how things are going to a small degree down there, you know, culturally.

The nimble and artful subjects of international business, managing the margins of contemporary global capitalism, ultimately commensurate the singularity of international experiences through the marketing and the circulation of their professional selves.

Intrinsic to this circulation, as constructed by the STSA process, is the cultivation of risk. The double sense of "cultivation"—signaling at once the nurturing of growth and the harnessing of that growth to managed ends—evokes precisely the ways the STSA trips to the margins are charged with a risk that must never fully recede. The high value trips are the ones that take MBAs to places they would not risk going on their own. The relative security of the bubble of privilege in which most STSA groups travel while in country, the network of professional counterparts in Mexico or South Africa or Brazil that they develop in the course of their trips, and the confidence of a partial expertise developed from firsthand experience of local places, currencies, foods, or other tokens of the exotic create a space of plausible legibility for both foreign sites and the MBA students as adepts of international management. Yet, even as they harness these place experiences to their own "stories," taking these with them as part of their professional selves, they leave aside, in the margins, the singularities they do not yet know how to manage—the things they hope to see "only once." Thus placed on the margins of the ledger, on the verge of legibility, they stand for the promise of risk and the potential for its management.

SIX

Partial Answers

THE USES OF ETHNOGRAPHIC CAPITALIST REALISM

> From Mike Graves's tall windows, which were draped in red velvet, the view of Shanghai was spectacular: the stately old Western-style buildings, the riot of modern skyscrapers, the familiar needle of the TV tower. But today Mike barely noticed it. Clenching a copy of his Chinese partner's proposal for another acquisition—it would be the company's fourth—he paced the floor and replayed in his mind that morning's unsettling phone call. (Xin and Pucik 2003, 27)

SO BEGINS A CASE STUDY—a signature component of MBA training. Business case studies are short narratives that explore a problem faced by managers in what is presented as a real-world business situation. Many cases challenge MBAs to develop a set of recommendations about what to do next and to defend those decisions against competing recommendations from their classmates. Case studies thus participate in the cultivation of a managerial perspective as they involve MBAs in taking on the vantage of a decision-making CEO or of an upwardly aspiring middle manager ("What would you tell the boss to do?"). Cases also embody and enact the compression of detail and fast-paced rhythm that is part of the managerial habitus explicitly shaped by MBA training.[1]

THE (PANIC-INDUCING) HOLD REAL LIFE HAS

Cases are constructed to convey too much information, often distilled into ten or so pages of text, sometimes with accompanying tables or graphs. Case assignments pop up regularly on syllabi requiring MBAs to prepare and submit written evaluations (solely or in teams) and to be ready to discuss the case and present and defend their analysis in class. Depending on the professor and the competitiveness of a given cohort, these can be panic-inducing ordeals in which mistakes or long pauses in formulating a response provide openings for criticism and upstaging by other students.

My own anxiety about the case method stemmed from my sense that there was often no single right answer—multiple strategies could be pursued and defended based on the information being presented. My initial conceit was that I was a relativizing anthropologist able to see a range of meaningful courses of action, whereas the MBAs were being trained to see a single maximizing way forward. That explained my indecisiveness, but was little comfort if I was called on in class. Even trying to take on the native's point of view, I could never detect a self-evidently best resolution to the cases.[2] It turns out that my anxiety and frustration were not the fruit of my nuanced anthropological perspective. While I am sure that I asked some questions and saw some alternatives that were less apparent to the MBAs and their professors, it is a hallmark of the business case method that there is typically no single correct answer. There is only the performance of wrestling with the open-ended complexity of a real-world case, and defending a decision as one that is plausibly best given the information available, the managerial criteria, and the time pressure to take some action.

The cases present simulacra of the world, and they do so in a double sense. On the one hand, they offer the sort of distilled complexity we have seen in other facets of MBA training: a boiled-down essentiality that both suits the busy workweek and short attention span of an overscheduled MBA and also performs a terse grappling with key information that is such a defining characteristic of an effective senior manager. But the cases also simulate an excess of information, a condition of uncertainty and potential risk, intended to evoke the lived quality of real-world, real-time business. They do so through a mythic paraethnographic voice gesturing to the points of excess that function poetically as indexes of the real.

I intend "paraethnographic" to signal a self-aware effort to evoke contextual sociocultural thickness as part of a strategic simulation of the real.[3] This is especially noticeable in international cases, such as the case above titled, with more than a whiff of orientalism, "Trouble in Paradise." The case presents a fictionalized depiction of the situation of a middle manager—Mike Graves—who represents his Ohio-based textile company, Heartland Spindle, in a joint venture with a Chinese partner. The opening paragraph sets the scene cinematically, as Mike's red velvet-framed view of Shanghai beholds a turbulent blend of tradition and modernity, stemming from a long history of Chinese engagement with the West.

The case turns around Mike's response to his partner's proposal to expand the business through acquisition of another Chinese textile producer. Mike's calls to his Ohio-based boss are met with criticism; ten years into this joint venture they expect something more than the 4% return on investment realized so far. The lower returns are due to repeated acquisitions, such as the one being proposed. Caught between the expectations from the home office and what he has learned about doing business with his Chinese partners, Mike is feeling very alone as he prepares to attend a banquet celebrating the tenth anniversary of the Chinese venture. The case follows Mike through the banquet, as his behavior is being carefully read for clues about Heartland's enthusiasm for the proposed acquisition, to a dinner with his wife at their house in an enclave community of expatriates, and into a meeting the following day with the CEO of the new acquisition target. At the close of the five-page case, Mike, wrestling with all he has seen and heard, contemplates whether to recommend the new acquisition to his boss, possibly risking his own job, or propose rejecting the deal, which might mean breaking up the joint venture.

. . .

This chapter examines the case method of MBA education as it is illustrative of the coproduction of the "real world" of business and the managerial skills and talents it is said to require. In this regard, the case method sits squarely within what other analysts have called the cultural circuit of capitalism and performative economics, as authoritative framings of the world—such as the action problems posed by the cases—shape the analytic habits and ensuing decisions of cadres of managers, who may themselves emerge as lightly fictionalized protagonists of new generations of case studies (cf. Callon 2007; MacKenzie and Millo 2003). In this chapter, I am especially interested in the tropes of ethnographic capitalist realism as deployed to depict international and cross-cultural business settings and in the ways specific cases play out in MBA classroom discussion.

INVENTING THE CASE METHOD

The case method in business education emerged out of the development of the curriculum at the Harvard Business School. It is an artifact of the crisis of legitimacy facing emerging university-level business curricula at the turn of the twentieth century, and of business schools' efforts to frame their contributions in terms of practical applications of classical learning as evident in other respected professional schools, especially law and medicine. But, unlike training in the law, which can make use of court cases and legal decisions, or medical training, which can make use of clinical records, "business" did not have a naturally occurring set of entextualized cases. So, part of the case method of business education is the invention of the genre of the business case study, meant to stand as an artifact conveying qualities of real-world business situations for the purposes of management training.

The genre conventions for telling a case story are deeply connected to the goals of MBA training and the crystallizing idea(l) of the manager. The case studies constituted a codified rendering of something called "business" that, through the formative rituals of the business schools, was connected to the production of business managers. And, since second-year students often served as research assistants in the production of early case studies, this connection was tight indeed. There is a circuit reminiscent of an Escher print (a hand holding a pencil sketching another hand that is itself in the process of sketching the first), as the cases, crucial to the production of managers, prepare and calibrate the managers to "real-world" situations that are selected and curated to fill the needs of the educational system producing the managers.

During the early years of university business training, businessmen were invited to meet with classes to discuss problems in their companies. These presentations served as "cases on the hoof" and sometimes included write-ups prepared by the visitors (Barnes, Christensen, and Hansen 1994, 43; McNair 1954). At Harvard, this was a second-year class in the MBA program implemented "to deal with top management problems" and also geared toward "integrating subjects" taught elsewhere in the curriculum (Copeland 1954, 26). The Harvard Bureau of Business Research was a hub for gathering data and documenting business problems, a process formalized under the leadership of the second HBS dean, Wallace Donham (1919–42). Donham had been trained at Harvard Law School and is credited with adapting the "problem method" of training from law to business (Copeland 1954, 25; David 1954, vii). By 1924, the Bureau of Business Research had twenty recent MBA graduates at work preparing cases (Barnes, Christensen, and Hansen 1994, 43).

By 1930, the system of case production was effectively industrialized and integrated with other productive processes at HBS. Faculty teaching loads were calibrated to allow time for research and case development, and a cadre of student research assistants were funded to do the legwork of case research under the supervision of faculty who curated the production and development of cases fulfilling needs identified in the MBA classrooms. Relatively standardized procedures for developing case studies were also taking shape, with a filing card system at the Office of Business Research tracking a network of business contacts and logging research visits to collect cases on specific themes. And, as we have seen in chapter 2, case development and the incorporation of new and updated cases in MBA syllabi became an index of currency: a derivation of the real world developed from within the MBA cultural circuit. Recall that John Fayerweather's inaugural IB publications included a book of cases (1960), and that his early essay in *The International Executive* introduced the managerial dilemmas of Harry Grey using the already established genres of the case method.

From its initial beginnings in practices of emulation to shore up the legitimacy of business education, by the 1930s the case method had become a distinct social fact, closely connected with the Harvard brand, but suffusing across MBA training. A series of publications on the case method, outlining the philosophy and the methods of producing and teaching cases, illustrate the coordinated rise of the case method with the institutionalization of MBA education. The dates of a sequence of volumes produced by Harvard Business School are instructive. In 1931, just as post-Crash commentary was championing the need for advanced business training to avoid another crash, *The Case Method of Instruction* was published under the editorship of Cecil E. Fraser, an instructor of Finance at HBS who had also served as Office Manager of the Harvard Bureau of Business Research. In 1954, in response to increasing postwar interest in business training, *The Case Method at the Harvard Business School* was published. The editor, Malcolm McNair, was a professor of marketing and managing director of the Bureau of Business Research. And, beginning in 1981, with subsequent editions following up to today, the Harvard Business School Press has published *Teaching and the Case Method*, a set of essays on pedagogical theory and practice related to the case method, developed in conjunction with faculty training seminars on case instruction offered by the Harvard Business School (Barnes, Christensen, and Hansen 1994).

The Myth of the Case Method

The three volumes in aggregate constitute a mythic folk history of the MBA case method crystallizing over the twentieth century.[4] Indeed, like other heroic folk tale cycles, the Harvard volumes include canonical tellings from previous texts, as selected essays from the 1931 volume are republished in 1954, extended quotes from both 1931 and 1954 appear in the editions published since 1981, and newer contributors are authorized by genealogical connections to the founders of the case method.[5]

The HBS cycle depicts the case method as crucial to the preparation of MBA managers. Indeed, the situations presented in the cases and the requirements of reading and responding to the cases in class are intended quite explicitly to exemplify the ideal of the manager. The case method is about "mastery of the art of decision making" (McNair 1954, 23). Case study serves the goal of educating the MBA student "to meet in action the problems arising out of new situations of an ever-changing environment. . . . Acquiring facility to act in the presence of new experience" (Dewing 1954, 2).

In his foreword to the 1954 McNair volume, then dean of the HBS, Donald David, introduced the case method as part of a decisive turning toward the social sciences in management training:

> The dependence of business upon science and technology is clear. In the social sciences we are accustomed to think of economics as our source discipline. But we must not conceive of business education as simply consisting of applied economics. We must look to all the social sciences for insight usable in defining the scope of administration and for aid in teaching those professional skills that will promote the attainment of good managerial results—sociology, psychology, anthropology, political science—these are as important to us now and for the future as is economics, the field from which we still need to derive a theory recognizably useful as an account of and guide to business activity. (David 1954, viii)

As Charles Gragg's contribution to the volume put it: "Business management is not a technical but a human matter" (Gragg 1954, 7). He continues,

> The work of a graduate school of business consequently must be aimed at fitting students for administrative positions of importance. The qualities needed by businessmen in such positions are ability to see vividly the potential meanings and relationships of facts, both those facts having to do with persons and those having to do with things, capacities to make sound judgments on the basis of these perceptions, and skill in communicating their judgments to others so as to produce the desired results in the field of action. (Gragg 1954, 8)

McNair's essay underscores the idea that mere technical knowledge and competence are not enough:

If knowledge of a few formulae and ability to manipulate a slide rule were enough to produce the right administrative action, then you may be sure that the demand for really good executives would not so greatly exceed the supply. Business can hire plenty of average-grade technicians who can figure the right answers to the problems that lend themselves to exact routines and procedures. But business, by and large, does not pay a very high price for that kind of ability. What business does pay a premium for, and what the business community as well as the social community vitally needs, is qualities of judgment and leadership. (McNair 1954, 23)

Cases are said to expose MBAs to the "raw material" of business decisions, and this evokes a visceral management experience. In the canonical framing of the case method, the experience-near ethnographic quality of the cases—they encourage including transcripts of "real conversation"—cultivates managerial capacities by provoking "pit-of-the-stomach" reactions. The student "feels" a need to immerse and learn about the situation. This is a fuller embodiment of management as lived, called forth by the hands-on engagement with singular complexity (Schön and Sprague 1954, 80f.).

An additional outcome of the case method is a sense of self-awareness on the part of the MBA students.

At some point, from continued emphasis on group as well as individual activity and from his written reports on cases as much as from his oral classwork, the student achieves insight into his personal make-up. As he airs his views, feelings, reactions, attitudes, and prejudices and sees them reinforced or rejected by thinking individuals around him, he has an opportunity to reevaluate and reappraise his own character and personality. (Schön and Sprague 1954, 81)

The case method is cast as prototypical of discussion-based teaching methods, with a goal of making classrooms into transformative communities of learning in which students become teachers and teachers students. The catechism for case method instruction exhorts faculty to leave behind pedagogical models of content transfer where they have information to transmit to receptive students. The focus is on the collaborative journey of learning. The HBS website today presents the case method as a signature component of its MBA training and tells applicants that 85% of the talking in a case-based classroom is done by students; "you'll be amazed at what you learn from exchanging ideas with your classmates."[6]

While this may sound rather crunchy and communitarian to be the signature pedagogical practice of the competitive world of MBA education—

more Freire than free market—keep in mind that the product of the case method crucible is a more self-aware, multifaceted, and agile manager. As we have seen, the decentering communal experience of grappling with (simulated) real-world complexities attaches to individual MBAs whose talents will enable them to work as productive team members and leaders of organizations, creating value by building relationships. There are strong parallels, then, between the payoff of the case method and the payoff of international MBA experience. STSA courses might be seen as immersive cases cultivating managerial qualities consistent with those evoked by the mythic paraethnographic realism of the case study.

The Functions of Excess

> A good case is the vehicle by which a chunk of reality is brought into the classroom to be worked over by the class and the instructor. A good case keeps the class discussion grounded upon some of the stubborn facts that must be faced in real life situations. It is the anchor on academic flights of speculation. It is the record of complex situations that must be literally pulled apart and put together again for the expression of attitudes or ways of thinking brought into the classroom. (Barnes, Christensen, and Hansen 1994, 44)

> Where truth is relative, where reality is probabilistic and where structural relationships are contingent, teaching and learning are most effectively accomplished through discussion. With intrinsically complex phenomena and the limited usefulness of simple theoretical relationships, little of value can be communicated directly from teacher to student. The learning process must emphasize the development of understanding, judgment, and even intuition. (McClough 1979 in Barnes, Christensen, and Hansen 1994, 38)

These elaborations of the case method cast the MBA classroom as a laboratory of reflexivity and relativism. The incommensurable excess of "real" business problems provokes the development of the value-adding excess of a good manager: talent, intuition, etc. Cases are intended to reflect the reality of human actions as an "intricate and disordered heteronomy of happenings." In developing a stock of teaching cases, "there should not be a single problem in use which is not capable of at least two intelligent solutions" (Dewing 1954, 3). "There is no single, demonstrably right answer to a business problem" (Gragg 1954, 11).

The case method thus enables a thoughtful embracing of uncertainty, with two promising career benefits for the MBA. First, the experience of the case method provides a head start in the development of business experience. Notwithstanding criticisms in the early decades of MBA education that no schooling could replace hands-on professional experience, by mid-century, the seasoning of simulation offered by the case method is held to provide a fast track toward professional insight and wisdom for aspiring MBAs. Proper training through the active learning of the case method leads to early professional maturity. The give and take of classroom discussion, the realization that others have ideas you have not even considered, the cultivation of new axes of personal relationships among students in the simulated professional setting of a case, and the recognition that the teacher does not have all the answers, are offered as accelerating the professional maturation of the MBA, more than offsetting the time lost in an academic rather than professional environment (McNair 1954, 8–13). An MBA student is not yet an expert, but thanks to exposure to the case method, "he" gains "composure in the midst of complexity" (Schön and Sprague 1954, 81).

Developing facility in making decisions under conditions of complexity and uncertainty is directly linked to another desirable quality of the effective manager: the ability to take risks. This is the second career benefit of the case method. McNair champions the case method as a way to develop the sort of "tough-mindedness" he says is necessary to counteract a malaise of uncertainty and timidity brought about by the complexities of the early Cold War era. After stressing the value of the case method in preparing students to make difficult decisions, McNair continues,

> if we are successful in developing and strengthening these tough-minded qualities, you won't always try to play it safe.... If you are really tough-minded, you will cultivate qualities of initiative and venturesomeness. You will not be afraid to act, even if you act on imperfect knowledge, for you will realize that all knowledge is imperfect and experimental rather than final. And you will not be afraid to take chances.... The essence of profit in a changing world is risk and uncertainty. Your objective should be, not the *avoidance of risk*, but the *intelligent management of risk*. (1954, 24; emphasis in original)

As it was in the mid-twentieth century, so is it early in the twenty-first. A handout circulated by the Haas School of Business with advice about the case method counsels MBAs to "take risks." "The case method represents a unique opportunity to take risks, make mistakes, and learn." "There is typically no 'right' answer; there are several thoughtful evidence-based solutions" (Purewal and Berman 2006).

The efficacy of business case studies stems from the ways they immerse the student in the context of the business problem being posed. Much of this is achieved through the paraethnographic voice of the case study genre, which includes scene-setting details that evoke the rhythms of corporate life, the stress of responsibility for decision-making managers, the intrusions of the exotic into international business contexts, as well as experience-near presentations of a managerial protagonist's point of view, including narrations of dialogue that simulate on-the-ground business interactions. Guides to the production of cases reveal the paraethnographic aims of the genre and the role of ethnographic excess in the case method.

The 1954 McNair volume, for instance, includes essays on the collection and writing of case studies, compiling best practices from the early decades of the Harvard model. These make a distinction between "field" and "armchair" cases. The latter are entirely fictional business problems framed from the comfort of a faculty member's office; the former, although they may be fictionalized for the purposes of confidentiality, are based upon field research. The distinction nicely echoes the mythos of field research in anthropology, where the move from armchair to field, associated with heroic ancestors like Bronislaw Malinowski, opened up access to realistic details, nuances, and intersubjective experience that are said to be the prized objective of best practices in the collection of a business case.

Researchers are advised that the business case should focus on routine challenges of business life rather than on exceptional or unusual circumstances. In their attention to these "imponderabilia of actual [business] life" (cf. Malinowski 1922), case researchers should balance cases between "specific and typical situations which confront people in administrative positions" and "newly developing practices and . . . problems not yet recognized by most business men" (Culliton 1954, 257f.). The case research method is generally a top-down process as researchers contact senior executives, working through contact cards at the Bureau of Business Research, alumni records, and contacts developed through supervising faculty. The value of working with senior managers is both substantive (cases are meant to evoke the experiences of senior managers and, according to the methods essays, senior executives are likely to know the full details of a situation) and pragmatic (senior executives are the ones able to give consent to the case research process).

The Harvard model of case research involves research assistants doing much of the actual research, guided by questions stemming from curricular needs framed by faculty. Researchers are expected to talk about developing cases with the professor to understand faculty expectations, but at the same time are told "do not overlook other things, including the possibility that what you thought you wanted either does not really exist or is in fact quite different from what you supposed" (Culliton 1954, 259). So there is an inductive, iterative component to the method of case research, reflecting the potential of cases to capture something more.

Case research centers on the interview. The researcher is advised to undertake some prior research and have a list of the topics "he" wants to cover. But there is also a call to balance that with what is described as a "wandering" interview, a less-structured format that "gives the researcher a chance to see what matters are most on the executive's mind, what the relations between him and his assistants are, and a myriad of other things which will contribute to the 'plusses' of his case" (Fayerweather 1954, 273).

I read these "plusses" to be precisely the thicker ethnographic elements of the case method telling. Fayerweather unpacks his point:

> The case writer does not merely record surface facts. He has to explore the situation being discussed and to do it with the same penetration that a management consultant would apply. Every statement made by the executive must immediately be analyzed by the research assistant for clues of further matters to be explored. (1954, 273)

As we know from chapter 4, Fayerweather drew from his experiences researching HBS cases in developing his approach to international business. There, too, he stressed the cumulative value of contextual information about foreign settings as essential to students' ability to "get" international business.

Part of the promise of the case method, then, is to evoke the imponderabilia of actual business practice, an excess that marks the space between the classroom and the lived reality of business. For Fayerweather, this includes some background information about the history of a company or an industry, as this can help to render the material as "a coherent whole." James Culliton recommends other observations of life in the office or on the plant floor as well as fortuitous conversations with other employees along the way. "Get material you may not need," he advises (1954, 261). Every written case involves a "compromise between voluminous information necessary to give a full picture and the comparatively brief statement which the student can be expected to digest in the time that he has allotted to the study of the case" (Fayerweather 1954, 274).

We are here back on the ground of the busy MBA and the ordeal of the fire hose of information. The written case is an icon of this excess and it is quite consciously overwritten in two regards. It is a gesture to the voluminous information that represents the salient complexities an executive must distill and make manageable. But the case is also salted with "irrelevant" information to further simulate the challenge a manager faces "to discriminate between useful and unnecessary information." This quasi-ethnographic rendering of excess is essential to the framing of international business contexts, where differences and distractions signal qualities of exceptional incommensurability and risk requiring the application of managerial talent.

WORKING THE CASES

"What is this case about?" Geraldo starts the class discussion about "Trouble in Paradise" by asking a student to summarize the case "without analysis." He calls on Chris, who says,

> Differences really, I guess, between business goals between China and US. China, I mean, the Chinese really stress acquisitions and growth, with the ROIs, return on investments, lower, whereas, the US, they want big returns on their investment and, I guess it seems as though they're really, the US is trying to help shareholders.

"Okay," Geraldo starts to break in, as Chris quickly adds, "China is more long-term."

"Let me stop you right there," says Geraldo as he pulls together the points so far.

Geraldo had kicked off the case discussion with a couple of framing comments. An old Adidas commercial from 2003 evoked the rivalry between the Chinese and US women's national soccer teams on the eve of the World Cup. The ad presents the Chinese athletes in matching red and black warm-up outfits standing in formation performing synchronized ball skills on the lawn of a training compound housing the US women. The US women, having been woken by the apparently early morning exercises of the Chinese, scramble out of their rooms and assemble loosely on the edge of the lawn in an assortment of practice clothes. Asked to summarize the sentiments evoked by the ad, the MBAs said it was about "different styles of competition," and suggested as a slogan for the ad: "Here's our game, can you top this?" and "Look out your window, because we're coming fast."

The video bears more analysis, and the MBAs' comments could use some polish, but the brief warm-up sets out some of the themes for the day: the rise of China, competitive relations between China and the United States, and a set of cultural differences that suffuse those relations. The ad highlights a "new competitive reality," says Geraldo, and it captures a sense of "pride," which he says he has noted when he's in China, adding, "This is all in the background of the case for today."

Geraldo also framed the case by locating it within the current module of the syllabus, which included a textbook reading on cross-cultural communication. A core takeaway from the chapter was that international managers should start from an assumption of difference, requiring a heightened awareness of different styles of spoken and written language use as well as nonverbal and other contextual channels of communication. The chapter includes quantitative data on linguistic diversity and cultural sensitivity, confronting MBAs with the realization that, while it may be emerging as a universal language of business, English is not the most widely spoken language, the United States lags far behind many other countries in terms of cross-cultural awareness and foreign language study, and the same English words and phrases may have different implications in different national settings. A case involving Bridgestone frames the chapter, which focuses especially on differences in communication practices between the United States and Japan, with examples from European cases illustrating that even "closer" business settings are impacted by cultural nuances in meaning.

Geraldo tells the class that the case highlights the most "salient communication differences between the United States and China," as well as "the importance of relationships. In international business it is very difficult to separate the business proposition from the relationships themselves." He adds that it is also a preview of an upcoming class session focused on the roles of the expatriate manager.

Five minutes into the case discussion, Geraldo has probably said too much—at least by the best practices described in the case method canon. But his work setting up the discussion discloses something more about the case method in practice. The carefully curated excess of the case study as a simulacrum of real work complexity is met and managed in the MBA classroom through a performance of framing and segmentation comparable to processes we have seen in other facets of the MBA experience. It seems fitting, then, that so much of the case method involves the strategic enlisting of MBA students in an always-partial engagement with the case. Other case discussions I have observed bear this out, as faculty proceed systematically through a stepwise analysis of delimited segments of the case, sometimes pushing against students' efforts to raise new points of discussion while they elicit more thoughts about a tightly circumscribed issue in the case. There is an active avoidance by faculty of students attempting any sort of conclusive analysis. In this light, the idea that the case study is an exercise in communitarian learning may mask the extent to which the wisdom of the crowd needed to crack the case serves as well as an index of the fundamental reality (= irreducible complexity) of the case as told. In this way, too, the case experience establishes the MBAs as always-partial adepts of complexity. As we shall see below, a core lesson of Geraldo's teaching of this case is that international managers, appropriately aware of their cross-cultural limitations, need to enlist the strategic support of a team of cultural specialists. It takes an MBA village.

Just the (Social) Facts

In the remainder of this chapter, I draw on observations of MBA case discussions to detail the case method in practice and particularly in relationship with themes of international and cross-cultural business. "Trouble in Paradise" will provide the overall arc for the discussion. Alongside that, I will offer detailed vignettes from a second case discussion, observed as part of a study abroad exchange between a US business school and a partner institution in Mexico.

Geraldo begins the "Trouble" case by asking for a just the facts ("no analysis") summary of the case. Chris's narration of the case is made partial by Geraldo's interruption. And Chris's push to get out his final (and most analytic) thought—"China is more long-term"—reflects a performative imperative for MBA students to make memorable contributions to case discussions. It also reflects the ways some of the takeaways from the case are already frontloaded—if not through Geraldo's setup, then through familiar Hofstedian shorthands for Chinese ("Confucian") cultural characteristics. Thus, Chris immediately scales the details of the case to reflect dyadic differences in national business culture.

These are social facts, in a double sense. They are social facts in the Durkheimian sense of broader collective patterns whose authority stems from outside of the individuals who may trade in them. They are social facts as well in the context of the classroom, insofar as they are socially produced through the scaffolded collective conversational performance of the MBA case discussion.

Geraldo summarizes Chris's contribution—the case is "about different objectives or goals between the Chinese business partner and the US business partner"—and then calls on another student, "What else?"

A second student offers, "You have a manager, expat, coming to the end of his assignment, and he has to decide what to do based on what to say to his manager at home in Ohio."

Another student adds, "Also about someone caught between two sides and how to explain to each side."

Geraldo jumps in. The case is "about being caught in the middle. Going back to another course I teach, we talk about the 'floating subsidiary dilemma' and the position the international manager finds himself or herself in. Common to international business. Less common in domestic." Geraldo goes on to talk briefly about different sorts of dilemmas or contrasts between "home and host objectives," before offering a global summary of the discussion so far, defining the case as about "the business objectives, how to resolve them, and being caught in the middle."

Summarizing and Scaffolding

This brief excerpt captures some of the rhythm of the discussion, which was an iterative process of contributions by students punctuated by summarizing and scaffolding interventions by Geraldo. The summaries function as strategic shorthands: at once validating student contributions and flagging the key themes on which Geraldo wants to build this case discussion. Along the way, he takes advantage of opportunities to review some more technical concepts in international business, and he does so in a way that evokes a world of specialized complexity beyond the limited taste of international business he can provide in this course. This burnishes his authority and also frames international settings as requiring advanced managerial capacities.

A similar process is evident in a discussion of a case focused on the Mexican cement company, CEMEX (Marchand, Chung, and Paddack 2002). The widely used case has made CEMEX a canonical example of the global expansion of a business based in an emerging economy. The case challenges students to make sense of the strategic decisions that drove CEMEX's success. From the 1980s through the early 2000s, CEMEX, founded in 1906, had grown through a set of aggressive acquisitions in Europe, Asia, North and South America, and the Pacific, achieving impressive rates of growth in its operating cash flow. CEMEX is also widely known for being an innovative early adopter of information technology in the stereotypically low-tech cement industry. The case concerned decisions about the next stages of growth for the company, given the rapid consolidation of the cement industry around five global firms. The instructor, Charles, was miked, making his staccato interventions to prod students' answers especially jarring.

"What are the issues in the case that we should address?" asks Charles.

"Growth and expansion" says one student.

Charles repeats this, writing furiously at a chalkboard, adding, "obviously, they are not the same. What else?"

"I think, 'technology,'" offers another student.

Charles: "Why?"

"Technology helps them achieve their expansion all around the world."

Charles: "Do you find that important because it is only a matter of technology, why should we focus on it?"

"Because when you are expanding you need good communication around the world."

Charles: "Because of communication, what else?"

Another student suggests that communication makes for greater efficiency.

Charles: "Why is efficiency a relevant point for you?"

"When you're more efficient, you can reduce costs."

Charles cuts him off: "That's a cookbook recipe," repeating in a sing-song cadence: "as long as you're efficient you can manage cost." A few more students attempt responses; when they stumble in reaction to Charles's interjections, he reframes the question and moves on to another student. Finally, he interrupts a stammering MBA to say, "We understand that we are in global processes around the world. And we understand that IT development is also happening everywhere else. WHY should it matter in this case, particularly?"

Oscar answers that "CEMEX got business purchasing standardization."

"Also McDonald's," interrupts Charles. "What's the difference?" As Oscar hesitates, Charles throws him a lifeline, "'Standardized'—great. Why?"

Charles seems to be batting away the contributions of the students; he certainly has me feeling that anything I might offer would be hopelessly incomplete. But, as his exchange with Oscar shows, he is retaining fragments of each contribution, building a record at the blackboard of ideas reclaimed and reframed from the discussion: efficiency, standardization, communication, control, decision-making, etc. Charles has a habit of murmuring to himself as he writes a term on the board; with his voice miked, the effect is akin to italicizing the key word in a given stretch of dialogue.

The discussion turns to CEMEX's performance in comparison with its multinational rivals, and Charles quizzes the MBAs on their reading of charts in the case, presenting detailed financial information about CEMEX and comparing some of those data to comparable information about the rival firms.

Charles: "How is CEMEX doing in comparison to its competitors? Is a 20% return on investment good?"

This stretch of the course becomes an exercise in reading and evaluating financial information, leading up to Charles suggesting that a 20% ROI for a firm in an emerging market is not particularly impressive. For all of its global expansion, the bulk of CEMEX's business is in Latin America. For a firm in a "mature market" an ROI of 4 or 5% might be expected. By that standard, some of CEMEX's Europe-based rivals, although they have lower ROIs than CEMEX, are performing better.

Charles uses a deft rephrasing of student comments and an arch tone to make each contribution seem partial and incomplete. When a student responds to his questioning about whether CEMEX is an industry leader by discussing a series of mergers and acquisitions, he cuts her off, saying "So, you are doing better than competitors because you are doing more acquisitions than them?!" Elsewhere he paraphrases student descriptions of what CEMEX is doing well—"market share" or "efficiency"—into a debate about the value of "size" versus "performance." The MBAs respond to Charles's gendered and sexualized repartee with laughter and even applause at one point. Beyond breaking the tension and giving some students the impression they are in the hands (or at the mercy) of a virtuoso case discussion leader, these interactional devices create performative spaces for additional class contributions and render the discussion a communal project.

Mapping the Players

Case discussions involve active framing by faculty, who underscore key words from the flow of student comments, and these become anchors and waypoints for the conversation. They are written on blackboards or anticipated on PowerPoint slides, and they are reframed into questions that shape the next leg of the class discussion or as cues for pedagogical digressions. These may involve introductions of quasi-technical terms, like "floating subsidiary dilemma," or they may involve hands-on practice in reading account statements, as when Charles takes the students through their paces in analyzing CEMEX's financial information. Depending on where a case falls in the arc of a syllabus, an instructor may use a case for a very focused practical assignment: in a marketing class, a case about a cell phone company entering the market provided an exercise in calculating specific elements of cost and pricing.

In the "Trouble" discussion, the sense of Mike Graves being "in between" must have been a target for Geraldo, because he moves to a slide that illustrates Mike's situation, caught between the home office and the Chinese partner in the joint venture. This is a common step in case discussions, as students are asked to review the different "players" in a case, commenting on their perspectives and interests. Of note here is that alongside text and boxes mapping out Heartland, the Chinese partner, and the prospective acquisition target, Geraldo added a figure that looked like a cumulus cloud. He told the class that this represented the impact of the "local government officials" in the case. Working with government is certainly a crucial component of doing business in China, and it is not surprising that Geraldo would anticipate this as part of the case analysis. But representing the government as a cloud suggests to my eye the exotic opacity of the Chinese business context, where certain elements defy any sort of stable knowing.

I will return to that below; for now, the MBAs have other things in mind. Before Geraldo can work through his map of the players, another student—who clearly has read the textbook chapter for today—breaks in to ask, "Would it be typical of a US expat in China not to speak the language at all?" Geraldo allows that this is "pretty typical in my experience," saying that he could supply examples from the executives he's taught in the business school's management academy. He then turns the question back to the MBAs to ask what their experiences have been. An MBA from Colombia tells the story of a French manager posted there who came with no Spanish, but picked up the language in a matter of months. A domestic MBA tells the story of his college roommate, who studied finance and Chinese. He was quickly hired and posted to China, primarily to serve as an interpreter for an expat manager who did not speak Chinese. This was not presented as a positive story. And a

Chinese student points out that a manager in the textile industry in eastern China was not likely to be fluent in English, but more likely to be bilingual in Japanese.

Geraldo breaks in here with another scaffolding and summarizing intervention. First he provides some geopolitical and geocultural context for China, noting the stronger influence of Japan and Korea in eastern China. Then, returning to the initial question, he says,

> to give a short answer, if I had to prepare you for this assignment I'd say "learn Chinese," or make sure your firm sends somebody who knows the local language. The reality is that it is a scarce . . . it is really hard to learn it. And if you have someone who is good in a number of markets, they may be sent there, not necessarily for the language capabilities but because of what they know about the business and doing business worldwide. Not that surprising. It does create problems, but there are managers who can be effective.

Geraldo's comments encapsulate the MBA curricular approach to international business issues. On the one hand is an acknowledgment of an ideal of deep linguistic and cultural competence, reflecting an enlightened sensitivity to why these things matter. This is consistent with the founding positions of Edward Hall and Fayerweather. On the other is the pragmatic reality of business practice, which inevitably falls short of that ideal. Brokering the space between these are "the managers who can be effective." MBA programs map out the vanguard of international business preparation, even as they facilitate the production of "good-enough" self-aware managerial talent. Case studies, STSA experiences, and connections to international MBA teams provide MBAs with a starter kit to the good-enough claim to be "good in a number of markets" and to "know . . . about doing business worldwide."

With that, Geraldo returns to his mapping of the players, asking the MBAs, "What are the salient cultural differences in the case?"

"Chinese colleagues save face in meetings," one student offers, reporting, "[they] took a more silent approach rather than speaking up."

Geraldo follows, "How do they explain it in the case?"

Another student paraphrases a line of dialogue from one of Mike's Chinese partners: "If you don't say anything, you won't get in trouble."

Geraldo breaks in to invoke an earlier time in IB education: "An old saying in Japan that we used to use in the '70s and '80s . . . 'The nail that sticks out gets hammered.'" He looks to a Japanese MBA student to validate this saying, and, after an additional example, says, "All of that to say that communication tends to be less direct on the Chinese side—as far as face-saving culture."

He turns quickly to elicit other "differences," cold-calling on another student, who says there "seems to be a lot more formality and respect shown to other people."

"How did that come out for you?" asked Geraldo. The student describes the banquet Mike attended, where there was a clear protocol of how seats were taken at the table, with "elders getting positions of honor."

Geraldo continued, "What are other examples of formality?" A student detailed the elaborate scene at the banquet, where an orchestra was playing and where the atmosphere was one of "pomp and circumstance." Geraldo rephrases this back to the students as "ceremony," and he reminds the MBAs of another detail somewhat buried in the case: Mike Graves was initially scandalized when he arrived in China to see that his predecessor had a special account for what seemed like extravagant lunches.

On this point, Geraldo suggests that "if we wanted to go further" we could use other cases to examine ethical differences in doing business across cultures, offering a brief commentary on the Foreign Corrupt Practices Act. As was the case with his earlier intervention, the effect is one of gesturing to an excess of nuance and complexity at stake in international business. This excess is more than can be contained in a single case discussion. Geraldo was likely plugging some of his other classes, and building up his authority in ways we've seen in chapter 2. He may well have been performing for me, as some of our conversations had addressed the constraints of teaching complex business themes in the boiled-down MBA curriculum. But I think these periodic gestures to excess are part of the pragmatic takeaway (or, perhaps better, the "leave behind") of international case teaching. For it is in the face of a welter of complexity that the students are challenged and taught to find more familiar grooves of analysis and, ultimately, action. To a large extent, these grooves were already in view prior to the case, thanks to the students' habituation to the codifying language of Hofstedian binary contrasts and the cultural distances of the CAGE framework. Thus, the students land very quickly on concepts like face-saving or long-term versus short-term perspectives in their comments. For his part, Geraldo calls them repeatedly back to a close reading of the paraethnographic data in the case, habituating the analytic move from simulated real-world practice to familiar slots of otherness.

After another student comments on Mike's apparent surprise at the role of government officials in the case, Geraldo remarks that "the strategy of the firm is being influenced by taking into account how the government official feels about the business," adding that this direct involvement of government officials is very different than a US context.

Cementing Differences

The CEMEX case does not deal as explicitly with cross-cultural experiences, but as an example of a corporation globalizing from a position in an emerging market, the case entails a decentering of a Euro-American perspective, one that takes on additional nuances in a case discussion at a Mexican business school. As Charles probes for MBAs' views on what CEMEX is doing well, one student says, "CEMEX applied First World technologies in Third World markets."

"And what do we expect of Third World markets?" asks Charles. "Are they risky?" His immediate point is to underscore that CEMEX's rate of return of 20% is expected for bearing the risk of operating primarily in emerging markets. He leads the students to see that as CEMEX ponders additional expansion into more "mature markets," their history of 20% growth is not likely to be sustained.

The case as Charles is framing it is about the ways CEMEX moves to become a global company, and he returns the discussion repeatedly to the counterintuitive success of a *Mexican* global company. About twenty minutes into the case, he shifts from eliciting different views of CEMEX's strengths (capacity, efficiency, etc.) to ask,

> What do you think about a Mexican company achieving this type of success against a French, a Swiss, and in the meantime eating an American company? How does it feel when you come from the US and see that an American company is being swallowed by a Mexican one?

The nervous laughter this elicits grows even sharper when he cold-calls a US student to ask if he could imagine himself being told what to do by a Mexican. (He responded with a quick-witted joke that he certainly could, based on his experiences today, and added that the growth of CEMEX was good because "competition brings out the best in everyone.")

Charles turns to a device he deploys a couple of times in the case discussion. "Give me some adjectives to describe the cement industry." He elicits a list—static, male, strong, old, boring, dangerous, dirty, dependent— interrupting twice to prime the pump by asking, "Would you say that it is sexy...?" and by asking for adjectives to describe consulting or finance and using those as a contrastive foil for eliciting students' views about cement. He then asks the students to consider these qualities in a Mexican context, asking them how they imagine a cement company would be run in a developing country like Mexico. The students described a "traditional," "family-controlled" administrative structure, a "repressive" culture of high authority with little tolerance for mistakes, and an organization that was very efficient and able to learn fast. Some Mexican students pointed to recent Mexican history to suggest that a Mexican business had to be flexible and able to adapt and survive during periods of economic and political crisis.

The comments strongly echo framings of Mexico that were wired throughout the STSA course (see chapter 5) regarding a set of culturally distinctive forms of practice that create value possibilities for Mexican businesses. The US MBAs are being groomed to see the potential in all of this, but the case discussion presents this as a nuanced reading likely to be missed by conventional analysts. At one point, Charles urges the MBAs to "think like an analyst," noting CEMEX's global expansion beginning in the late 1980s and asking them leadingly, "Would an analyst in the late '80s consider Mexico a logical candidate for economic growth?"

Many of the cultural qualities of Mexican business are suffused with a sense of the past—marked as "traditional" or as reflecting savvy business agility shaped in the crucible of the gritty Third World past. Charles drives the point home when he later asks the students to imagine what business was like in a Mexican cement company in the mid-1980s. Images of paper records, corded phones, poor communication across company plants, and slow processes of consultation between delivery drivers and managers are intended to help the students discuss the value added by adopting cutting-edge information technology; they also complete the exotic bona fides of Mexico as an emerging economy.

Although this cultural otherness is not written into the CEMEX case, Charles evokes a cloud of difference through a device that would be at home in an ethnographic interview or focus group: eliciting a componential inventory of Mexican distinctiveness. Much as cases themselves are produced through paraethnographic practices and include thick(ish) descriptions of business contexts, the case discussions I observed often approximated ethnographic interviews, as faculty and sometimes other students engage students with relevant industry experience or with relevant cultural competence to elicit crucial information. In addition to the componential inventory of attributes evoking the qualities of the Mexican construction industry (standing in this STSA context for Mexican business in general), Charles relied on a student who reported that he had experience in the construction industry and drew on other students with experiences in software development to discuss the information technology side of the case.

Of Culture and Coaching

In the "Trouble" case, Geraldo next turns to elicit from students the primary tensions between Heartland and the Chinese partners. Heartland seeks a 20% ROI from their business in China, much higher than the 4–5% the joint venture is currently achieving. (Note how similar figures in the CEMEX case routinize expectations about "emerging" and "mature" economies.) From the material presented in the case, it is also clear that Heartland wants to limit further acquisitions and focus on producing higher-end retail products. This would involve investing in newer machinery, which would allow the production of higher quality textiles and also enable Heartland to reduce their "headcount." The students stressed the "short-term" focus and impatience of the US company. Geraldo continued to probe with questions about Heartland's "market focus" until he established that Heartland was primarily focused on producing in China for a US market, and that their interest in shifting to higher-end products would mean a continuation of the United States as their primary market, rather than producing for Chinese consumers.

At this point, Geraldo steers the discussion to the Chinese partners and government officials, effectively assigning them a single perspective. Citing comments made at the banquet, the students report that "stability and growth in employment" are their primary goals, also glossed as "keeping the government happy." The Chinese "side" is satisfied with a 5 or 6% ROI. One MBA says, "[The] Chinese seem to be more about creating harmony than they are about change or revamping the system. Long-term harmony kind of wraps up the whole outlook." Geraldo pushes back against a sense of resistance to change—change "is happening very rapidly there"—and reframes the comment, saying it is "more about preserving harmony among the stakeholders in the business." A Chinese student comes at it a bit differently, suggesting that the Chinese partners in the joint venture "want to contribute to the local economy before they get their profit." Geraldo's summary distills this into a general international management takeaway: "so we see that there are pretty big differences in terms of their goals and objectives."

Here, about halfway through the ninety-minute class, Geraldo turns the discussion to decisions and actions. Mike is coming to the end of his time in China. What can he do, what are his options to resolve this conflict, and what would you have done differently in Mike's place? The conversation moves through a variety of strategies.

The first recommendation is that Mike should have kept his manager at home more "educated" along the way.

Geraldo: "What does 'educated' mean?"

"Share some of things that he learned about the culture … what the Chinese partners' goals are."

Geraldo takes the students through a listing of Mike's options at this point. One MBA suggests that he try to "steer the Chinese partners" toward an arrangement closer to what Heartland wants.

"How would you do that?" asks Geraldo, to which the student says that "informally and behind the scenes" Mike should start to stress the ways new technology could benefit the firm, aiming for a middle-ground arrangement where the new acquisition could go hand in hand with addressing some of Heartland's priorities. A few other students jump in to sketch out arrangements that would have a commitment to increasing ROI to something less than 20% and a reduction of staff without becoming "a hatchet man." These echo platitudes from MBA negotiation modules encouraging "win-win" arrangements and promoting your suggestions without tearing down other proposals. These suggestions peter out as Geraldo pushes for nuts-and-bolts details.

Two other students introduce themes that will occupy the discussion for the rest of the session. One student observes that, whatever the initial agreement on the joint venture, the partners seem to want different things from the relationship today. Another student, from China, says that it is important for Mike "to identify who the key decisions-makers are in the Chinese group."

Geraldo takes up the second point: Who would you approach, how would you get access, what are the risks or sensitivities connected to reaching out to high-level senior officials? Geraldo sounds out some of these themes, but explicitly encourages the MBAs in the class to ask the Chinese student for advice on identifying whom to talk to. He asks a similar question of a Japanese student—"How would you do it in Japan?"—and then goes through a series of other countries represented by international MBAs in the class. "I want to be able to influence in a legal way, in an acceptable way, in an appropriate way, a local government official. Who can I find as a coach?"

Geraldo is introducing the idea of a "coach"— a position akin to a mentor that appears across management training publications. In this case, Geraldo is using the challenges facing Mike Graves to illustrate the importance of cultivating a relationship with a culturally adept local advisor who can offer insights and bridge relationships in ways that might minimize the pitfalls of cultural differences. Geraldo frames some of his interactions with international MBAs as if he were asking them who might be a good coach in Japan, China, etc. But an additional result of the conversation is that the international classmates are framed as themselves potential coaches for the domestic MBAs. There is an awkward silence as some of the international MBAs are put on the spot. That is broken with laughter when an MBA student from Japan suggests sheepishly that the perfect local coach would be someone from the Japanese trading company he works for. Geraldo points out that local business partners as well as industry associations connecting various expatriate managers can be vital resources for sharing information and facilitating interactions with local governmental bureaucracies. He ties things together with an extended anecdote about an STSA course he recently led to China.

Geraldo's Trip to the Chinese Central Bank

Geraldo had met a well-placed official with the Chinese Central Bank at a conference and he wanted to use that contact to line up a visit to the bank for his class. Geraldo's contact responded enthusiastically to his email proposing a meeting and said he would be delighted to meet with the students at their hotel. Geraldo sent a series of follow-up emails diplomatically indicating that they would prefer to meet at the bank offices, but received no further communication on the matter. Stymied, he reached out to a contact at the consulate, who "gave me some very good coaching," explaining the bureaucratic and security concerns entailed by the visit. The consulate official encouraged Geraldo to talk directly by phone to the bank official. Geraldo enlisted the help of a Chinese MBA student who was also serving as one of the trip leaders for the STSA. "I'm not the smartest guy," Geraldo told the class, "but I know when someone has skills that I don't have." The student was able to get the bank official's mobile number from his assistant, and the direct phone call from the student succeeded in opening the doors for the bank visit.

Geraldo offered this as an example of finding a "creative solution" when there appeared to be no way forward. His point, he insisted, was not specific to the Chinese context. The managerial challenge is learning "[how] it works in that system and using networks, contacts, coaches to get things done. . . . I want you to be thinking about a wealth of opportunities rather than one way to do this or that this is an insurmountable problem." He continued,

> Within a world of hierarchies and status differences and educational levels and coming from a rich country, medium country, small country . . . whatever, there's a wealth of talent and resources that's captured in each individual. And sometimes that's not utilized because we let the hierarchy put us off or we let distance get in the way. I've seen some incredible cases in international business and in my travels where what we would consider to be a low-level production worker can effect a huge amount of change if it's done in the right way that goes around all the bureaucracies and hierarchies.

Geraldo recounted times when his senior position as a business school professor has opened doors. But the generic managerial point was that relationships matter, that moving a relationship "to a more productive space" requires working according to local cultural norms, and that it "takes time and effort and ability to see where resources can be utilized to get things done." And, as the broader class discussion makes clear, the resources and the ability to see them are being coproduced in the international classroom milieu. As a perfect kicker to the anecdote, Geraldo tells them that they learned during their visit that the bank official had fond memories of a time early in his career when he was a visitor in residence at their business school.

This is part of the lesson for Mike Graves, who is criticized for not developing effective relations with his Chinese partners, being out of touch with local government officials, and being too comfortable in his gated community of expat managers. A student builds on this to suggest that Mike should have developed a long-term coaching relationship, and Geraldo responds to her by talking about the desirability of hiring a local manager and right-hand person who "knows both sides" and can work closely with the expatriate.

Another student breaks in to say that "you definitely want both sides to understand and to see it from both sides, and communication is central," but once both sides understand, "you can talk all you want, you still have two completely opposing views," stemming from what seem to be conflicting goals for the joint venture. The student is returning to the win-win scenario that came up earlier and talking about delicately balancing fixed and variable costs in a way that could accommodate the new acquisition and some automation without drastically cutting employment.

Geraldo pushes him for some specific options that he might propose, and in the process it becomes clear that the student is holding constant the current fifty/fifty arrangement in the joint venture. "What if that's not written in stone? What if that contract is ending tomorrow? What options are there?" Geraldo and the MBAs work through a number of hypothetical transformations of the joint venture. Alongside maintaining the status quo, they explore rebalancing the partnership, including splitting the partnership so that Heartland might focus on production for export to the high-end US market, while the Chinese partner could pursue local business in coordination with their goal of building "a national brand."

Geraldo supplies this last detail, telling the students that the information was "hidden in the case." In fact, the words "national brand" are italicized on the third page of the case. They appear in the remarks by the top executive on the Chinese side of the joint venture at the ceremony marking the tenth anniversary of the partnership. He describes their goal of becoming a national brand in conjunction with the announcement that they are "preparing our fourth acquisition, which is expected to raise our production capacity by 40%. The number of our employees will grow to nearly 3,500." In the case narrative, Mike is gobsmacked by this announcement of a fourth acquisition, which stirs him from an internal monologue that nicely serves the purpose of summarizing some of his problems establishing effective managerial communications with Chinese managers. Against the home office's interest in increasing ROI by limiting new acquisitions, and shedding employees through automation, the numbers in the paragraph (40% increase in production capacity; 3,500 employees) certainly seem salient.

It may be that the MBAs overlooked the national brand aspirations, although there were some references in the case discussion to the local/national focus of the Chinese partners. As significant, I think, is that the detail was cast as "hidden" in the discussion: a managerial Easter egg to be detected through sensitive attention to ceremonial practices and by looking beyond the immediately commensurable numbers to detect motive and intent. It requires no great hermeneutic effort to see the italicized words at the end of the third full paragraph on page three. But among the takeaway lessons of the case is that Mike has done a poor job understanding the strategic goals of his partners. The MBAs' classroom analysis performs a success where Mike failed, based in detecting the nuances otherwise hidden to Mike and other less-sensitized managers.

The third option for changing the JV is "ending the marriage." The MBAs debate a number of ways the partnership might end "with everyone happy." They anticipate that it would be very difficult for the Chinese partner to buy out Heartland's share of the business, since Heartland would want some return on their initial investment and "it would take the Chinese partner years to make that up with 5% or 6% ROI." There is no single decision being recommended here, but the discussion makes clear the multiple tradeoffs, and perspectives of each side of the partnership. Geraldo pulls together this segment of the discussion by characterizing the changing nature of doing business in China. A decade or two ago, he says, it might have been impossible for a US firm to go it alone in China. The fifty/fifty joint venture is an artifact of that time. However, things have changed, he reports, and "across many industries, it is now possible to go it alone. That may be one of the opportunities here."

Here, the challenges of the case point out a new range of possibilities and new risk/reward profiles for the sort of action that may soon be under the purview of the emerging MBAs. Geraldo pulls the session to a close by underscoring the topic of the module: communication. The main takeaway is more and better communication. Mike should obtain a clearer strategy for Heartland's involvement, and he should be more familiar with the strategy and goals of their partners. Geraldo is working through his own list of takeaways and squaring this with class discussion by calling back to students' comments and by gesturing to the graphical record of the discussion evident in the notes on the board. Geraldo brainstorms some ways US-based executives might be more involved in the partnership and notes that a well-executed visit from the boss could enhance Mike's status in the eyes of his Chinese partners. A final set of comments warns MBAs not to get too comfortable in an expat assignment. Residential enclaves like Mike's can isolate managers and prevent them from getting to know local stakeholders. He ends the class by calling for a round of applause "for a very good discussion."

The CEMEX Dude

In the CEMEX case discussion, Charles has evoked the stolid dullness of the cement industry and connected a sense of "unsexy" tradition to a broader quality attached to the Mexican business environment—at least in the 1980s, that is, before the liberalization of the economy. CEMEX had diversified since its founding, and by the 1980s the company was involved in hotel management, petrochemicals, and a number of other fields. Yet, beginning in the late 1980s, the firm's CEO made a strategic decision to shed its diversified industries and focus more fully on cement. The final third of the case discussion focused on why this was successful.

On the face of it, the decision to focus on cement made little sense. A Third World company in a mature industry, focused on a commodity with little product differentiation is not a recipe for growth. Charles shifts the conversation to the benefits of CEMEX's investments in information technologies. Accurate real-time information enabled CEMEX to minimize waste and keep costs down, offer precise delivery times, and react quickly to changing customer needs. This is the CEMEX success story of building brand equity and brand loyalty by offering superior customer service. The core of their success was taking an industry based in a very basic and primitive commodity, and developing a brand differentiated by customer experience.

Charles slows down the discussion to ask how specifically CEMEX's IT platform worked. The IT platform ran through the truck drivers, the students report.

"How easy is it to train truck drivers?" asked Charles. "Don't forget, we are in Mexico. We are not dealing with Swiss, French ... well, they're not really that good [laughter]—not dealing with, let's say, modern-oriented truck drivers."

Charles calls on a student who refers to the case document to report that CEMEX devoted a lot of training to their employees, particularly at their newly acquired companies, and also that CEMEX removed "traditional senior management" when they encountered managers who were skeptical of the innovations.

This is part of the story, but Charles still wants to focus on the (Mexican) truck drivers. How does CEMEX achieve their commitment to the new system? He goes back to MBAs who have been involved in software development to elicit their experiences working with clients. He seems pleased when they report that the challenge of software development is that most clients can't really articulate what they want. Charles turns back to the truck drivers to ask, "What does it take for a truck driver to think to link these two concepts—customer satisfaction and information technology?" Charles is leading the MBAs to describe an incentive system that CEMEX put in place connected to customer reviews and reflecting the improved logistics and service enabled by the IT platform. Along the way, he takes them through a digression imagining the experiences of a truck driver.

Charles asks, "What does a truck driver usually think when he is delivering cement? That he's fulfilling a customer need? What do they usually think?"

He cold-calls a student who says: "I don't know, probably nothing."

Charles moves to another student, who offers, "Just earning money."

Charles interrupts her saying, "'I'm doing my job. I'm merely doing my job.' Why would it be so different? . . . What type of ideas, of new concepts would the truck driver need in order to build that brand equity, that customer loyalty? . . . What would make a difference for a truck driver in order to understand that he's not merely doing his job, but satisfying customer needs?"

This stretch of the class is notable not only for the thought experiment of imagining a cement truck driver's experience and point of view, but especially for the brute elemental wage-laborer sensibilities they ascribe to the drivers: seemingly unable to think beyond a paycheck and quitting time. CEMEX connected their newly developed IT platform to a reengineering of their personnel, all in the service of building brand equity through improved customer service. This is one component of a broader standardized corporate culture that has come to be known as the "CEMEX way."[7] As Charles elicits the story from the MBAs, while other industry competitors were trying to cut costs and marginally improve their product, CEMEX "realized that by changing from a product to a service industry it could differentiate itself."

The case discussion is moving the MBAs through the strategic decisions undertaken by the CEMEX CEO. Charles's questions continuously reframe the problem as seen through the eyes of a manager contemplating a counter-intuitive course of action. Charles reviews the history of CEMEX's expansion, which involved assessments of target markets and strategic decisions to expand first into markets in developing countries, and especially, but not exclusively, Spanish-speaking markets, seen as being "closer"—in Hofstedian and CAGE framework terms—to CEMEX's experiences in Mexico. The case quotes a CEMEX manager describing their focus on markets with "chaotic distribution logistics and primitive information technology." Expansion into developed economies was a second wave of growth for CEMEX.

Charles draws the discussion together:

> We come to my earlier point: how easy, how practical is it to bring ideas and business practices that were developed in a Mexican company and take them to developed countries? What are the hard points there? What are the main challenges that you face there?

He cuts off a student who starts to talk about changing the objectives of the cement industry. "How is CEMEX perceived in Indonesia?" A number of students call out: "As a Third World company." The challenge for CEMEX is to remake its identity from a Third World to a global company. Charles reviews how they do this. He asks students to look at CEMEX's website and the ways the site's design and especially its use of English perform a certain global identity. He also asks the Mexican MBAs if they know anyone who works for CEMEX and how they would describe CEMEX employees. (He throws in a Mexican Spanish pun changing the "CEMEX way" to the "CEMEX guey" [i.e., CEMEX dude].) Tentatively at first, the MBAs describe CEMEX managers as well-educated and arrogant. This is "not your typical Mexican worker," says Charles, stressing that this came about because the CEO "chose to do this . . . chose to push people to change."

Reengineering the Social

Both case discussions feature ideals of managers involved in reengineering social relations to enable global business success. In the "Trouble" case, it involves what Mike *ought* to have done to establish more productive relationships with his Chinese partners and to enable Heartland to operate more independently in the changing Chinese business landscape. In the CEMEX case, the CEO is celebrated for having accomplished the social work of redesigning a corporate culture—from management to truck driver. These changes unlock new value potential in the stolid commodity of cement by building new relations with customers and with global partners.

Like the real or hypothetical managers in the cases, the case discussions position the MBAs as simulated protagonists as they perform the orientation of the probing, active, socially embedded, fiscally accountable manager. Some of this is modeled by Geraldo and Charles, who, in their different ways, interrupt and interrogate the students, and point them to all that they do not know.[8] But they also point the MBAs to one another, as the case and its various analyses cohere as coproduced social facts. In that coproduction, the MBAs inhabit various managerial subject positions, from a distant clinical analysis of the business venture (in which employees work only for a paycheck, as in the CEMEX drivers, or figure euphemistically as a "headcount" to be reduced by automation in the Heartland case), to closer attention to the affective world of managerial capitalists. The examination of the simulated world of the case calls these cosmopolitan managerial subjects into being.

SEVEN

Frontiers of Capitalism

IN 2008, I ATTENDED A CONFERENCE for business faculty and administrators focused on best practices in international business programs. The goal of the conference, according to the organizers, was to examine "emerging developments in international business and their implications for IB education." From keynote remarks underscoring the business catechism that all business is global, to surveys of the rise of the BRICS countries and other "emerging" economies, to sessions devoted to the design and management of short-term study abroad courses, the conference embodied the boom in international business education in the United States. And yet, there was a sense of challenge and change looming over the conference. It wasn't the financial crisis; although things were beginning to unwind, the scale of the problem was not in plain view until later that year. The challenge, rather, was from the vibrant diversity of global business. A key takeaway from the conference, underscored in postconference summaries, was that global changes in business-as-usual require transformations in business education.

In previous chapters I have focused on the ways US business curricula construct international space as an unavoidable and necessary space of difference, an enduring zone of risk to be managed, and a resource for the production of managerial subjects able to transit difference and decompose the risk of distance to render it manageable. Successful management requires the cultivation of a habitus that routinizes the ceaseless engagement with risk and difference and their conversion into value. The ceaseless engagement with risk and difference requires its ceaseless production, and, in this regard, business schools are engaged in a continuous quest for new margins, making the periphery core to contemporary capitalism. This concluding chapter examines this through the phenomena of "bottom of the pyramid"

(BoP) business strategies—focused on producing the "marketness" of the global poor.

BoP and related discourses of social entrepreneurship have taken on new prominence in the years since the financial crisis of 2008. From one vantage, this makes no sense. Cultural differences and immiseration, particularly when combined, pose a pairing of heightened risk and limited reward that would reasonably be shunned by most business strategists. And cautionary tales abound (e.g., Karamchandani, Kubzansky, and Lalwani 2011; Rangan, Chu, and Petkoski 2011; Simanis 2012). Yet modules on social entrepreneurship—sometimes connected to STSA courses—and specialized MBA concentrations are among the trends in MBA education over the past decade. Similarly, the global paracurriculum of MBA education now includes initiatives like the Global Social Venture Competition, founded at the Haas School of Business at UC Berkeley and expanded into a network of hosting and participating business programs in the United States, Europe, Asia, Africa, and Latin America. And MBA student blogs and other promotional materials featuring MBA experiences are filled with declarations of MBA students' commitments to twinning "doing good and doing business."

The moral promise of capitalism is one side of a very old story. Capitalist discipline, worldly success as a reflection of a righteous inner state, and the ideal of markets as moral machines maximizing and efficiently distributing the benefits of human progress—these are tropes and alibis found in missionary sermons, neoliberal policy tracts, and MBA core economics classes. Contemporary MBA programs harness this core claim of capitalism to the production of modern managerial talent.

SCALING DIFFERENCE

My concluding discussion begins with this redemptive production of local subjects for global projects, understanding by "local subjects" the nascent MBA entrepreneur as well as the denizens of the bottom of the pyramid. By focusing on this coproduction, we can better examine the mutually constituting relationship between local and global and the work that needs to be done to achieve the complex connections between phenomena of different scale integral to such voicings of globalization. In conventional business-speak, *scale* and *scalability* often refer to the possibilities and challenges of expanding production processes and connecting markets across the globe.

Anthropological discussions of scale call attention to the ways the local places being linked together are produced, or at least transformed, by the larger processes that connect them. This, as we have seen in chapter 4, helps correct a traditional disciplinary blind spot in which the small-scale communities that were the focus of anthropology over much of the twentieth century were too often cast in relative isolation. And the descriptive shorthand of "scale" helps to mark both the inequality of such connections and the ways these inequalities contribute to a sense of a similar set of localities/markets/BRICS (and "poor entrepreneurs") available for incorporation within larger-scale processes. These examinations of scale raise a chicken-and-egg question about the local markets and the larger processes.

In chapter 1, I reviewed a range of work by anthropologists who have drawn ethnographic attention to the codependency of the local and the global and particularly the ways framings of one entail framings of the other. What I aim to underscore here is the way the transformation of the redeemed BoP subjects also relies upon and participates in the production of scalar connections. Thus approached, the question becomes less "local versus global" than understanding the ways contemporary efforts to embrace the local elicit processes that produce the articulation across both scales.

TWO PARABLES OF SOCIAL ENTREPRENEURSHIP

I. Cabbages to Market

The culminating session of the 2008 conference included a pair of presentations focused on "the bottom of the pyramid." The term comes from the influential book, *The Fortune at the Bottom of the Pyramid: Eradicating Poverty through Profits* (Prahalad 2005). The title refers to a socioeconomic pyramid representing income distribution across the world's population. As rendered by Coimbinatore Prahalad, at the narrow top of the pyramid sit 75–100 million people with annual purchasing power of greater than $20,000. In the middle tiers of the pyramid, with purchasing power of between $1,500 and $20,000 per year are some 1.5–1.75 billion people. And at the bottom of the pyramid are more than 4 billion people living on less than $2 per day. In Prahalad's view, the BoP presents a business opportunity: there is money to be made, and lots of it, if only firms can see the poor for what they really are: a "latent market for goods and services." In the eyes of BoP theorists, the poor are organic entrepreneurs, value-conscious consumers, who will respond to the right opportunities placed before them. Indeed, the BoP message has a redemptive function, enabling a fuller realization of the entrepreneurial dignity of the poor by connecting them to markets to which conventional business wisdom condemns them to have no access. In Prahalad's view, the marketplace confers "self-esteem" and "dignity" (2005, 5).

One of the cases was presented by Anju, director of an organization I'll call Social Entrepreneurship International (SEI), devoted to work focused primarily on agriculturalists in India. Anju began by declaring her organization's approach to the poor "as entrepreneurs." SEI started work focused on poverty in the United States, but soon expanded their focus internationally. This was cast as a "natural" progression, and it sets up a tension between the global category of "the poor" and the necessity of engaging the poor in local contexts. Indeed, after specifying her group's focus on people living on less than $1 per day, and particularly on subsistence farmers, Anju turned to the importance of local contexts. She noted with pride that even the most senior SEI staff spends extensive time with their impoverished "clients." "My personal target," she said, "is to talk to at least 100 families a year, on their farms. Go out and really walk the farms and talk to our clients, to listen and problem-solve at that level."

The organization uses a family-focused methodology that enables them to realize increases in income of about $150 in one growing season, $300 in the second, "and it is onward and upward from there." This miraculous transformation stems from a sober assessment of the "assets" of the very poor: "land and the lowest labor costs in the world," by which Anju was referring to the family as a unit of production.[1] Note that "listening and problem-solving" involve recasting their experiences within a new comparative and analytic framework. The primary constraint to "capitalizing" on these assets is lack of access to water.

Here is where SEI enters the picture. Their intervention involves reengineering a set of irrigation technologies—treadle pumps for groundwater and drip irrigation systems—to make them affordable and scalable for poor customers. This is a page directly from the BoP literature, which encourages businesses to think in terms of smaller, low-margin products, like single-use shampoo packages, to serve poor customers unable to invest in larger units. Although conventional business thinking might counsel against single-use packaging because of the low profit margin, Prahalad's message is that the fortune at the bottom of the pyramid is found when a low per unit margin is multiplied by billions of new customers.

In the case of SEI, this takes the form of a suite of products engineered to be low-cost and scalable. Drip irrigation kits for a kitchen garden, available for a few dollars, might help a family achieve food security. Drip irrigation sets for larger fields, available for $5, enable a family to produce a small surplus for sale. Treadle pumps, produced by SEI for a fraction of the hundreds of dollars they conventionally cost, enable the expansion of surplus production. The SEI product line structures a narrative of entrepreneurial development, moving farmers step-wise from marginal subsistence to profitable surplus. This is a redemptive myth of capitalism. The hold it has on a business school view of the (rest of the) world was nicely indexed by the very first question raised after the presentation, which asked if SEI had to engage in "barter" relations with their clients to help bridge their conversion into market-based entrepreneurs.

There is more than a whiff of the miraculous in this telling as Anju describes rocky, desolate areas yielding bumper crops of cabbage and cucumbers. But the miracle is incomplete. "You can grow all the cabbage you want in the world," said Anju. "You don't have an income until you have a marketplace to sell them in." She now reframes the elemental needs of a farmer: access to water is not enough; they also need markets. Water enables growth; markets provide a "fair price." This is a vital link in the story. Because the redemptive transformation of the subsistence farmer requires more than the "natural" urge to capitalize on his assets; it requires a different sort of reengineering, now at the level of the social.

This takes two forms in stories like Anju's. One involves scaling up from the entrepreneurial producer to form alliances of producers who collaborate in the effort to bring their crops to market. At the same time, in addition to culminating the redeemed productive experience, markets serve another moralizing function: disciplining the farmers to channel their entrepreneurial energies in ways rewarded by the market. In Anju's words,

> Market research is a huge part of what we do. Even though we talk about water as our entry point into farm families, the truth is "markets" is the entry point into the areas that we work. Because we want to see what the market will bear, what the demand is, and then we advise farmers what to grow.

There is a vast literature on the moral attributes of markets. In the MBA cosmology, markets do the moralizing work of harnessing baser human drives to the approximation of social perfection by commensurating and coordinating dispersed productive activities (e.g., Fourcade and Healy 2007). From an anthropological perspective, markets are embedded social institutions, and through them any and all acts of commensuration are deeply social processes (Espeland and Stevens 1998; Granovetter 1985; Polanyi 1957). In the redemptive BoP myth, the market marks two phases of the conversion at stake. Entrepreneurs are most fully expressed through their articulation with the market. This is a realization of an elemental core entrepreneurial spirit. Moreover, this connection with the market is generative of further transformation as the moral sway of market demand reshapes the local efforts of the entrepreneur.

II. The Social Application

An MBA class preparing for a 2007 STSA trip to India has invited an outside speaker, Karen, to discuss social entrepreneurship. Karen is an MBA who has started her own management consulting firm specializing in microfinance. She begins by defining social entrepreneurship as "using a business vehicle to execute a social mission." Social entrepreneurship is aimed at solving a problem and she specifies that the problem being addressed is a result of "social market failure." By this she means "government is not getting something done."

Into the breach step strategically focused social entrepreneurs, introducing business activities that also restructure and repair the social as a market. Karen was careful to point out that this was not the same as business practices that might have socially beneficial impacts, such as creating jobs, as a by-product. Social entrepreneurship involves business activities built around a strategic focus on an identified social problem. This point proved contentious in the classroom as MBA students repeatedly pressed their case that capitalism was an engine of social good. Karen did not disagree, but she insisted that social entrepreneurship involved business practices aimed not primarily at developing an identified business opportunity but at reengineering the social fabric using business as a driver of change. "What is the problem you are trying to solve?" she challenged the MBAs.

The professor intervened to connect the conversation to the familiar trope of a value chain, suggesting that social entrepreneurship involves "looking for opportunities to create social value throughout the value chain." He asked Karen for examples. She describes a problem in "the dairy sector," where powerful middlemen perpetuate the marginalization of local producers, creating barriers between them and the market. "What we do in social entrepreneurship," Karen explained, "is target places in the value chain that need to be developed" in order to "identify gaps" and "create competitive markets."

Karen's example is structurally close to the situation described by Anju, although it is inverted in revealing ways. Anju narrates an organic scaling up from the elemental basics of agricultural production, through the small producer's achievement of surplus to sell, to the crucial articulation with the market. Karen moves from the outside in, effectively decomposing Indian society by isolating a "sector" of the economy, and further isolating specific links in that value chain. Like Anju, Karen is telling a story promising the transformation of the local entrepreneurial subject through the engineering of the social as a market.

The outcome of such an analysis—marketness—is given in the first move. By identifying an industry "sector," by approaching the "small producers" as such, Karen has broken down the problem into parts that can only be recombined in the production of new forms of scalar articulation. As global adepts, MBAs are schooled to be experts in a strategic framing of international business contexts that is inseparable from the generation of scalar potential. In contexts like the Indian ones under discussion here, the decomposing analysis of social entrepreneurs turns symptoms of third-worldness ("a social market failure") into business potential. Reengineering the social redeems weaknesses in the value chain. Karen described a "boot camp" she runs for local entrepreneurs, training them "to scale their projects" or to "box up" their innovations so they can be replicated by others.

But Karen's framing also provokes the transformation of the global MBA subject, challenged to recast a business opportunity as an engine to redeem a social problem. Karen talked about the rising tide of financial support from corporate leaders for her work and similar initiatives. Part of this name-dropping was in line with other strategies we have seen of indexically establishing business authority in MBA classrooms. Yet, Karen was telling a different story—one that invited the MBAs into a different sort of connection.

> The project I'm working on now is with three independent investors. Two made their money in Silicon Valley, one came from Goldman Sachs . . . and [they] believe in the power of social entrepreneurship in the social application

as well. [Unlike classic development work funded through bilateral government relations,] more and more we are seeing in this field that the funders are living, they are people that have made a lot of money, and they are seeing philanthropy as kind of a second career. And what resonates with them is using business practices, using entrepreneurship.

Karen was tracing a new arc of success, where accomplishments in business were the condition of possibility for a fuller extension of entrepreneurial talent through "the social application." She was presenting these budding MBA managers a glimpse of their aspirational futures.

The MBAs had futures on their minds as well. They asked Karen where she would place India relative to the United States in terms of "social enterprise consciousness." "Would you say it's like ten years behind the US, on par with the US ...?" "I think they're ahead in some ways and in some ways they're behind," replied Karen. She noted that India has a more developed legal infrastructure for social enterprise, and she suggested that the proximity and visibility of India's "social problems" (she described views of poverty and hardscrabble toil from elite hotel rooms), and the rapid pace of change, made it a place more conducive to putting the ideals of social enterprise into practice. At the same time, she suggested that India was ten years behind in the development of its entrepreneurial sector. She gushed about the "state of the art" amenities of an elite Indian business school campus (where the US MBAs would be visiting as part of their upcoming trip, and which would soon be hosting the regional finals of the Global Social Venture Competition), and she praised the "incredibly high caliber professors and students" there. But she complained that rather than applying their talents to the work of social enterprise, "these guys are all going back to family businesses that have grown to be large biotech or IT businesses."

Just prior to this turn in the discussion, Karen had been describing the broader Indian socioeconomic context to the MBAs. "What is interesting about India now is it's incredibly dynamic, very much in transition. A lot of new wealth, a new middle class, a lot of really talented human input. Educated people." She said there was a growing consciousness about social entrepreneurship, and she described a range of projects and discussed plans to begin an Indian MBA concentration in social enterprise. "India is ripe!" she exclaimed.

The lag in development of Indian leaders in social entrepreneurship created an opportunity for the US MBAs to do the picking. In this light, the "second careers" of CEOs who had made their money in the past few decades is not a hobby for the early retirement of Masters of the Universe; it is a leading edge of global capitalist engagement, presented as a model for the aspiring MBAs.

NEW ECONOMIES ARISING

How to Grow Again was the title of a 2011 issue of the *McKinsey Quarterly*, a publication of the famed management-consulting firm, McKinsey & Company. Founded in the 1920s, McKinsey's story matches that of the MBA: deeply networked into the emerging twentieth-century myth of insightful creative managerial talent, explicitly focused on recruiting young MBAs from top programs as the MBA brand ascended in the 1950s and 1960s, representative of the elite Masters of the Universe swagger of the go-go 1980s, diligently expanding its "global footprint" with the establishment of the McKinsey Global Institute in the 1990s, and positioning itself as a leader in social entrepreneurship through a variety of social sector initiatives since the 2000s.

I subscribed to the *Quarterly* as a "premium member" soon after I started this project in 2006. The premium membership, I was told, would provide me "exclusive access to business strategies from McKinsey & Company." It also gave me access to the publication's online archive. By keeping abreast of the *Quarterly* along with a couple of other leading industry publications, I sought to supplement my immersion in the business culture of MBA programs and check the alignment of MBA discourses with the expertise McKinsey was offering to executives. When the "exclusive" content of the *Quarterly* became free in 2010, I was glad to be relieved of the subscription cost, and interested to see McKinsey change their model. In an environment of low-cost digital publishing, with no shortage of business advice online, widely circulating their content helped reinforce the authoritative McKinsey brand. Printed copies of the *Quarterly* continued to arrive through 2011. The *How to Grow Again* issue was among the last; it caught my eye as it seemed to signal a shift from the recovery, rebalancing, and rethinking that marked so much of the literature during the depths of the financial crisis. Also, the cover.

The cover art (by Daniel Bejar) for the *How to Grow Again* issue features a tree cut off at the trunk and at one of its branches, with a handful of tentative green leaves sprouting from a spindly lower branch. The image, of course, conveys the trauma of the financial crisis, and the title struck me for its parallels with self-help headlines of "how to love again" in the face of fear and uncertainty after the tragedies of heartbreak or loss. The McKinsey editors get right to the point: "The global economy is growing again, but it sure doesn't feel like a normal recovery." Growth is slow, risks connected to sovereign debt are concerning, and projections for the coming decade vary widely. "In a world where future prospects are so uncertain," McKinsey is offering nervous senior executives advice.

The postcrisis environment, they counsel, sets new conditions for, and new patterns of, growth. A McKinsey survey of leading firms reveals three insights. First, the most successful companies have a multipronged strategy emphasizing growth along more than one dimension.[2] Second, companies from emerging economies are growing more quickly. Third, smaller companies (with revenue <$1 billion) are growing through increases in market share to a greater extent than larger companies. There is no single takeaway from all of this, but the authors emphasize the importance of a flexible multidimensional business strategy, they encourage larger, more established firms to try to think like their younger smaller competitors, and they gesture to emerging markets as a continuing source of opportunity, business innovation, and market dynamism. I take McKinsey's postcrisis advice as an opportunity to pull forward three points that speak to core themes in contemporary MBA training.

The first of these has to do with the representation of emerging markets as new horizons of opportunity. The McKinsey commentary from 2011 casts emerging markets as partially sheltered from the financial crisis, or at least as spaces of enduring value potential. And they do this by shifting the frontiers. As the pull quote from one of the articles puts it: "Over the next 15 years, 400 cities that most executives have never heard of will power global growth. Are you ready?" (Dobbs, Remes, and Smit 2011). The story here is twofold. On the one hand is a narrative we have seen evidence of already regarding the iterative embracing of clusters of emerging markets (e.g., BRICS, CIVETS, MINTs). The business literature has been periodically filled with the promise of these virtual regions as the next frontiers of global capitalism, sometimes pairing clear-eyed warnings of the failure of one with expressions of faith in the next. For a recent example, consider a 2016 publication from the Wharton School, titled "Have the BRICS Hit a Wall? The Next Emerging Markets."[3] The text details the disappointing performances of Brazil, Russia, and China over the past few years. India receives more nuanced treatment as a BRICS country "worth holding on to." But a Wharton faculty member "cautions that India has 'a long list of things' it needs to accomplish, including reforms, opening up its economy and investing in infrastructure." Without missing a beat, the next paragraph continues,

> Meanwhile, one can hear the rumblings of new economies arising. For example, in September American cereal giant Kellogg announced a $450 million joint venture with Tolaram Africa Foods to create breakfast foods and snacks for the West African market. Johan Burger, director of the NTU-SBF Centre for African Studies at Singapore's Nanyang Business School, calls the deal "a very clear indication that there are companies that have come to realize . . . Africa presents a lot more than meets the eye."[4]

The essays in the 2011 *McKinsey Quarterly* make an additional point, gesturing not beyond the BRICS, but deeper within them. "Is your emerging-market strategy local enough?" asks one of the essays (Atsmon, Kertesz, and Vittal 2011), and a couple of the pieces point to mid-size cities and subnational regional clusters as "growth opportunities" to be realized if executives abandon their "one-size-fits-all approach." "There is no such thing as an effective country-wide strategy," cautions one of the executives featured in the volume. We have come a long way from Levitt's globalization of markets!

Such ceaseless production of horizons of difference is a steady task of international MBA training. In addition to participating in the professional boundary-making that defines and authorizes the fields of business, international business curricula in MBA programs produce boundary lines demarcating spaces of difference and incommensurable excess that realize their value through MBAs' abilities to transit and connect them (cf. Preda 2009). They join in a continuous enchantment of the local as an ever-receding horizon of possibility requiring globally adept managers.

Adept management requires forging articulation across scales. This introduces my second point. The McKinsey article urges executives to focus on the "granularity" of growth.[5] "Granularity" suggests the subdivision of data from coarse to fine categories; the trope is itself a powerful illustration of the technique of moving across scales in a way that conditions scalar articulation. A related McKinsey discussion calls for executives to "'de-average' their views of markets" to examine the component segments of bottom-line performance data (Baghai, Smit, and Viguerie 2007). In this regard, the call for granularity is another voicing of the techniques of decomposition that saturate MBA training. As we have seen, the disassembling of the parts enacts a theory about the composition of the whole. And the manager able to take a granular approach is already committed to the recombination of the whole.

As the correlated managerial jargon of "drilling down" or making a "deep dive" into the data discloses, this is a scale-making commitment. "Diving" for granularity may be a mixed metaphor, but the connection of part/whole relations with the agentive transiting of surface and deep/hidden levels brings the point home. Indeed, layered on to their advice about emerging markets, local frontiers are the sites of granularity, to be connected to global business strategy through managerial action. The promise of granular analysis is that the new knowledge, the newly confronted difference, can be scaled back up to connect with broader global flows (cf. Rockefeller 2011).

Granular, scale-making action requires creativity, insight, and talent. This is my third point. The McKinsey study underscores the need now, more than ever, for strategically talented leadership. "It takes a mix of leaders and talent to pursue a variety of growth strategies simultaneously. Few executives can do it all" (Herrmann, Komm, and Smit 2011). MBA programs have positioned themselves as incubators of talent calibrated specifically to a host of global challenges. "Talent" is semantically empty—evoking a quality rather than a substance. It implies an incommensurable excess that goes beyond technical skill, as in the common assertion that business management involves a mix of science and art. It is, then, of a qualitative kind with the spaces of difference that managerial talent is marshaled to access and transact. In this regard, we can see the reciprocal constitution of global business space and global business talent as both are articulated (in all senses of the word) in MBA education.

Gordon's Warning: Managing the Bottom of the Pyramid

In late 2007, Gordon was frightening his Global Marketing class. He had set aside Porter's diamond for PowerPoint slides showing Gini[6] indices and graphs of inequality around the world. Part of his story was familiar from STSA courses and the BoP literature: there are a vast number of potential consumers around the world and they present an emerging business opportunity. But Gordon also talked about the political economy of contemporary multinational firms as compressed product life cycles, increasing costs of research and development, and other factors created pressure for companies to get into overseas markets quickly. This was the work his students would be doing, and Gordon's warning was that they would find themselves in a situation of heightening contradictions driven by frictions between local and global processes.

According to Gordon, global business had created a "winner takes all society," resulting in concentrations of wealth among the elite and expanding markets for highly skilled workers, and stagnation or declines among the poorest and least skilled. Globalization, in other words, entailed "high social and economic costs" and exacerbated social differences, leaving some more able to respond to new opportunities than others. Gordon allowed that the movement of factory work to places like China or India created new economic opportunities for unskilled poor. But those benefits were dwarfed by the accumulation of wealth at the top end, and, Gordon warned, "problems arise when they start to see visual differences." He sketched similar challenges in the United States where the loss of manufacturing jobs combined with reductions in the social safety net around pensions or healthcare was creating growing resentment around inequalities.

Gordon was committed to globalization and its benefits, but was challenging his students to see that globalization to date had created new stresses that would need to be dealt with by the global managers of the future. He described the impact of globalization on China by invoking industrialized, commercial, Westernized cities along the coasts and a relatively unchanged interior. I had heard similar characterizations in other business schools, particularly among MBAs returning from study trips to China, where part of the takeaway was a sense of an unexplored hinterland yet to be tapped. Four years later, this was an integral part of the postcrisis promised land heralded by McKinsey.

Although I did not encounter many other structural critiques of global inequality in the MBA classes I visited, Gordon's warning shared in a more general unease that suffused the halls of capitalist reproduction in MBA programs, particularly in regard to global business. This was a sense of a world always on the cusp of its undoing. Managing global capitalism requires working between two sorts of destruction. The first is the specter of truly unmanageable difference—a potential always lurking in radical otherness and the extremes of immiserating inequality. On the other side is the excess of global integration leading to the monstrous flatness that would erase the value-generating potential of manageable (granular) difference. MBA programs are engaged in the world-sustaining task of producing difference and the talent to manage it.

SCALING THE MBA

With the advantage of hindsight, that meeting of Gordon's class was one of the two most prescient moments that I recorded during my time among the MBAs. The other was a reference in one of the first MBA economics classes I observed in 2006 to Robert Shiller's identification of a housing bubble under way since the late 1990s. The immediate aim was to introduce the concept of the market as a self-correcting price-setting mechanism. Class discussion tempered some of Shiller's claims, addressing the difficulties comparing housing prices across the 1960s and the present, given that cultural norms about house size and layout had changed dramatically over that time, and reviewing some current articles describing slowdowns in certain sectors of the housing market connected to new single-family and luxury home construction. We also took the conversation as an exercise in reading the four quadrant graphs that appear in the *New York Times* to chart the performance of a given economic sector over a given time frame, relative to a given benchmark. With one or two exceptions, all of the examples reported for the housing sector in fall 2006 were doing better over that past week than the Standard and Poor's 500.

The financial crash shifted the contours of MBA education, depressing domestic demand somewhat, intensifying the development of MBA specializations outside of the field of finance (like social entrepreneurship), and prompting discussions of ways of further compressing MBA training, including the predictable forays into online and "blended" education. The preparation of global managers remains a core part of MBA strategy through the curricular practices I have discussed above. And the recovery from the recession has spurred new international managerial imperatives, as low interest rates in the United States have encouraged continued and increasing investments in emerging markets, and downturns in familiar "emerging markets" have kept international MBAs exploring new frontiers and fishing holes. The current moment of "slowbalisation" announced by the *Economist* in January 2019, and underscored by other characterizations of "globalization in transition," seems designed for the artful agile entrepreneurial managers envisioned by contemporary MBA programs.[7]

This has surely exacerbated the heightened inequality Gordon was calling to our attention in 2007, and connecting those dots converges with other trends leading to the protectionist and antiglobalist positions connected (unevenly, and with outcomes as yet unclear) with the political developments related to the Brexit vote and the election of Donald Trump. Gordon was clear that the social costs of globalization impacted Europe and the United States as well as developing economies. That impact has been widely cited as an underlying cause of Trump's support among his base: working-class whites, who have been unable to respond to what Gordon cast as the unequally available opportunities of globalization.

Though it may dismay putative "antiglobalists," the assertion of national boundaries and other particularizing tendencies can be seen as continuous within the longer arc of neoliberal globalization discussed here, in which a leading edge has become the reenchantment of the local. Business faculty I spoke with since the 2016 US elections anticipated little change to their core messages about global or international business, locating the current moment as a pendulum swing entirely within the frame of globalization. Indeed, in January 2017, one was already using news items regarding proposed protectionist policies in a core global economy module for MBAs.

This book tells the story of the refiguring of the world of global capitalism through the MBA curriculum. It remains a story of globally expansive capital, but one premised on a world crosshatched with challenging differences, in which value is produced by converting the risks of difference into a manageable future. Within this ever more minutely mapped terrain of global distinctions, MBA programs are engaged in the coproduction of an up-to-date vision of the world and the managerial qualities adequate to its challenges. This is scaling work: engaging salient specificities and harnessing risk to the end of marketness. The work constructs the MBAs as partial adepts of the margins being generated, and enlists them in a relational imperative to engineer the scalar connections of global capitalism. These aspiring masters of the world embody the latest iteration of the resilient figure of the MBA, reflecting the world they have a hand in making, prospecting for risks they require, and managing the margins in coordination with a recalibration of themselves.

NOTES

CHAPTER 1. WALL STREET GOES TO THE ENDS OF THE EARTH

1. For some insightful work on this process of financialization, see Knorr Cetina and Preda 2005; LiPuma and Lee 2004; Miyazaki 2013; Preda 2009; Riles 2010; and Thrift 2005. For neoliberalism, see Harvey 2005; Hayek (1944) 2007; and Mirowski and Plehwe 2009. For a discussion of how certain habits of finance thinking push business practices toward international settings, see chapters 4 and 5.

2. This was part of the narrative at the apparent end of the Cold War.

3. As a Latin Americanist, I chafe at the designation "American" to refer to the United States, recognizing that this is but part of the Americas. I use quotes to mark this as a native term, and also note here that the ascendance of US business is one of the conditions that enables the appropriation of the hemispheric label.

4. According to the National Center for Education Statistics, tables 323.10 and 324.10.

5. Ricardo restates, at the level of the country, Smith's point that by pursuing their own interests, individuals advance the interests of society, "Under a system of perfectly free commerce, each country naturally devotes its capital and labour to such employments as are most beneficial to each. This pursuit of individual advantage is admirably connected with the universal good of the whole" (Ricardo 1817, 7.11).

6. And while neoliberal political conventions promote skepticism about "society"—particularly as a collective object of interest for classical liberal social policies—they have been entirely congenial to more fragmented modes of belonging through official multiculturalism and ideas of civil society composed of smaller scale interest groups (e.g., Hale 2006; Orta 2013).

7. This is noted with alarm by some IB scholars, such as Buckley, who see it "under threat," particularly in the United States, where the trend toward infusion has dulled the edge of any disciplinary mission to the field (2005, 6).

8. http://mba.haas.berkeley.edu/academics/culture.html (accessed March 20, 2015).

9. A national network of federally funded CIBERs (Centers for International Business Education and Research) was an important resource in this broader immersion in international business education.

10. In addition to Datar, Garvin, and Cullen 2010, see, for instance, Aspen Institute 2008; Damast 2008; Mintzberg and Danos 2011; Petriglieri 2012.

11. That said, Trump-era policies of travel bans and other restrictions on foreign visitors to the United States have created tensions for US MBA programs, which have relied for more than a generation on robust cohorts of international MBA applicants. MBA faculty I spoke with are concerned that fewer international applicants will seek graduate business education in the United States, electing to attend programs elsewhere in the world. And some report that international MBAs currently in the United States are uncomfortable participating in the sorts of international MBA study abroad trips discussed in chapter 5 because of concerns over problems with leaving and reentering the United States.

12. And they are likely to make those arguments in the *Journal of International Business Studies* or at the meetings of the Academy of International Business.

CHAPTER 2. FAST SUBJECTS: THE RITUALS
OF MBA TRAINING

1. For discussions of the construction and mobilization of authoritative expertise in business practices, see also Clark and Thrift 2005; Lezaun and Muniesa 2017; Preda 2002; Riles 2010; Santiso 2003, esp. ch. 5.

2. https://www.tuck.dartmouth.edu/mba/blog/what-does-24-7-learning-mean (accessed October 19, 2016).

3. Some programs include these invited talks and professionalizing events as formal credit-bearing parts of the curriculum.

4. See Navarro 2008 for a critical inventory of the core curriculum of the top fifty US MBA programs.

5. Many instructors' versions of business cases are available with teaching notes—outlines of key themes, recommendations for how to structure the class time, sample analyses of the business problem—prepared by the original authors of the case or by selected industry leaders.

6. Porter's diamond adapts to the analysis of a national business environment, another strategy shorthand he had made famous a decade earlier. Porter's "five forces" (bargaining power of suppliers, bargaining power of buyers, interfirm rivalry, threat of new entrants, threat of substitute products) offered a framework for assessing a firm's position and optimal strategy within its industry (Porter 1979; cf. McDonald 2017, 413ff.).

7. The "planner" is also the villainous alternative in Hayek's case for the liberating promise of the free market ([1944] 2007).

8. For a different use of the term, see Block 1990.

9. Man/Woman or Actor/Actress are examples, and it is not coincidental that gender hierarchies provide many examples of this whole/part relationship.

10. In chapter 3, we will see the development of the MBA anchored in a recognition of the firm as a bundle of social relations requiring management. This reframing as a bundle of cash flows offers a stark illustration of the changing managerial imperatives under neoliberalism.

11. My comments on marginal analysis and value-chain analysis are informed by the courses I observed as well as Albaum, Duerr, and Strandskov 2005; Bartlett, Ghoshal, and Birkinshaw 2003; Landsburg 2005; and Wild, Wild, and Han 2006.

12. The naturalness of these concepts is further evoked by the use of the symbol π to represent "profit": as if the calculation of "profit," itself contingent on the selection of a range of motivated counting criteria, were as inherent in the world as the geometric ratio of π.

13. This five-to-ten-year time horizon was one I heard frequently, in reference both to the career aspirations of MBA students as well as actionable projections of the future in analysis of emerging economies or trending market sectors.

14. It seems an apt reflection of the late capitalist, you-are-your-own-brand moment, that managers, once framed as making whole workers damaged by corporate industrialization, are now focused on cultivating and actualizing themselves (cf. Gershon 2017).

15. Arbitrage involves taking advantage of simultaneous differences in pricing for a given asset or item in different markets. The inefficiency of markets (which should reflect a single value) and the correlated risks for market actors are the conditions of possibility for arbitrage, which requires the opportunistic exploitation of the inefficiency by a savvy investor identifying a less risky course of action.

CHAPTER 3. ACCOUNTING FOR BUSINESS

1. For histories of the development of business education, see Benson 2004; Cruikshank 1987; Daniel 1998; Graham 1933; McDonald 2017.

2. Columbia, Cornell, Dartmouth, Harvard, NYU, Northwestern, Ohio State, Tulane, University of California, Berkeley, University of Chicago, University of Illinois, University of Nebraska, University of Pennsylvania, University of Texas, University of Wisconsin–Madison, and Yale.

3. Admissions Test for Graduate Study in Business.

4. Graduate Management Admission Test.

5. Barnes, Christensen, and Hansen describe the early curriculum as a "potpourri" of courses, many borrowed from other departments of the university: "There were three required courses; Principles of Accounting, Commercial Contracts, and Economic Resources. Other offerings were German, French, Commercial Correspondence, Fire Insurance, Economic Resources of Eastern Asia, and Railroad Operations" (1994, 40).

6. Regarding professional societies, the Society for the Advancement of Management (1912), American Marketing Association (1915), American Accounting Association (1916), Administrative Management Society (1919), American Management Association (1923) (Daniel 1998, 73).

7. Early courses at Harvard had used cases in commercial law borrowed from the law school, and developed the practice of inviting businessmen to serve as "walking cases" for the classes (Cruikshank 1987; McNair 1954).

8. Historian Nils Gilman (2006, 112) writes, "In Drucker's view, the problem with both liberalism and socialism was that they defined men's social status in terms of their 'mechanical' (economic) function, rather than any higher spiritual values."

9. http://www.druckerinstitute.com/peter-druckers-life-and-legacy/druckers-career-timeline-and-bibliography/ (accessed October 15, 2016).

10. This review of Drucker's personal and intellectual biography draws from the work of Gabor 2000; Gilman 2006; Hoopes 2003; and Immerwahr 2009.

11. "Foundational" fields were defined as "economics, accounting, statistics, business law, finance, marketing, and production or industrial management" (Daniel 1998, 151).

12. The joke also references contemporary debates about the role of the Federal Reserve in determining monetary policy after years of artificially low interest rates during World War II.

13. The experiences of university faculty teaching returning GIs in the postwar years seems to have sharpened this sense of the immaturity and dearth of life experience of typical college undergraduates.

14. The proceedings of the conference, focused on doctoral training in US business schools, are known as the "Arden House Report."

15. The implications of this recommendation have been significant as it consolidates an anti-intellectual worldview, alienates research faculty from the MBAs they teach, and silos professional training from the cutting edges of research in business practice and history.

16. Consider, for instance, Six Sigma: a statistically driven quality control process developed by Motorola in the mid-1980s. It prescribes a set of manager-led steps for process improvement with a goal of fewer than 3.4 defects per million. See discussions of Deming and Juran, below.

17. That the reports were received as a scathing rebuke of business education must not have helped (Daniel 1998).

18. "The American Universities Field Service," http://calteches.library.caltech.edu/133/1/Field.pdf (accessed September 29, 2011).

19. These figures are taken from the 2018 award cycle and reflect a decline from previous funding cycles in total funding and in the number of centers supported. In 2014, the same total funding allocation ($4.57 million) supported seventeen CIBER centers; in 2010 an allocation of $12.75 million funded thirty-three centers nationally.

1. My own view is that the anthropological concept of culture remains a useful analytic tool for making sense of a human capacity to experience the world as meaningful in ways that are shared with others, and the record of anthropological study documenting the variation of human cultural forms across space and time is an (imperfect) archive worth continued development. See Orta (2004b) for an earlier position of mine on the utility of reclaiming classic and even outdated work in anthropology as resources for theorizing an anthropology of the contemporary global moment.

2. See Trouillot (2001) and Rockefeller (2011) for two efforts to critically identify and check this trend.

3. Margaret Mead and Ruth Benedict may be the best known of this group, which also included Cora Du Bois, Edward T. Hall, Clyde Kluckhohn, and Alfred Kroeber.

4. Hall described Boas, Benedict, Mead, Sapir, and Kardiner as his influences of the time and also pointed to his work experiences in the 1930s on Navajo and Hopi reservations in the Southwest and his experiences leading an African American regiment during the World War II as contributing to his concern with the challenges of intercultural communication (E. Hall 1992; see Pusch 2004; and Rogers, Hart, and Miike 2002 for additional biographical details).

5. Hall moved to positions at the Illinois Institute of Technology (1963–67) and at Northwestern University (1967–77), where he held appointments in Anthropology and at the College of Business.

6. The qualifier "good-enough" is used in medical anthropology, inspired by Scheper-Hughes's (1992) discussions of a "good-enough ethnography." These uses often underscore an engaged activist imperative to do the ethnographic work, avoid the tentative half steps of excessive critical reflexivity or disciplinary formalism, and embrace the power of ethnography as a positive contribution to humanistic ends (cf. Eaton 2011).

7. This also seems to have been a time of rich interdisciplinary collaboration. John Fayerweather, a founding figure in the field, notes that many of his collaborators in the 1950s were not in business schools (1994, 7).

8. The Academy's journal, *The Journal of International Business Studies*, began publication in 1969.

9. Mexico, Central Africa, India, Turkey, France.

10. A section in the 1960s textbook, *Management of International Operations*, for instance, underscores the importance of local language learning (Fayerweather 1960, 17).

11. Kluckhohn's work is also cited appreciatively by other business management theorists of culture, such as Geert Hofstede. See below, page 118.

12. The mid-century sense of a "small world" would soon be formally debuted and branded through the Disney-designed Small World attraction at the 1964 World's Fair.

13. The one item they report universal consensus on among the managers surveyed is their disagreement with the proposition that "anyone can be a manager."

14. It bears pointing out that their research sample was derived largely from international management training courses, indicating that the respondents were already participants in a circulating rhetoric of international business and framings of country-level difference.

15. In his 1997 biographical essay, he cites the experience of taking his family to three different countries as shaping his eventual insights into country-level cultural differences.

16. Hofstede cites this and related dimensions (e.g., "short-term orientation") as characteristic of US business leaders and as a cause of the 2008 financial crisis that could have been predicted from his earlier studies (Hofstede, Hofstede, and Minkov 2010, 326).

17. As McSweeney notes, Hofstede initially controlled for "organizational culture" by arguing that it was homogeneous across IBM internationally. Later, in the face of the growing vogue in organizational culture-talk within management studies, he framed organizational culture as separate from his object of study because it was a different order of phenomenon and, in any event, more transitory than the supposedly more determining national cultural characteristics he has analyzed (Hofstede, Hofstede, and Minkov 2010, 346; McSweeney 2002, 96f.).

18. For an example of an especially prolific critic from within the field of cross-cultural management, see McSweeney 2002.

19. Although the United States was not included in the initial "international" survey, Hofstede negotiated with IBM to have the questionnaires administered to a sample of US employees (Hofstede 1984, 42).

CHAPTER 5. MANAGING THE MARGINS

1. CliffsNotes are student study guides presenting literature or other works in a condensed booklet format.

2. Other issues she raised included the role of family structure and the organization of the firm, as family groups in some countries often constitute somewhat self-contained lending institutions.

3. This is not to argue that some places stand outside of globalization, which might be better approached as a skein of asymmetrically entangled local vantages in which translocal contexts are undeniable and irreversible (Orta 2004a; Tsing 2005; Wilk 1995). Nor am I suggesting that some firms fail a test of "real globalization." I am interested, rather, in the ways the idea of global business, and the qualities of international business spaces, are conjured through the staging of "international" content in MBA curricula.

4. Initially intended to pluralize the acronym, the "S" in BRICS became "South Africa" in 2010.

5. Purchasing power parity assesses the relative value of different currencies by comparing the cost of a hypothetical basket of goods in each country. It is an alternative to comparing economies through a third commensurating value such as US dollars (as would be the case in GDP rankings).

6. The alternative sorting in international business fields is to be lumped with all generic "others" in the "ROW" column—Rest of the World.

7. Some obsolescence is built into the designation as "emerging" economies; the financial crisis of 2008 has changed things as well.

8. Bangladesh, Egypt, Indonesia, Iran, Korea, Mexico, Nigeria, Pakistan, Philippines, Turkey, and Vietnam.

9. Colombia, Indonesia, Vietnam, Egypt, Turkey, and South Africa.

10. Respectively, Mexico, Indonesia, Nigeria, and Turkey, and Mexico, Indonesia, South Korea, and Turkey.

11. The acronyms also take on geopolitical flesh in the form of the annual BRICS summit, which, since 2009 has brought Brazil, Russia, India, China, and South Africa (since 2011) together.

12. As noted above, reviews of MBA curricula in the wake of the financial crisis have stressed the importance of experiential learning opportunities like the STSA courses. Some programs now make such courses a required component of MBA training.

13. One of the recommendations following the 2008 financial crisis is for MBA curricula to do just this (Datar, Garvin, and Cullen 2010).

14. These characterizations are, necessarily ephemeral—and that contributes to the attraction of the cycle of BRICS, MINTs, CIVETS, and other targets of STSA programming as a series of dynamic, precarious, and relatively manageable spaces of global capitalism.

CHAPTER 6. PARTIAL ANSWERS: THE USES OF
ETHNOGRAPHIC CAPITALIST REALISM

1. For a discussion of the case "genre" in legal training, see Mertz (2007); as part of his history of the Harvard Business School, McDonald (2017) underscores the ways case teaching standardizes uncritical understandings of what doing business means.

2. In an early description of the aims of ethnography, Bronislaw Malinowski challenged anthropologists to "grasp the native's point of view, his relation to life, to realize his vision of his world. We have to study man, and we must study what concerns him most intimately, that is, the hold life has on him" (1922, 25; see also Allen 1988).

3. Here, I depart slightly from other uses of the term to discuss the extension of ethnography in collaborations between anthropologists and professional neighbors (e.g., Holmes and Marcus 2008).

4. There is surely a less Harvard-centric version of the story to be told, and it bears noting that many business schools across the United States and worldwide have their own case study publication program.

5. Thus, an oft-cited essay in the 1954 volume "Wisdom Can't Be Told" by Charles I. Gragg, is introduced with a note reporting that Gragg was a student in Professor Arthur Stone Dewing's class. Dewing himself contributed an influential essay to the 1931 Fraser volume, which was reprinted in the 1954 volume edited by McNair. Dewing, Gragg, and others from the 1931 and 1954 volumes are cited in the 1987 volume, which also includes another essay of Gragg's, "Teachers Also Must Learn."

6. https://www.hbs.edu/mba/academic-experience/Pages/the-hbs-case-method.aspx (accessed January 22, 2017).

7. Note the parallel with the "Toyota way" that stood for Japanese distinctiveness and competitive economic success since the 1980s. The CEMEX way is similarly part of a broader branding effort of the Mexican business context.

8. "Don't give me words, give me data from the case!" yelled Charles when they were going over CEMEX's financials.

CHAPTER 7. FRONTIERS OF CAPITALISM

1. We've heard a version of this paean to the productive family in emerging markets in the context of the STSA program to Mexico.

2. They list portfolio growth, increases in market share, and mergers and acquisitions, and note that the strongest companies were focusing on at least two of the three.

3. http://knowledge.wharton.upenn.edu/article/98411/.

4. The authors of a 2018 book by the McKinsey Global Institute and published by Harvard Business Review Press would agree. *Africa's Business Revolution: How to Succeed in the World's Next Big Growth Market* presents Africa as poorly understood, but offering "exciting opportunities to build large, profitable businesses" for those "looking to access new growth markets" (Leke, Chironga, and Desvaux 2018).

5. The 2011 essay builds off a 2007 publication of the same name, and nicely embodies the ways the business cognoscenti (MBA programs included) took on the financial crisis as a serious challenge, but one to which they already had many of the answers.

6. The Gini index is a statistical representation of income inequality within a given population, used to compare degrees of inequality across nations.

7. At around the time of the *Economist* headline, the McKinsey Global Institute released a report titled "Globalization in Transition: The Future of Trade and Value Chains" aimed at helping policy makers and business leaders prepare to engage with the opportunities and challenges of "globalization's next chapter" (Lund et al. 2019).

REFERENCES

AACSB International Globalization of Management Education Task Force. 2011. *Globalization of Management Education: Changing International Structures, Adaptive Strategies, and the Impact on Institutions.* Bingley, UK: Emerald Group Publishing.

Abdelal, Rawi E. 2006. "Journey to Sakhalin: Royal Dutch/Shell in Russia (A)." HBS No. 704-040. Boston: Harvard Business School Publishing.

Abend, Gabriel. 2014. *The Moral Background: An Inquiry into the History of Business Ethics.* Princeton, NJ: Princeton University Press.

Albaum, Gerald, Edwin Duerr, and Jesper Strandskov. 2005. *International Marketing and Export Management.* 5th ed. New York: Prentice-Hall.

Allen, Catherine J. 1988. *The Hold Life Has: Coca and Cultural Identity in an Andean Community.* Washington, DC: Smithsonian Books.

Appadurai, Arjun. 1996. *Modernity at Large: Cultural Dimensions of Globalization.* Minneapolis: University of Minnesota Press.

Appiah, Kwame Anthony. 2007. The Ethics of Identity. Princeton, NJ: Princeton University Press.

Applbaum, Kalman. 2003. *The Marketing Era: From Professional Practice to Global Provisioning.* New York: Routledge.

Aspen Institute. 2008. "A Closer Look at Business Education: Finance Faculty Reflect on the Financial Crisis." Washington, DC: The Aspen Institute Center for Business Education.

Atsmon, Yuval, Ari Kertesz, and Ireena Vittal. 2011. "Is Your Emerging-Market Strategy Local Enough?" *McKinsey Quarterly* 2011 (2): 50–61.

Baghai, Mehrdad, Sven Smit, and S. Patrick Viguerie. 2007. "The Granularity of Growth." *McKinsey Quarterly* 2007 (2): 41–51.

Barnes, Louis B., Carl Roland Christensen, and Abby J. Hansen. 1994. *Teaching and the Case Method: Text, Cases, and Readings.* Cambridge, MA: Harvard Business School Press.

Bartlett, Christopher A., and Sumantra Ghoshal. 2000. "Going Global: Lessons from Late Movers." *Harvard Business Review* 78 (2): 132–42.

Bartlett, Christopher A., Sumantra Ghoshal, and Julian Birkinshaw. 2003. *Transnational Management: Text and Cases*. 4th ed. Boston, MA: McGraw-Hill/Irwin.

Benson, P. George. 2004. "The Evolution of Business Education in the U.S." *Decision Line* 35 (1): 17–20.

Berle, Adolf A., and Gardiner C. Means. (1932) 1991. *The Modern Corporation and Private Property*. Reprint, New Brunswick, NJ: Transaction Publishers.

Block, Fred. 1990. *Postindustrial Possibilities*. Berkeley: University of California Press.

Bourdieu, Pierre. 1977. *Outline of the Theory of Practice*. Translated by R. Nice. Cambridge: Cambridge University Press.

Bourdieu, Pierre, and Loic Wacquant. 2001. "Neoliberal Newspeak: Notes on the New Planetary Vulgate." *Radical Philosophy* 105: 1–6.

Boyer, Dominic. 2008. "Thinking through the Anthropology of Experts." *Anthropology in Action* 15 (2): 38–46.

Bright, Charles, and Michael Geyer. 1987. "For a Unified History of the World in the Twentieth Century." *Radical History Review* 1987 (39): 69–91.

Buckley, Peter, ed. 2005. *What Is International Business?* Houndmills, UK: Palgrave Macmillan.

Callon, Michel. 2007. "An Essay on the Growing Contribution of Economic Markets to the Proliferation of the Social." *Theory, Culture & Society* 24 (8): 139–63.

Carroll, Thomas H. 1959. "A Foundation Expresses Its Interest in Higher Education for Business Management." *Academy of Management Journal* 2 (3): 155–65.

Cefkin, Melissa, ed. 2010. *Ethnography and the Corporate Encounter: Reflections on Research in and of Corporations*. New York: Berghahn Books.

Chandler, Alfred. 1977. *The Visible Hand: The Managerial Revolution in American Business*. Cambridge, MA: Harvard University Press.

———. 1984. "The Emergence of Managerial Capitalism." *Business History Review* 58 (4): 473–503.

Christensen, Clayton M., Michael Raynor, and Rory McDonald. 2015. "What Is Disruptive Innovation?" *Harvard Business Review* 93 (12): 44–53.

Clark, Gordon L., and Nigel Thrift. 2005. "The Return of Bureaucracy: Managing Dispersed Knowledge in Global Finance." In *The Sociology of Financial Markets*, edited by Karin Knorr Cetina and Alex Preda, 229–49. Oxford: Oxford University Press.

Copeland, Melvin T. 1954. "The Genesis of the Case Method in Business Instruction." In *The Case Method at the Harvard Business School*, edited by Malcolm P. McNair, 25–33. New York: McGraw-Hill.

Crane, Richard Teller. 1901. *Utility of an Academic or Classical Education for Young Men Who Have to Earn Their Own Living and Who Expect to Pursue a Commercial Life*. Chicago: Inland Press.

Crennan, Charles Holloway. 1923. "Human Nature in Business." In *Psychology in Business*, edited by Charles Holloway Crennan and Forrest Alva Kingsbury. Philadelphia: The American Academy of Political and Social Science.

Cruikshank, Jeffrey L. 1987. *A Delicate Experiment: The Harvard Business School 1908–1945*. Boston: Harvard Business Review Press.

Culliton, James W. 1954. "Writing Business Cases." In *The Case Method at the Harvard Business School*, edited by Malcolm P. McNair, 256–69. New York: McGraw-Hill.

Damast, Alison. 2008. "B-Schools and the Financial Bust." *Business Week* 24: 40–45.

Dane, Erik, and Michael G. Pratt. 2007. "Exploring Intuition and Its Role in Managerial Decision Making." *Academy of Management Review* 32 (1): 33–54.

Daniel, Carter A. 1998. *MBA: The First Century*. Lewisburg, PA: Bucknell University Press.

Daniels, John D. 2003. "Specialization to Infusion: IB Studies in the 1990s." In *Research in Global Strategic Management. Volume 8, Leadership in International Business Education and Research*, edited by Alan M. Rugman, 29–46. Bingley, UK: Emerald Group Publishing.

Datar, Srikant, David A. Garvin, and Patrick Cullen. 2010. *Rethinking the MBA: Business Education at a Crossroads*. Cambridge, MA: Harvard Business School Press.

David, Donald K. 1954. "Foreword." In *The Case Method at the Harvard Business School*, edited by Malcolm P. McNair, vii–x. New York: McGraw-Hill.

Denny, Rita M., and Patricia L. Sunderland, eds. 2015. *Handbook of Anthropology in Business*. New York: Routledge.

Dewing, Arthur Stone. 1954. "An Introduction to the Use of Cases." In *The Case Method at the Harvard Business School*, edited by Malcolm P. McNair, 1–5. New York: McGraw-Hill.

Dirlik, A. 1999. "Globalism and the Politics of Place." In *Globalisation and the Asia-Pacific: Contested Territories*, edited by Kris Olds et al., 39–56. London: Routledge.

Dobbs, Richard, Jaana Remes, and Sven Smit. 2011. "The World's New Growth Frontier: Midsize Cities in Emerging Markets." *McKinsey Quarterly* 2011 (2): 46–49.

Donham, Wallace Brett, and Alfred North Whitehead. 1931. *Business Adrift*. New York: Whittlesey House, McGraw-Hill.

Downey, Greg, and Melissa S. Fisher. 2006. "Introduction." In *Frontiers of Capital: Ethnographic Reflections on the New Economy*, edited by Melissa S. Fisher and Greg Downey, 1–30. Durham, NC: Duke University Press.

Drucker, Peter Ferdinand. 1942. *The Future of Industrial Man: A Conservative Approach*. New York: John Day Company.

———. 1946. *Concept of the Corporation*. New York: John Day Company.

———. 1950. "The Graduate Business School." *Fortune* 42: 92–116.

Dumont, Louis. 1977. *From Mandeville to Marx*. Chicago: University of Chicago Press.

Durham, Elizabeth. 2016. "The 'Good-Enough Anthropologist.'" *Somatosphere: Science, Medicine and Anthropology*, August 26. http://somatosphere.net/2016/08/the-good-enough-anthropologist.html.

Eaton, David. 2011. "Good-Enough Anthropology: Reflections on Becoming a Medical Anthropologist." *Krober Anthropological Society Papers* 100 (1): 87–94.

Economist. 2019. "Slowbalisation: The Steam Has Gone Out of Globalisation." January 24.

Escobar, Arturo. 1995. *Encountering Development: The Making and Unmaking of the Third World.* Princeton, NJ: Princeton University Press.

Espeland, Wendy Nelson, and Mitchell L. Stevens. 1998. "Commensuration as a Social Process." *Annual Review of Sociology* 24: 313–43.

Fassin, Didier. 2001. "Culturalism as Ideology." In *Cultural Perspectives on Reproductive Health,* edited by Carla Obermeyer, 300–317. Oxford: Oxford University Press.

———. 2010. "Noli Me Tangere: The Moral Untouchability of Humanitarianism." In *Forces of Compassion: Humanitarianism between Ethics and Politics,* edited by Erica Bornstein and Peter Redfield, 35–52. Santa Fe, NM: School for Advanced Research Press.

Fayerweather, John. 1954. "The Work of the Case Writer." In *The Case Method at the Harvard Business School,* edited by Malcolm P. McNair, 270–76. New York: McGraw-Hill.

———. 1959. *The Executive Overseas: Administrative Attitudes and Relationships in a Foreign Culture.* Syracuse, NY: Syracuse University Press.

———. 1960. *Management of International Operations: Text and Cases.* New York: McGraw-Hill.

———. 1969. *International Business Management: A Conceptual Framework.* New York: McGraw-Hill.

———. 1994. "A Personal Odyssey through the Early Evolution of International Business Pedagogy, Research and Professional Organization." *Journal of International Business Studies* 25 (1): 1–44.

Foster, Robert John. 2008. *Coca-Globalization: Following Soft Drinks from New York to New Guinea.* New York: Palgrave Macmillan.

Fourcade, Marion, and Kieran Healy. 2007. "Moral Views of Market Society." *Annual Review of Sociology* 33: 285–311.

Fraser, Cecil Eaton. 1931. *The Case Method of Instruction.* New York: McGraw-Hill.

Frederick, William C. 1964. "The Cultural Matrix of Business Education." In *Professional Education for Business,* edited by John J. Clark and Blaise J. Opulente, 1–13. Jamaica, NY: St. John's University Press.

Friedman, Jonathan. 1995. "Global Systems, Globalization, and the Parameters of Modernity." In *Global Modernities,* edited by M. Featherstone, S. Lash, and R. Robertson, 69–90. London: Sage.

Fukuyama, Francis. 1992. *The End of History and the Last Man.* New York: Free Press.

Gabor, Andrea. 1990. *The Man Who Discovered Quality: How W. Edwards Deming Brought the Quality Revolution to America.* New York: Penguin Books.

———. 2000. *The Capitalist Philosophers.* New York: Times Books.

Gershon, Ilana. 2016. "'I'm Not a Businessman, I'm a Business, Man': Typing the Neoliberal Self into a Branded Existence." *Hau: Journal of Ethnographic Theory* 6 (3): 223–46.

———. 2017. *Down and Out in the New Economy: How People Find (or Don't Find) Work Today*. Chicago: University of Chicago Press.

Ghemawat, Pankaj. 2007. *Redefining Global Strategy: Crossing Borders in a World Where Differences Still Matter*. Boston: Harvard Business School Press.

———. 2011. "The Cosmopolitan Corporation." *Harvard Business Review* 89 (5): 92–99.

Gilman, Nils. 2006. "The Prophet of Post-Fordism: Peter Drucker and the Legitimation of the Corporation." In *American Capitalism: Social Thought and Political Economy in the Twentieth Century*, edited by Nelson Lichtenstein, 109–32. Philadelphia: University of Pennsylvania Press.

Gordon, Robert Aaron, and James Edwin Howell. 1959. *Higher Education for Business*. New York: Columbia University Press.

Gragg, Charles I. 1954. "Tough-Mindedness and the Case Method." In *The Case Method at the Harvard Business School*, edited by Malcolm P. McNair, 6–14. New York: McGraw-Hill.

Graham, Jessie. 1933. *The Evolution of Business Education in the United States and Its Implications for Business Teacher Education*. Los Angeles: University of Southern California Press.

Granovetter, Mark. 1985. "Economic Action and Social Structure: The Problem of Embeddedness." *American Journal of Sociology* 91 (3): 481–510.

Grindle, Merilee. 2007. *Going Local: Decentralization, Democratization, and the Promise of Good Governance*. Princeton: Princeton University Press.

Guyer, Jane I. 2004. "Anthropology in Area Studies." *Annual Review of Anthropology* 33: 499–523.

Haire, Mason, Edwin Ernest Ghiselli, and Lyman W. Porter. 1966. *Managerial Thinking: An International Study*. New York: John Wiley & Sons.

Hale, Charles. 2006. *Más que un Indio: Racial Ambivalence and the Paradox of Multiculturalism in Guatemala*. Santa Fe, NM: SAR Press.

Hall, Edward T. 1960. "The Silent Language in Overseas Business." *Harvard Business Review* 38 (3): 87–96.

———. 1992. *An Anthropology of Everyday Life: An Autobiography*. New York: Doubleday.

Hall, Sarah. 2008. "Geographies of Business Education: MBA Programmes, Reflexive Business Schools and the Cultural Circuit of Capital." *Transactions of the Institute of British Geographers* 33: 27–41.

Halsey, Frederic M. 1918. *Investments in Latin America and the British West Indies*. Special Agents Series, 169. Washington, DC: US Department of Commerce.

Hanlon, Gerard. 2016. *The Dark Side of Management: A Secret History of Management Theory*. New York: Routledge.

Hannerz, Ulf. 1989. "Notes on the Global Ecumene." *Public Culture* 1 (2): 66–75.

Harvey, David. 1989. *The Condition of Postmodernity*. Cambridge: Blackwell.

———. 2005. *A Brief History of Neoliberalism*. Oxford: Oxford University Press.

Hayashi, Alden M. 2001. "When to Trust Your Gut." *Harvard Business Review* 79 (2): 58–65.

Hayek, Friedrich. (1944) 2007. *The Road to Serfdom*. Edited by Bruce A. Caldwell. Chicago: University of Chicago Press.

Hegeman, Susan. 1999. *Patterns for America: Modernism and the Concept of Culture*. Princeton, NJ: Princeton University Press.

———. 2012. *The Cultural Return*. Berkeley: University of California Press.

Herrmann, Katharina, Asmus Komm, and Sven Smit. 2011. "Do You Have the Right Leaders for Your Growth Strategy?" *McKinsey Quarterly* 2011 (2): 22–26.

Ho, Karen. 2005. "Situating Global Capitalisms: A View from Wall Street Investment Banks." *Cultural Anthropology* 20 (1): 68–96.

———. 2009. *Liquidated: An Ethnography of Wall Street*. Durham, NC: Duke University Press.

Hofstede, Geert. 1984. *Culture's Consequences: International Differences in Work-Related Values*. Abridged ed. Newbury Park, CA: Sage.

———. 1997. "The Archimedes Effect." In *Working at the Interface of Cultures: Eighteen Lives in Social Science*, edited by Michael Harris Bond, 47–61. London: Routledge.

———. 2001. *Culture's Consequences: Comparing Values, Behaviors, Institutions and Organizations across Nations*. 2nd ed. Thousand Oaks, CA: SAGE Publications, 2001,

Hofstede, Geert, Gert Jan Hofstede, and Michael Minkov. 2010. *Cultures and Organization: Software of the Mind*. New York: McGraw-Hill.

Holmes, Douglas R., and George E. Marcus. 2008. "Cultures of Expertise and the Management of Globalization: Toward the Re-Functioning of Ethnography." In *Global Assemblages, Technology, Politics, and Ethics as Anthropological Problems*, edited by Aihwa Ong and Stephen J. Collier, 235–52. Oxford: Blackwell Publishing.

Hoopes, James. 2003. *False Prophets: The Gurus Who Created Modern Management and Why Their Ideas Are Bad for Business Today*. New York: Basic Books.

Immerwahr, Daniel. 2009. "Polanyi in the United States: Peter Drucker, Karl Polanyi, and the Midcentury Critique of Economic Society." *Journal of the History of Ideas* 70 (3): 445–66.

Jack, Gavin, and Robert Westwood. 2009. *International and Cross-Cultural Management Studies: A Postcolonial Reader*. Basingstoke, UK: Palgrave Macmillan.

James, Edmund J. 1893. *The Education of Business Men in Europe*. New York: American Bankers' Association.

Javidan, Moansour, Mary Teagarten, and David Bowen. 2010. "Managing Yourself: Making It Overseas." *Harvard Business Review* 88 (4): 109–13.

Jensen, Michael C., and William H. Meckling. 1976. "Theory of the Firm: Managerial Behavior, Agency Costs and Ownership Structure." *Journal of Financial Economics* 3 (4): 305–60.

Johnson, Joseph French. 1906. "The Business School and What It Should Do." *New York Times*, September 15, 9.

Juran, Joseph M. 1956. "Improving the Relationship between Staff and Line: An Assist from the Anthropologists." Selected Papers no. 2. TPOK/Juran Institute.

Retrieved on July 31, 2017. https://www.yumpu.com/en/document/view/5989050/improving-the-relationship-between-staff-and-line-juran-institute.

———. 1957. "Cultural Patterns and Quality Control." Selected Papers no. 4. TPOK/Juran Institute. Retrieved on July 31, 2017. https://www.yumpu.com/en/document/view/37642677/cultural-patterns-and-quality-control-j-m-juran-juran-institute.

———. 1964. *Managerial Breakthrough: A New Concept of the Manager's Job.* New York: McGraw-Hill.

Kahneman, Daniel, and Gary Klein. 2010. "Strategic Decisions: When Can You Trust Your Gut?" *McKinsey Quarterly* (March).

Karamchandani, Ashish, Mike Kubzansky, and Nishant Lalwani. 2011. "The Globe: Is the Bottom of the Pyramid Really for You?" *Harvard Business Review* 89 (3): 107–11.

Kluckhohn, Clyde. 1951. "The Study of Culture." In *The Policy Sciences*, edited by Daniel Lerner and Harold D. Lasswell, 86-101. Stanford, CA: Stanford University Press.

Knorr Cetina, Karen, and Alex Preda, eds. 2005. *The Sociology of Financial Markets.* Oxford: Oxford University Press.

Knowledge@Wharton (blog). 2011. "The New BRICs on the Block: Which Emerging Markets Are Up and Coming?" January 19. http://knowledge.wharton.upenn.edu/article/the-new-brics-on-the-block-which-emerging-markets-are-up-and-coming/.

Korn, Morgan. 2011. "Goldmans' Jim O'Neill: 'Our Future Prosperity Depends on China.'" *Yahoo Daily Ticker* (blog). December 22. http://finance.yahoo.com/blogs/daily-ticker/goldman-jim-o-neill-future-prosperity-depends-china-133813261.html.

Landsburg, Steven E. 2005. *Price Theory and Applications.* 6th ed. Mason, OH: Thomson South-Western.

Lederer, William J., and Eugene Burdick. 1958. *The Ugly American.* New York: Norton.

Leke, Acha, Musta Chironga, and George Desvaux. 2018. *Africa's Business Revolution: How to Succeed in the World's Next Big Growth Market.* Boston: Harvard Business Review Press.

Levitt, Theodore. 1983. "The Globalization of Markets." *Harvard Business Review* 61 (3): 92–102.

Lezaun, Javier, and Fabian Muniesa. 2017. "Twilight in the Leadership Playground: *Subrealism* and the Training of the Business Self." *Journal of Cultural Economy* 10 (3): 265–79.

Lieber, Nick. 2016. "The Selling of the American MBA." *Bloomberg BusinessWeek*, March 18.

LiPuma, Edward, and Benjamin Lee. 2004. *Financial Derivatives and the Globalization of Risk.* Durham, NC: Duke University Press.

Lund, Susan, James Manyika, Jonathan Woetzel, Jacques Bughin, Mekala Krishnan, Jeongmin Seong, and Mac Muir. 2019. *Globalization in Transition: The Future of Trade and Value Chains.* McKinsey Global Institute.

MacKenzie, Donald. 2006. *An Engine, Not a Camera: How Financial Models Shape Markets*. Cambridge, MA: MIT Press.

MacKenzie, Donald, and Yuval Millo. 2003. "Constructing a Market, Performing Theory: The Historical Sociology of a Financial Derivatives Exchange." *American Journal of Sociology* 109 (1): 107–45.

Madsbjerg, Christian, and Mikkel B. Rasmussen. 2014. *The Moment of Clarity: Using the Human Sciences to Solve Your Toughest Business Problems*. Boston: Harvard Business Review Press.

Malinowski, Bronislaw. 1922. *Argonauts of the Western Pacific*. London: Routledge and Kegan Paul.

Marchand, Donald A., Rebecca Chung, and Katarina Paddack. 2002. "CEMEX: Global Growth through Superior Information Capabilities (Abridged)." *IMD* No. 084. Lausanne, Switzerland: International Institute for Management Development.

Marx, Karl, and Friedrich Engels. 1970. *The German Ideology, Part 1*. New York: International.

———. 1977. "The Communist Manifesto." In *Karl Marx: Selected Writings*, edited by David McLellan, 219–47. Oxford: Oxford University Press.

McDonald, Duff. 2017. *The Golden Passport: Harvard Business School, the Limits of Capitalism, and the Moral Failure of the MBA Elite*. New York: Harper Collins.

McNair, Malcolm Perrine. 1954. *The Case Method at the Harvard Business School: Papers by Present and Past Members of the Faculty and Staff*. New York: McGraw-Hill.

McSweeney, Brendan. 2002. "Hofstede's Model of National Cultural Differences and Their Consequences: A Triumph of Faith—a Failure of Analysis." *Human Relations* 55 (1): 89–118.

Mead, Margaret, ed. 1953. *Cultural Patterns and Technical Change*. Paris: UNESCO.

Mertz, Elizabeth. 2007. *The Language of Law School: Learning to "Think Like a Lawyer."* New York: Oxford University Press.

Miller, Daniel, ed. 1995. *Worlds Apart: Modernity through the Prism of the Local*. London: Routledge.

———. 1997. *Capitalism: An Ethnographic Approach*. New York: Bloomsbury.

Mintz, Sidney. 1985. *Sweetness and Power: The Place of Sugar in Modern History*. New York: Penguin.

Mintzberg, Henry, and Paul Danos. 2011. "Business Education: Would the Economy Be Better Off without MBA Students." *Economist*. Accessed November 29, 2012. http://www.economist.com/debate/days/view/900.

Mirowski, Philip. 2014. *Never Let a Serious Crisis Go to Waste*. London: Verso.

Mirowski, Philip, and Dieter Plehwe, eds. 2009. *The Road from Mont Pelerin: The Making of the Neoliberal Thought Collective*. Cambridge, MA: Harvard University Press.

Miyazaki, Hirokazu. 2013. *Arbitraging Japan: Dreams of Capitalism at the End of Finance*. Berkeley: University of California Press.

Nader, L. 1972. "Up the Anthropologist—Perspectives Gained from Studying Up." In *Reinventing Anthropology*, edited by Dell H. Hymes, 284–311. New York: Pantheon Books.

Navarro, Peter. 2008. "The MBA Core Curricula of Top-Ranked US Business Schools: A Study in Failure?" *Academy of Management Learning & Education* 7 (1): 108–23.

New York Times. 2011. "DealBook Special Section: Wall Street Goes to the Ends of the Earth." *New York Times*, September 29. https://dealbook.nytimes.com/2011/09/29/morning-take-out-336/.

O'Connor, Ellen S. 1999. "The Politics of Management Thought: A Case Study of the Harvard Business School and the Human Relations School." *Academy of Management Review* 24 (1): 117–31.

O'Neill, Jim. 2001. "Building Better Global Economic BRICs." Goldman Sachs Global Economics Papers No. 66.

Ong, Aihwa. 2006. *Neoliberalism as Exception: Mutations in Sovereignty and Citizenship*. Durham, NC: Duke University Press.

Orta, Andrew. 2004a. *Catechizing Culture: Missionaries, Aymara, and the "New Evangelization."* New York: Columbia University Press.

———. 2004b. "The Promise of Particularism and the Theology of Culture: The Limits and Lessons of 'Neo-Boasianism.'" *American Anthropologist* 106 (3): 473–87.

———. 2013. "Forged Communities and Vulgar Citizens: Autonomy and Its *Limites* in Semi-neoliberal Bolivia." *Journal of Latin American and Caribbean Anthropology* 18(1): 108–33.

Ortiz, Horatio 2014. "The Limits of Financial Imagination: Free Investors, Efficient Markets, and Crisis." *American Anthropologist* 116 (1): 1–13.

Peck, Jamie, and Adam Tickell. 2002. "Neoliberalizing Space." *Antipode* 34 (3): 380–404.

Peirce, Charles S. 1955. *Philosophical Writings*. Edited by Justus Buchler. New York: Dover Publications.

Person, Harlow. 1920. "The Basic Elements and Their Proper Balance in the Curriculum of a Collegiate Business School: Discussion." *Journal of Political Economy* 28 (2): 109–12.

Petriglieri, Gianpiero. 2012. "Are Business Schools Clueless or Evil?" *Harvard Business Review Blog Network*. Accessed November 14, 2017. https://hbr.org/2012/11/are-business-schools-clueless.

———. 2016. "In Defense of Cosmopolitanism." *Harvard Business Review* 94 (12).

Pierson, Frank Cook. 1959. *The Education of American Businessmen: A Study of University-College Programs in Business Administration*. New York: McGraw-Hill.

Pletsch, C. E. 1981. "The Three Worlds, or the Division of Social Scientific Labor, circa 1950–1975." *Comparative Studies in Society and History* 23 (4): 565–90.

Polanyi, Karl. 1957. *Trade and Markets in the Early Empires*. New York: Free Press.

Porter, Michael E. 1979. "How Competitive Forces Shape Strategy." *Harvard Business Review* 59 (2): 137–45.

———. 1990. "The Competitive Advantage of Nations." *Harvard Business Review* 68 (2): 73–91.

Prahalad, Coimbinatore K. 2005. *The Fortune at the Bottom of the Pyramid: Eradicating Poverty through Profits.* Upper Saddle River, NJ: Prentice-Hall.

Preda, Alex. 2002. "Financial Knowledge, Documents, and the Structures of Financial Activities." *Journal of Contemporary Ethnography* 31 (2): 207–39.

———. 2009. *Framing Finance: The Boundaries of Markets and Modern Capitalism.* Chicago: University of Chicago Press.

Purewal, Jesse, and Adam Berman. 2006. "Making the Case Method Work for You." Haas School of Business, University of California Berkeley, July 31.

Pusch, Margaret D. 2004. "Intercultural Training in Historical Perspective." In *Handbook of Intercultural Training,* edited by Dan Landis, Janet M. Bennett, and Milton J. Bennett, 3rd ed., 13–36. Thousand Oaks, CA: Sage Publications.

Rafael, Vicente L. 1994. "The Cultures of Area Studies in the United States." *Social Text* 41: 91–111.

Rangan, V. Kasturi, Michael Chu, and Djorjiji Petkoski. 2011. "Segmenting the Base of the Pyramid." *Harvard Business Review* 89 (6): 113–17.

Riaz, S. 2009. "The Economic Crisis as a Time for IB to Lead." *AIB Insights* 9 (3): 4–7.

Ricardo, David. 1817. *Principles of Political Economy and Taxation.* London: John Murray.

Riles, A. 2010. "Collateral Expertise: Legal Knowledge in the Global Financial Markets." *Current Anthropology* 51 (6): 795–818.

Rivera Cusiqanqui, Sylvia. 2012. "Ch'ixinakax Utxiwa: A Reflection on the Practices and Discourses of Decolonization." *South Atlantic Quarterly* 111 (1): 95–109.

Robock, Steven H. 2003. "Indiana University as a Pioneer in the Internationalization of Business Education." In *Research in Global Strategic Management. Volume 8, Leadership in International Business Education and Research,* edited by Alan M. Rugman, 3–18. Bingley, UK: Emerald Group Publishing.

Rockefeller, Stuart A. 2011. "Flow." *Current Anthropology* 52 (4): 557–78.

Rogers, Everett M., William B. Hart, and Yoshitaka Miike. 2002. "Edward T. Hall and the History of Intercultural Communication: The United States and Japan." *Keio Communication Review* 23: 3–26.

Rosenzweig, Philip M. 1994. "National Culture and Management." HBS Cases 9-394-177. Boston: Harvard Business School.

Rugman, Alan M., and Alain Verbeke. 2004. "A Perspective on Regional and Global Strategies of Multinational Enterprises." *Journal of International Business Studies* 35 (1): 3–18.

Sahlins, Marshall. 1974. *Stone Age Economics.* New York: Aldine.

———. 1988. "Cosmologies of Capitalism: The Trans-Pacific Sector in the World System." *Proceedings of the British Academy* LXXIV: 1–51.

———. 1999. "Two or Three Things I Know about Culture." *Journal of the Royal Anthropological Institute* 5 (3): 399–421.

Santiso, Javier. 2003. *The Political Economy of Emerging Markets: Actors, Institutions and Financial Crises in Latin America*. New York: Palgrave.

Scheper-Hughes, Nancy. 1992. *Death without Weeping: The Violence of Everyday Life in Brazil*. Berkeley: University of California Press.

Schmitt, Jeff. 2017. "Business Schools with the Best MBA Cultures." Poets & Quants, February 13. Accessed March 18, 2017. http://poetsandquants.com/2017/02/13/business-schools-best-mba-cultures/.

Schön, Donald R., and Philip Sprague. 1954. "What Is the Case Method?" In *The Case Method at the Harvard Business School*, edited by Malcolm P. McNair, 76–81. New York: McGraw-Hill.

Schurz, William Lytle. 1921. *Bolivia: A Commercial and Industrial Handbook*. Department of Commerce, Special Agents Series 208. Washington, DC: Washington Government Printing Office.

———. 1941. *Latin America, a Descriptive Survey*. New York: E. P. Dutton.

Shankar, Shalini. 2015. *Advertising Diversity: Ad Agencies and the Creation of Asian American Consumers*. Durham, NC: Duke University Press.

Simanis, Erik. 2012. "Reality Check at the Bottom of the Pyramid." *Harvard Business Review* 90 (6): 120–25.

Sorkin, Andrew Ross. 2011. "For Deals, Wall Street Goes East." *New York Times*, DealBook Special Section: Wall Street Goes to the Ends of the Earth, September 29. https://dealbook.nytimes.com/2011/09/28/for-deals-wall-street-goes-east/.

Stachowicz-Stanusch, Agata. 2009. "Culture Due Diligence Based on HP/Compaq Merger Case Study." *Journal of Intercultural Management* 1 (1): 64–81.

Stiglitz, Joseph E. 2003. *Globalization and Its Discontents*. New York: W. W. Norton.

Susman, Warren. 1984. *Culture as History: The Transformation of American Society in the Twentieth Century*. Madison: University of Wisconsin Press.

Szanton, David L. 2004. *The Politics of Knowledge: Area Studies and the Disciplines*. Berkeley: University of California Press.

Thrift, Nigel. 1999. "The Globalization of the System of Business Knowledge." In *Globalisation and the Asia-Pacific: Contested Territories*, edited by Kris Olds et al., 57–71. London: Routledge.

———. 2000. "Performing Cultures in the New Economy." *Annals of the Association of American Geographers* 90 (4): 674–92.

———. 2005. *Knowing Capitalism*. London: Sage.

———. 2006. "Re-Inventing Invention: New Tendencies in Capitalist Commodification." *Economy and Society* 35 (2): 279–306.

Trouillot, Michel-Rolph. 2001. "The Anthropology of the State in the Age of Globalization: Close Encounters of the Deceptive Kind." *Current Anthropology* 42 (1): 125–38.

Tsing, Anna Lowenhaupt. 2000. "Inside the Economy of Appearances." *Public Culture* 12 (1): 115–44.

———. 2005. *Friction: An Ethnography of Global Connection*. Princeton, NJ: Princeton University Press.

———. 2013. "Sorting Out Commodities." *Hau: Journal of Ethnographic Theory* 3 (1): 21–43.

United States, Bureau of Education, and National Education Association of the United States. 1919. *Business Education in Secondary Schools*. Washington, DC: Government Printing Office.

United States Senate, Committee on Education and Labor. 1885. *Report of the Committee of the Senate upon the Relations between Labor and Capital*. Vol. 2. Washington, DC: Government Printing Office.

Urciuoli, Bonnie. 2008. "Skills and Selves in the New Workplace." *American Ethnologist* 35(2): 211–28.

Van Maanen, John. 1983. "Golden Passports: Managerial Socialization and Graduate Education." *The Review of Higher Education* 6 (4): 435–55.

Veblen, Thorstein. 1918. *The Higher Learning in America: A Memorandum on the Conduct of Universities by Business Men*. New York: B. W. Huebsch.

White, Harrison C. 1981. "Where Do Markets Come From?" *American Journal of Sociology* 87 (3): 517–47.

Whyte, William H. (1956) 2013. *The Organization Man*. Philadelphia: University of Pennsylvania Press.

Wild, John J., Kenneth L. Wild, and Jerry C. Y. Han. 2006. *International Business: The Challenges of Globalization*. 3rd ed. Upper Saddle River, NJ: Pearson.

Wilk, Richard. 1995. "Learning to Be Local in Belize: Global Systems of Common Difference." *Worlds Apart: Modernity through the Prism of the Local*, edited by Daniel Miller, 110–33. London: Routledge.

Williams, Brett. 2005. *Debt for Sale: A Social History of the Credit Trap*. Philadelphia: University of Pennsylvania Press.

Wolfe, Tom. 1987. *The Bonfire of the Vanities*. New York: Farrar, Straus and Giroux.

Womack, James P., Daniel T. Jones, and Daniel Roos. 1991. *The Machine That Changed the World: The Story of Lean Production*. New York: HarperCollins.

Xin, Katherine, and Vladimir Pucik. 2003. "HBR Case Study: Trouble in Paradise." *Harvard Business Review,* August, 27–37.

Zaloom, Caitlin. 2004. "The Productive Life of Risk." *Cultural Anthropology* 19 (3): 365–91.

INDEX

Academy of International Business, 90, 92, 105

accounting: in contemporary MBA core curriculum, 23, 28, 33, 35; in early MBA curriculum, 76, 209n5, 210n11; international content in 129–130; reinforcing lessons from economics, 51

Admissions Test for Graduate Study in Business (ATGSB), 64

American Accounting Association, 210n6

American Association of Collegiate Schools of Business, International, 64

American Bankers Association, 74

American Dream, 76

American Universities Field Service, 89–90, 106

anthropology: of business practices 14–16, 106–109; and business training, 101–104, 118–120, 166, 211n5; of capitalism 12–16; and the concept of culture, 9, 98–100, 118, 211n1; and globalization, 9, 99–100; medical 104, 211n6. *See also* culture; Hall, Edward T.; Hofstede, Geert

Applbaum, Kalman, 9–10

arbitrage, 58, 138, 209n15

Arden House Report. *See* Ford Foundation

area studies, xii, 90–91, 101, 143. *See also* American Universities Field Service; CIBER Program

Argentina: as a developing country, 110–113, 120, short term study abroad trips to, 141, 142, 156. *See also* short-term study abroad courses (STSA)

art (and science): and decision-making, 166; of management 21, 32, 55–57; and managerial talent, 203; and science, 129, 154. *See also* curriculum; talent

Benedict, Ruth, 118, 211n3, 211n4

Bennington College, 77, 101

Berle, Adolph, and Gardiner Means, *Modern Corporation and Private Property*, 50, 71–72, 83

Boas, Franz, 99, 100–101, 211n4

bookkeeping, 62–63

Booth School of Business. *See* University of Chicago

Bottom of the Pyramid (BoP): definition, 194–195; economic inequality and risk, 147, 203–204; in global marketing courses, 52, 203–204; and scale, 193–194; and social entrepreneurship, 192–197

Brazil: and BRICS, 137–138, 141, 201, 213n11; and Hofstede's country scores, 116–117; and MBA program marketing, 6; and short-term study abroad, 141, 142, 144, 147–148, 152, 154, 157–159. *See also* BRICS; short-term study abroad courses (STSA). *See also under* Hofstede, Geert and country scores

Brexit, 20, 21, 205

BRICS, 45, 137–139, 141, 143, 147–148, 192, 194, 201–202, 212n4, 213n14. *See also* virtual regions

Haas School of Business. *See* University of California, Berkeley
Hayek, F. E., 4, 78, 208n7
Hewlett-Packard, 15, 39
Hofstede, Geert: and anthropology, 118, 120, 211n11; country scores, 116–19; *Culture's Consequences*, 110, 115–17, 120–22, 212n19; dimensions of culture, 114–15, 116–120, 121, 151, 174, 180, 212n16,17
Hoover, 8

IBM (International Business Machines Corporation), 75, 115–16, 118, 120, 112n17,19. *See also* Hofstede, Geert
Illinois Institute of Technology, 211n5
India: and BRICS, 137–38, 201, 211n9, 213n11; in early international business literature, 103, 112–13, 117, 120; example in MBA class, 31, 40, 204; MBA students from, 6, 96–97, 155–56; and short term study abroad classes, 130, 139–42, 144, 145, 147, 149–51, 153–55; and social entrepreneurship, 195–200. *See also* short-term study abroad courses (STSA)
Indiana University, 89
intercultural communication, 101, 107, 211n4. *See also* Hall, Edward T.
Institute for Advanced Study, 66
The International Executive, 105, 106–7, 165
international MBA students, 5, 55, 59, 96–97, 129, 130, 155–56, 184–85, 208n11
International Monetary Fund (IMF), 91
Iran, 33, 213n8
Italy, 8, 95, 112–13

James, Edmund J., 66, 74
Japan, 39, 85–88, 90, 103, 112–13, 117, 131, 173, 179, 184–85, 214n7
Johnson, Joseph French, 64–65, 69, 72–73
Juran, Joseph M., 86–87

Kluckhohn, Clyde, 108, 118, 211n3,11

labor: family labor as asset of the poor, 195; low cost internationally, 139, 195; and marginal analysis, 46–47; and Porter's "Competitive Advantage of Nations,"

34; relations with management, 72–73, 75, 78, 83–84; wage laborers depicted in case study, 190
Latin America: case studies and, 106–109, 177; focus of MBA student organization, 29, 94; in Hofstede's country surveys, 120; as a market, 41; MBA students from, 156, 178, 193; as a regional culture, 95, 102, 112–113; short term study abroad trip to, 158, as site of developing countries, 113. *See also* short-term study abroad courses (STSA). *See also under* Hofstede, Geert and country scores
Levitt, Theodore, 2, 8–10, 91–2, 125, 202
Liberalism, 16–17, 78, 210n8
London Business School, 89

MacKenzie, Donald, 14, 58
Malinowski, Bronislaw, 13, 170, 213n2
managerial capitalism, 4, 11, 17, 20, 33, 45, 71–72, 76, 121
Managerial Thinking, 110–15, 120–21
margin: of commensurability, 57, 58–59, 88, 104–105; defined, 46; international spaces as, 2–3, 127–129, 137, 141, 145–160, 192, 206; low-margin products, 195–196; marginal analysis, 46, 51; marginal cost, 47–52; marginal production, 46; marginal revenue, 46–52; marginal thinking, 51–52; profit margin, 46; scalable, 51
marketing: and anthropology, 14–15; and globalization, 8–10, 40, 53–54, 203; in MBA core curriculum, 28, 33, 35, 45,178, 210n11; and short-term study abroad, 142, 148–149
marketness, 38–42, 125, 193, 198, 206
markets: and arbitrage, 57–58, 209n15; emerging, 1–3, 58–59, 134, 137–139, 177, 181, 201–206; financial, 40–41, 135–138; global, 8–11, 72, 91, 136, 157, 194, 203–206; in MBA core classes, 35–44, 47–51, 57–58; moral, 193, 196–197; neoliberalism and, 7–8, 10–12, 90–91. *See also* Bottom of the Pyramid (BoP); emerging economies; globalization; marketness, neoliberalism

Marshall Plan, Economic Cooperation Administration, 89, 100
Marx, Karl, 7
Master of Science in Commerce, 63–64
Masters of the Universe, 1, 3–4, 12, 18, 84, 200, 213
Mayo, Elton, 75, 79, 84
McKinsey and Company, 143, 200–204, 214n4,7
McNair, Malcolm P. 165–169, 170, 210n7, 214n5
Mead, Margaret, 86–87, 211n3, 4
Medill, Joseph, 68, 72
mergers and acquisitions: after the financial crisis, 214n2; and corporate culture, 15; globalization and, 2, 4, 177; impact on markets, 48, 177; neoliberal models of the firm, 12, 121
Mexico: BRICS/MINTs/CIVETS, 138, 211n9, 213n8,10; and CEMEX case study, 182–183, 188–91; example of country-level culture, 95, and Fayerweather, 105–109; short term study abroad trip to, 127, 141, 144, 145–147, 150, 151, 157, 214n1. *See also* short-term study abroad courses (STSA)
microfinance, 142, 143, 144, 145, 147, 197
MINTs, 45, 137–138, 201, 213n14. *See also* virtual regions

National Education Association, 63, 64
Neoliberalism: ascendance of in the 1980s, xii, 3, 90, 146; and contemporary anthropology, 12–14, 98–100; contrast with mid-century capitalism, 11–12, 52, 209n10; and dominance of economistic rhetoric, 9, 33, 61, 193; and Hayek, 78; localizing and standardizing, 7, 10–11, 16–17, 92, 206. *See also* globalization; neoliberalism; scale
New Deal, 77, 146
new economy: managerial subjects of, 11–12, 27, 55, 155
New York University, 63, 64, 72, 77, 79, 89, 209n10
Nigeria, 34, 117, 138, 213n8,9
Northwestern University, 70, 209n2, 211n5

Ohio State University, 209n2
operations management, 39–40, 53, 87–88
Organization Man, 84, 111
organizational culture. *See* culture

paracurriculum, 26, 29, 53, 83, 130, 142, 193
paraethnography, 162, 168, 170, 180, 182
Pareto Principle, 86
Person, Harlow, 73
Peru, 141, 142, 144–145, 147, 148–149, 152
Pierson Report. *See* Carnegie Foundation
Porter, Michael E., 6–7, 34–35, 54, 203, 208n6
Prahalad, C. K. *See* Bottom of the Pyramid (BoP)
Profit. *See* margin
Program in Economic Development and Administration. *See* Ford Foundation
psychology: and business approaches to cultural difference, 101, 110, 116; and connections between management and personal fulfillment, 84; early inclusion in business education 73, 75–76, 166

qualisign, 45, 59

return on investment (ROI), 172, 177, 183, 184, 187–188
Ricardo, David, 6, 34, 207n5
risk: and arbitrage, 57, 209n15; and corporate culture, 15; cultivated in MBA programs, 23, 26, 57–58, 59, 129, 141, 148–151, 159–160, 169, 192–193; cultural difference and, 58–59, 98, 104, 124–25, 192–93; finance, 36, 43–44, 51, 135–37; and the firm, 43; and international business, 2, 7, 12, 33–34, 53, 57, 58–59, 91, 128, 134–37, 138–39, 141, 146, 172, 181, 184, 188, 192–193; managing the future, 26–27, 43, 46, 73, 155; policy risk, 133; risk premium, 44, 135; as a qualisign, 59
rootedness, 124–126. *See also* Ghemawat, Pankaj
Royal Dutch Shell (case study), 33–34. *See also* case study method
Rugman, Alan M., 92, 123
Russia, 33–34, 137–38, 201, 213n11

Sahlins, Marshall, 16–17, 98
scale: anthropological concept of culture
    98–100; and, and country-level detail,
    133–134, 174; global-local, 9–10, 53,
    193–194, 202–203; and market, 40–41,
    194–197; and value chain, 52–53
self-actualization, 56, 111, 115, 209n14
semi-globalization, 92, 124, 125. *See also*
    Ghemawat, Pankaj
short-term study abroad courses (STSA):
    and BRICS, 139, 143; and MBA curricu-
    lum, 19, 89, 127–128, 140, 192; MBA
    student reflections on, 145–160, 204;
    preparatory classes, 139–145; and risk,
    148–151; and the staging of interna-
    tional difference, 128–129, 142–153
Six Sigma, 210n16
Smith, Adam, 7, 138, 207n5
social entrepreneurship, 3, 21, 144–45, 193,
    194–200, 205
Soviet Union, 74, 131
Spanish American War, 63
statistics (data analysis): as management
    tool, 83; in MBA core curriculum, 28,
    33, 35, 36, 210n11
stock market, 30, 50–51, 156–57
strategy: in MBA core curriculum, 22, 30,
    35, 54, 130–33; international/global, 10,
    26, 27, 31–32, 34–35, 40, 53, 61, 125,
    130–33
Structural Adjustment Policies, 91
supply and demand, 35, 42
supply chain, 12, 52
System: A Magazine of Business. See Busi-
    ness Week

talent: cultivated in MBA programs 20–21,
    26, 32–33, 54–60, 73, 79, 82, 163, 168,
    199–200, 203–204; and culture, 125;
    and international business, 26, 133,
    142, 145, 154, 172, 186, 193, 203–204;
    and risk, 57–59, 172. *See also* art;
    curriculum
Taylor, Frederick W., 68, 69–70
teams, MBA project: and international
    students, 59, 126, 130, 155–156, 179; and
    the MBA paracurriculum, 28–29, 30,
    32, 42, 94; and short-term study abroad,

127, 140, 142–145, 147–151, 152–156;
    simulating business life, 30, 32, 93
Third World, 2, 181–82, 189–91, 198
Thrift, Nigel, 7, 14, 26, 27
time: as dimension of cultural difference,
    95, 102–103, 106, 123, 156; MBAs as
    adepts of the future, 43, 129, 146–147;
    pace of MBA curriculum, 27–28, 32,
    130, 136, 141, 171; and space compres-
    sion, 26–27; value of money, 43–44,
    50–51
Toyota Way, (*kaizan*; just in time produc-
    tion), 87, 214n7
transitioning economies. *See* emerging
    economies
"Trouble in Paradise" (case study), 162,
    172–175, 178–181, 183–188, 191. *See also*
    case study method
Trump, Donald J.: *The Apprentice*, 56;
    election as US President, 20, 21–22,
    205–206, 208n11
Tsing, Anna L. 12, 17, 52
Tuck School of Business. *See* Dartmouth
    College
Tulane University, 90, 209n2
Turkey, 55, 211n9, 213n8,9,10

United Nations, 99
US Department of Commerce (Special
    Agents Series), 88–89
US Department of State, Foreign Service
    Institute, Point IV Training Program,
    101, *See also* Hall, Edward T.
University of California, Berkeley, Haas
    School of Business, 15–16, 63, 69, 193,
    207n8, 209n2
University of Chicago, Booth School of
    Business, 63, 65, 69, 209n2
University of Illinois, 65, 209n2
University of Wisconsin, 63, 65, 209n2
University of Pennsylvania, Wharton
    School, 63, 64, 66, 74, 75, 139, 201–202,
    214n3
University of Texas, 209n2

value chain, 12, 52–53, 156–158, 197–198,
    209n11
Veblen, Thorsten, 67

Founded in 1893,
UNIVERSITY OF CALIFORNIA PRESS
publishes bold, progressive books and journals
on topics in the arts, humanities, social sciences,
and natural sciences—with a focus on social
justice issues—that inspire thought and action
among readers worldwide.

The UC PRESS FOUNDATION
raises funds to uphold the press's vital role
as an independent, nonprofit publisher, and
receives philanthropic support from a wide
range of individuals and institutions—and from
committed readers like you. To learn more, visit
ucpress.edu/supportus.